The New Foundling Hospital for Wit

(6 Parts in 3 Volumes, 1768–73)

Edited by

Donald W. Nichol

The New Foundling Hospital for Wit

(6 Parts in 3 Volumes, 1768–73)

Volume 2

Parts 3 (1769) & 4 (1771)

Edited by

Donald W. Nichol

Routledge
Taylor & Francis Group
LONDON AND NEW YORK

First published 2006 by Pickering & Chatto (Publishers) Limited

Published 2016 by Routledge
2 Park Square, Milton Park, Abingdon, Oxon OX14 4RN
711 Third Avenue, New York, NY 10017, USA

Routledge is an imprint of the Taylor & Francis Group, an informa business

BRITISH LIBRARY CATALOGUING IN PUBLICATION DATA
The new foundling hospital for wit, 1768–1773
1. English literature – 18th century 2. English wit and humor
3. Satire, English
I. Nichol, Donald W.
827.6'08

ISBN-13: 978-1-85196-808-4 (set)

New material typeset by P&C

CONTENTS

CHRONOLOGY

1769 Almon publishes *The New Foundling Hospital for Wit*, Part 3; Gray's *Ode for Music* on Duke of Grafton's installation as Chancellor of Cambridge; Garrick's Shakespeare Jubilee in Stratford-upon-Avon all but rained out; 'Junius' letters start to appear, anonymously attacking Grafton and George III; Burke's *Observations on the Present State of the Nation*; James Cook on HMS Endeavour lands in New Zealand; James Watt patents steam engine.

1770 Lord North follows Grafton as Prime Minister (to 1782); Almon found guilty of seditious libel for selling a copy of John Miller's *London Museum* containing Junius's *Letter to the King*; fined and made to post £800 bond; publishes *Trial of John Almon*, including trial copy of the *Letter*; continues to report Commons debates for *London Evening-Post* in violation of parliamentary privilege; Wilkes released from prison; Burke's *Thoughts on the Causes of Present Discontents*; Lord North repeals Revenue Act but imposes duty on tea; Boston Massacre exacerbates tension in the American colonies; the next *New Foundling Hospital for Wit* likely delayed by Almon's legal and financial problems.

1771 The Printers' Case: Almon and Wilkes help Miller *et al.* establish principle that newspapers are allowed to report parliamentary debates once and for all; Wilkes elected Sheriff of London and Middlesex; Thomas Gray (b. 1716) dies in Cambridge; Tobias Smollett (b. 1721) dies following publication of *Humphry Clinker*; Burke appointed agent to New York; Benjamin West's painting, *The Death of Wolfe*; Almon publishes Part 4 of *The New Foundling Hospital for Wit*.

THE NEW FOUNDLING HOSPITAL FOR WIT, PART 3 (1769)

The frontispiece to Part 3 is the most audacious of the six. A blindfolded 'Farmer' George III, tethered to a nose-ring, is led by his mother, the Princess Dowager, who is making a come-hither gesture to her alleged lover, the Earl of Bute, identified by his tam, tartan and large boot. He responds with an equally provocative sexual gesture. The *double entendre* in the legend on the royal residence at 'Kew' was intended to fuel the rumour that George III was under the baleful influence of his dominating mother and her Scottish lover (*CPDBM*, vol. 4, no. 4245), hence Bute's rise to power. As history has not provided us with any solid proof of an affair, it seems more likely that the two were victims of a smear campaign.

In 'City Latin' (1), Bonnell Thornton applies his skills for textual emendation and satirical exegesis to the inscription 'if it may be called Latin' for the cornerstone to the new Blackfriars Bridge, and inadvertently reveals George White as *Agricola Candidus*, the hitherto unknown author of *The High Mass* (1746) and *The Latin Mercury*.

The extraordinary events surrounding Wilkes's return from France, his successful election campaigns in Middlesex (whose results were rejected by parliament) and his imprisonment form the backdrop to 'The Times' (35), 'Imitation' (36) and 'Epistle to John Wilkes' (37). The 'Parody on Cato' (51) applies Addison's tragedy to Sergeant John Glynn's victory over the incumbent, Sir William Proctor, in Middlesex, proving even Wilkes's lawyer could now get a seat in parliament. The victory is celebrated in the updated version of 'Chevy Chase' (55).

For readers unsure as to who stands for which party, we are given a list (64): the first name to appear in the *North Briton* column, 'P. D. of W.' – the Princess Dowager of Wales – is not likely to be counted as a Wilkes supporter. Arthur Murphy's *Auditor* (like Smollett's *Briton*) supported Bute's Treaty of Paris, the Peace negotiated by the Duke of Bedford and Henry Fox in 1763. On the other side, Wilkes's *North Briton* numbered the Dukes of Cumberland, Newcastle and Devonshire amongst supporters for extending the war. The appearance of the Earl of Talbot's horse, which advanced its rear end embarrassingly close to George III at his coronation, may also have reminded readers of the duel Wilkes fought with Talbot in 1762. Further down the list, Samuel Martin also faced Wilkes's pistol in 1763, only this time Wilkes nearly bled to death. Samuel Johnson's inclusion on the opposite side from his former pupil Garrick and Wilkes did not prevent him from joining the roster of *NFHW*, Part 5. Both Whiggish *North Briton* Charles Churchill and Tory *Auditor* William Hogarth died in 1764, suggesting that this list was drawn up half a dozen years before it appeared here. Another Tory *Auditor* was Wilkes's former Hell-Fire Club sponsor, Sir Frances Dashwood. The two had become estranged by political exigencies after Dashwood accepted Bute's offer to join his government as Chancellor of the Exchequer.

Two 'Notes' on Churchill's poems were bound to create a stir, especially between Buckinghamshire and Bath. The first, '*an explanatory Note of a Passage in* Mr. Churchill's Candidate', quotes a line that Dashwood probably no longer found funny: that he would handle 'A nation's reckoning, like an alehouse score' (71). Following on the 'Curious Description of West Wycombe' (*NFHW*, 1: 42), the description of Medmenham Abbey broke the code of secrecy surrounding Hell-Fire Club gatherings. Churchill and Wilkes seem to be the only members to have committed any Medmenham mayhem, however briefly, to print. The second, '*Notes on* Mr. Churchill's *Fragment of a Dedication*' (89), provided Wilkes with a new opportunity to assail William Warburton. In a long tirade, Warburton's only son is ridiculed as '*Potter*'s earth' (94), using Quin's quip on God's handwriting to add insult to injury. Now the secrecy surrounding Potter's epigram in Part 1 (1: 10) is revealed: he himself is the boy's father. Potter (d. 1759) was no longer around to confirm or deny the allegation.

Wilkes's two birthday poems to his daughter Maria (77, 78) are so utterly bad that, had they been published forty years earlier, they might have ended up beside the worst lines by Sir Richard Blackmore in Pope's *Peri Bathous* (1728). Even allowing for the fact that the second poem was '*Wrote in Prison*', it seems unlikely to this editor that Wilkes played a major part in composing *An Essay on Woman*, which, for all its salacious content seems much more smoothly written. A fiery columnist, even a fine classical translator, Wilkes was not doomed to be a poet.

The text for this first edition of *The New Foundling Hospital for Wit*, Part 3 (*ESTC* t139946), is reproduced from a copy held by Cambridge University Library (shelfmark Forster.d.81).

The New Foundling Hospital for Wit

Part 3 (1769)

To my children, Leila Evelyn Aitken Nichol
Susannah Marion Aitken Nichol
& Robert James Aitken Wingate Nichol

Frontispiece to part III.

You have got him Ma'am, in the right Kew.

THE

NEW FOUNDLING HOSPITAL FOR WIT.

BEING

A COLLECTION

OF

SEVERAL CURIOUS PIECES

IN VERSE AND PROSE.

Many of which were never before Printed.

WRITTEN BY THE

Earl of CHESTERFIELD,
Earl of CARLISLE,
Earl DELAWARR,
Lord LYTTELTON,
Lord HARVEY,
Lord CAPEL,
Lady M. W. MONTAGUE,
Sir CHARLES HANBURY WILLIAMS,
Sir WALTER RALEIGH,
Rt. Hon. CH. TOWNSHEND,
JOHN WILKES, Esq;
D. GARRICK, Esq;
B. THORNTON, Esq;
Mrs. LENOX,
Mr. RT. LLOYD,
Mr. W. KENRICK,
Mr. J. CUNNINGHAM;

AND OTHER EMINENT PERSONS.

PART THE THIRD.

LONDON:
Printed in the Year MDCCLXIX.

CONTENTS.

CONTENTS.

Poetical

CONTENTS.

An

CONTENTS.

CITY LATIN;

O R,

Critical and political remarks on the Latin inſcription on laying the firſt ſtone of the intended new bridge at Black Friars. Proving almoſt every word, and every letter of it to be erroneous, and contrary to the practice of both ancients and moderns in this kind of writing: interſperſed with curious reflections on antiques and antiquity, with a plan or pattern for a new inſcription. Dedicated to the venerable ſociety of antiquaries. By the Rev. BUSBY BIRCH, *L. L. D. F. R. S. F. A. S. F. G. C. and M. S. E. A. M. C.* i. e. *member of the ſociety for the encouragement of arts, manufactures, and commerce.*

Quis expedivit Salmaſio ſuam Hundredam,
Picamque docuit verba noſtra conari? MILT.

THOUGH I cannot but applaud the zeal and affection, which our worthy citizens of London have expreſſed towards the GREAT MINISTER, in their Inſcription on laying the firſt ſtone of the intended new bridge, yet I could wifh they had been contented with expreffing it in their own native language; which will probably laft as long as the bridge, though built on *Elliptic* arches.

There were doubtlefs among them perfons of fufficient abilities for fuch a tafk: witnefs the late addrefs of the lord mayor and aldermen; witnefs the addrefs of the common council; witnefs the addrefs of the merchants; all which, we may venture to fay, have not been outdone by the addreffes of any other mayors, aldermen, and corporations, or even of our two univerfities. Where then was the neceffity that the infcription in queftion fhould be couched in an unknown tongue? Unknown we may call it to moft of our citizens, whofe knowledge in Latin fcarce extends further than the famed Afhley's motto, *pro bono publico*; though it muft be allowed, that many of them are converfant in the French, Spanifh, Italian, German, High Dutch, Low Dutch, and Hebrew.

I know not, whether this Latin infcription (if it may be called Latin) was drawn up by the reverend ordinary of Newgate, or my lord mayor's chaplain, or the mafter of Merchant Taylors, or Paul's fchool, or even the Charter-Houfe; but the following remarks will, I think, fufficiently prove the author to be wholly ignorant of *Claffical Latinity*, and an intire ftranger to the ufual ftile of *Infcriptions*.

But

But it will be neceſſary, in order to refreſh the reader's memory, that I ſhould tranſcribe this inſcription, together with its *Engliſh* tranſlation, as it has appeared in the public papers: though there is great reaſon to imagine, that it was originally firſt drawn up in *Engliſh*, by ſome learned *deputy* or other, and afterwards *done into Latin*, as the phraſe is; which, if this be the caſe, will readily account for the many *Angliciſms* that occur in it.

Ultimo die Octobris, anno ab incarnatione
MDCCLX.
auspicatissimo principe GEORGIO Tertio
regnum jam ineunte,
pontis hujus, in reipublicæ commodum,
urbisq; majestatem,
(late tum flagrante bello)
a S. P. Q. L. suscepti,
primum lapidem posuit
THOMAS CHITTY, Miles,
Prætor:
ROBERTO MYLNE, Architecto.
Utque apud posteros extet monumentum
voluntatis suæ erga virum,
qui vigore ingenii, animi constantia,
probitatis & virtutis suæ felici quadam contagione,
(favente Deo
faustisque GEORGII Secundi auspiciis)
imperium Britannicum
in Asia, Africa, & America,
restituit, auxit, & stabilivit,
necnon patriæ antiquum honorem & auctoritatem
inter Europæ gentes instauravit;
cives Londinenses, uno consensu,
huic ponti inscribi voluerunt nomen
GULIELMI PITT.

Englished

Englished thus.

On the laſt Day of October, in the year 1760,
and in the beginning of the moſt auſpicious reign of
GEORGE the Third,
Sir THOMAS CHITTY, Knight, Lord Mayor,
laid the firſt ſtone of this bridge,
undertaken by the Common Council of London,
(amidſt the rage of an extenſive war)
for the public accommodation,
and ornament of the city:
ROBERT MYLNE being the Architect.
And that there might remain to poſterity
a monument of this city's affection to the man,
who, by the ſtrength of his genius,
the ſteadineſs of his mind,
and a certain kind of happy contagion of his
probity and ſpirit,
(under the divine favour
and fortunate auſpices of GEORGE the Second)
recovered, augmented, and ſecured,
the Britiſh empire
in Aſia, Africa, and America,
and reſtored the ancient reputation
and influence of his country
amongſt the nations of Europe;
the citizens of London have unanimouſly voted this
bridge to be inſcribed with the name of
WILLIAM PITT.

Ultimo Die Octobris.

The last day of October: This is a very bald expreſſion, and but little removed from a down-right *Angliciſm*. *Die Octobris* XXXI. would have been more in the inſcription taſte, which delights in theſe capital numerals. But, if they muſt have it *the* LAST *day*, *poſtremo* is undoubtedly the claſſical word; and, as elegance of conſtruction ſhould be particularly regarded in theſe little things, it ſhould alſo have been placed after *Die Octobris*, and not before it. *Die Octobris poſtremo.* It is ſttange, that when *poſtero*, or *poſteriore*, might have ſerved inſtead of a better word, that the author ſhould unluckily pitch upon poor *Ultimo*.

Anno ab Incarnatione.

If our author had known any thing of preciſion, he would certainly have added N. S. J. C. *i. e. Noſtri Salvatoris Jeſu Chriſti*, which would likewiſe have looked very pretty, ſince nothing in works of this kind is ſo pretty as ſingle capitals. But why could not ſimply *Anno Domini* have ſerved his turn, as brevity is no leſs to be conſulted in inſcriptions? I ſuppoſe he was afraid, leſt poſterity ſhould miſtake it for the *year of the lord* mayor. However, if the author had been the leaſt acquainted with the cuſtom of the *Romans* on theſe occaſions, he might have borrowed a very elegant phraſe from them, I mean, *Anno Urbis Conditæ*, which

which would have preferved to pofterity the precife æra when the city of *London* was firft built; and this, there is no doubt, might have been accurately fixed by the *Antiquarian* fociety, affifted in their enquiries by the ruins of the city-gates.

MDCCLX.

It may feem odd, that I fhould find fault with thefe innocent letters; but precifenefs obliges me to point out, that they are never applied in this manner in *Latin* infcriptions. Had the author but dipped into *Montfaucon*'s or *Graevius*'s *Antiquities*, or even *Stow*'s *Survey of London*, he would have found, that, inftead of CC, he fhould have ufed CIↃ; and the leaft obfervation would have informed him, that a point or dot was neceffary after fome of the letters, as thus M.D CIↃ.LX. The virtuofo's eye muft be as much hurt by the vulgar MDCCLX, as it would be by the barbarous *Arabic* numerals 1760.

Aufpicatiffimo Principe GEORGIO *Tertio Regnum jam ineunte.*

Aufpicatiffimo (the moft aufpicious) befides being a moft egregious Anglicifm, is, at beft, but a very doubtful compliment to his prefent majefty. I have looked into *Holyoak*'s dictionary, as it is vulgarly called, though the firft, and beft impreffion, properly ftiles it, *Vocabularium a Sancta Quercu*. There I find *Aufpicatus* [ab *Aufpicium*] *aufpicious*, malo fenfu frequenter ufitat. Omen aufpicatum, *i. e.* corvorum, CIC. Aufpicata Mulier,

lier. PLAUT. **A bad Woman.** Now, among the moſt numerous and moſt illuſtrious tribe of *iſſimi*, could not the author have culled out ſome choice epithet of the ſuperlative degree, that would not be liable to a double meaning? Surely he might have met with *pick and chuſe* in abundance from the dedications to foreign potentates; ſuch as in thoſe to the *French* king, *Chriſtianiſſimo*, to the *Spaniſh*, *Catholiciſſimo*, to his holineſs the pope, *Sacro-Sanctiſſimo*. But the epithet, that might at once have occurred to our author, as moſt ſuitable to his preſent majeſty's character, (and, I am ſure, every one will agree with me) is . . . . OPTIMO.

To proceed . . . . Our author is ſo deſirous of ſetting down at length, what ought to be expreſſed in figures only (contrary to the known rules of inſcription-writing) that here again he muſt ſubſtitute Georgio *tertio*, inſtead of Georgio III. as he would needs have ultimo die Octobris, in the room of *die Octobris* XXXI. I aſk him, did he ever ſee Tertius or Secundus upon an halfpenny, a coin the neareſt approaching to the copper medals of the Cæſars? No. Even Charles the Second, who would not ſtile himſelf either II. or Secundus (for fear, I ſuppoſe, of offending the Puritans) elegantly ſtamped himſelf, on his earlieſt coins, *Carolus a Carolo*; and I could not have blamed our author, if, inſtead of lengthen-

ing

ing out III. to *Tertio*, he had further extended it into *Georgio a Friderico a Georgio a Georgio.*

Regnum jam ineunte.

It is hoped, that the news-papers, magazines, and other faithful hiſtories of the preſent times, will convince poſterity that his majeſty king *George the Third* was, on the laſt day of *October*, 1760, actually in the kingdom; otherwiſe, from the above expreſſion, they might naturally conclude the contrary, ſince *regnum jam ineunte* can only be conſtrued, *juſt now coming into the kingdom*; and ſhould the unfortunate *Tertio* in the line above happen to be defaced or worn out, poſterity will be apt to imagine, that the bridge begun to be built at the time that *George the Firſt* landed on the Engliſh ſhore from Hanover.

Pontis hujus, in reipublicæ commodum urbiſque majeſtatem.

Here again my friend Holyoak muſt be called in to inform our author, that the prepoſition *in*, with an accuſative caſe following it, generally ſignifies *againſt*, and not *for*; ſo that the ſenſe of this paſſage might be, that the bridge was ſet on foot *to the detriment of the publick, and derogatory of the majeſty of the city of* London. Nor would this interpretation appear ſtrange, conſidering the great diſputes that have ariſen about the form and conſtruction of its arches. But allowing this ſentence to bear a good meaning, it is certainly neceſſary

ceſſary to make a ſlight tranſpoſition of the words thus .... *In Reipublicæ Majeſtatem, Urbiſque Commodum* ... for every one muſt agree with me, that the bridge is undoubtedly erected *for the accommodation of the city.*

Before I have done with this paſſage, I muſt remark, that every *claſſic* eye muſt be offended with ſeeing *reipublicæ* ſpelt at length, and made only one word of; whereas it ought to have been ſplit in two, or, at leaſt, contracted to *reip.* or *reipubl.* or to *Rpublicæ,* or ſimply *R. P.* which latter is perhaps the moſt elegant way of writing it, as it is certainly the moſt ancient, and (what muſt further recommend it) conſiſts only of capitals.

Latè tum flagrante Bello.

What muſt poſterity ſuppoſe from this ſentence (which is put in a parentheſis, and might indeed be better omitted) but that the bridge was built purely *on account of the war?* And can they conceive any other reaſon, but that it was merely deſigned for the conveniency only of the trained-bands croſſing the water? Otherwiſe, what ſignifies it, whether the bridge was built in war-time or in peace? Suppoſe our worthy citizens had ſet about it at the time of the laſt dreadful fire by St. *Magnus* church, the inſcription, in that caſe, might have run .... *Latè tum flagrante* IGNI ... and this too with ſome ſhadow of a meaning, as it might have been ſuppoſed, that the eſpouſers of *Black Friars* bridge thereby meant to expreſs their ſecret

ſecret wiſh, that the fire might reach as far as its antagoniſt, the temporary-bridge. But, after all, what has *tum* to do in this paſſage? Is it placed there to ſignify, that the war raged on the laſt day of *October* particularly, or at the very inſtant of my lord-mayor's laying the firſt ſtone?

Pontis hujus . . . . . .
a S. P. Q. L. *ſuſcepti.*

Here the author has for once aukwardly attempted to copy the uſage of the ancients on their publick inſcriptions. Every ſchool-boy can tell him, that S. P. Q. R. ſignifies the whole ſtate of *Rome*, that is, the ſenate and the people: But let us examine, whether S. P. Q. L. comprehends the whole city of *London*. Now it is well known, that the commonwealth of *Rome* was made up only of two bodies, to wit, the ſenate and the people; whereas the city is compoſed of,

1. The lord-mayor, or *prætor*.

2. The aldermen, or *aldermanni*, (there being no *Latin* term equal to their dignity.)

3. The common council men, or *Communis Concilii Fratres*.

4. The ordinary freemen, or *Liberti*.

Therefore the above capitals are not ſufficient to denote this extenſive corporation, but they ſhould ſtand thus:

a P.

a P. A. C. C. F. L. Q. L.

i. e. *Prætore, Aldermannis, Communis Concilii Fratribus, Libertisq; Londinensibus.* And how much more noble do these numerous capitals look (P. A. C. C. F. L. Q. L.) than the sneaking S. P. Q. R. of the *Romans!*

But what are we to understand by *Pontis suscepti?* Let us again consult *Holyoak*, and he will inform us, that *suscipere opus*, or *suscipere negotium*, may signify *to undertake any work* or *business*; but *suscipere onus*, or *suscipere pontem*, must have a different construction; and *Pontis a S. P. Q. L. suscepti*, in this place, can only be understood, *that the lord-mayor, aldermen, common council, and citizens, took up the bridge on their shoulders, and carried it clean off.*

Primum Lapidem posuit
THOMAS CHITTY, *Miles*,
Prætor:
ROBERTO MYLNE, *Architecto.*

The superficial common scholar will hardly conceive that any mistakes can possibly have been made in this plain and simple sentence; but any one, who is conversant in the method of inscriptions, will discover many blunders.

I am credibly informed, that the first plate, on which the inscription was engraved, was obliged to be laid aside on account of the engraver, who

did

did not underſtand *Latin*, cutting the line . . . *Thos. Chitty Miles*, (as if it was Mr. *Thos. Chitty Miles*) inſtead of, *Thomas Chitty*, Miles, *a knight*: And no wonder, that the ignorant artiſt ſhould commit ſuch a blunder, when the manuſcript had it originally *Thos.* a barbarous abbreviation of *Thomas*, and the word *Dominus*, as *Latin* for *Sir*, (i. e. *Knight*) inſtead of *Miles*. But does not any one ſee, that *Chitty* ſhould have been *Chittius*, or rather *Chitteius*, as in the next line *Mylne* ſhould be *Mylneio*, *Thomas Chitteius*, *Roberto Mylneio*? It is, indeed, a pity, that theſe words will not bear to be converted into true *Latin*, like my friend *Holyoak* into *Sancta Quercus*; or, as the Rev. *George White* ſtiled himſelf *Agricola Candidus* *. But, as this cannot be, they ought, at leaſt, to have a *Latin* termination; and every judge of antiquity will agree with me, that, without this addition, theſe names will ſound no better than the familiar appellations of *Tom Chitty* and *Bob Mylne*.

* This excellent genius formerly publiſhed a *Latin* news-paper, and ſtiled himſelf by the name above-mentioned. He was, indeed, obliged to have recourſe to the *Greek* language, as well as the *Latin*, on this occaſion. Finding out, that *George*, or rather *Georgus*, would in *Greek* characters be Γεωργος, and then finding out (in *Schrevelius's Lexicon*) that this meant *Agricola*, he very happily firſt *græcized*, thence *latinized*, his *pronomen* into that excellent appellation.

Utque

Utque apud Posteros extet Monumentum Voluntatis suæ ergà Virum.

Voluntatis suæ: It is hard to determine, whether this means the *Bridge*'s affection, or *Thomas Chitty*'s and *Robert Mylne*'s, whose names immediately go before; but it is obvious, that in the first line, the author has a double meaning, and intends a compliment to one of the city structures ... *Ut apud Posteros extet* MONUMENTUM; *that the* MONUMENT *may stand to posterity.* In return for this patriotic wish, I would propose, that, as some have idly conceived a prejudice against *Elliptic* arches (the most strong and beautiful of any) this line should be fixed on the center arch, with a slight alteration,

APUD POSTEROS EXTET PONS.

Qui Vigore Ingenii, Animi Constantiâ,
Probitatis & Virtutis, suæ felici quadam Contagione.

The first line might have been this, that, or t'other; but, in the name of *Latin*, what is this *felici quadam Contagione?* . . . By a certain kind of a sort of an happy contagion .... of what? ... *Probitatis & Virtutis suæ* . . . his own probity and virtue. Stay ... I shall wear out poor *Holyoak*, having used him at, and ever since I left, school .... but no matter ... let me see . . . oh . . . *Contagio*, f. [*a* contactus, *contangere*] *Contagion* ... Now for his instances . . . *Abisis* contagionem spirat, TER. and many others, not

one

one of which but gives the word in a bad ſenſe. But even allowing that *Contagio* may be taken in a good ſenſe, as it is qualified with the epithet of *felix*, the line, after twiſting and winding it which way you pleaſe, can only be underſtood, that Mr. Pitt *caught the happy contagion of his own probity and ſpirit*. But the author undoubtedly intended an inuendo by this paſſage, that the lord-mayor, aldermen, and the reſt of the citizens, were *infected* with the ſame probity and ſpirit.

Imperium Britannicum
in Aſiâ, Africâ, et Americâ,
reſtituit, auxit, et ſtabilivit.

From the order of the words, and from the common method obſerved in inſcriptions, poſterity will doubtleſs conceive, that the author meant to particularize the different ſucceſs of our arms in different parts of the globe; and they will naturally underſtand this paſſage as follows:

In Aſiâ reſtituit,	*In Africâ auxit,*	*In Americâ, ſtabilivit.*

that is, he reſtored the *Britiſh* empire in *Aſia*, he augmented it in *Africa*, he ſecured it in *America*. Every body knows, that inſcriptions ſhould be as plain as poſſible, and the leaſt liable to have their ſenſe miſtaken: I therefore cannot ſuppoſe, that our author ſhould depart from this known rule, but rather imagine, that ſome officious would-be-critic foiſted in this line about *Aſia*,

Africa, and *America*, becauſe *Europe* happens to come in the next ſentence, and he was willing to have all the four quarters of the globe together. I am convinced, that our author would rather have brought in all the four winds, and have written it, *In Euro, in Boreâ, in Auſtro*, &c. Or had he ſaid, *cum in Aſiâ, tum in Africâ, et Americâ reſtituit, auxit, et ſtabilivit*, there could have been no room to doubt of its meaning.

Necnon patriæ antiquum Honorem et Auctoritatem inter Europæ Gentes inſtauravit.

A little lad, a relation of mine, who is in the third form at *Weſtminſter* ſchool, happened to call upon me juſt as I had finiſhed my laſt remark. I ſet him to conſtrue this paſſage. He began . . . *Nec non*, alſo . . . *inſtauravit*, he, he, he, [reſtored, child ?] reſtored . . . *antiquum honorem*, the ancient honour . . . *et auctoritatem*, and the authority . . . [good boy ! wonderful !] . . . *patriæ* . . . [well !] of their countries . . . [*their* countries, child ?] . . . . Yes, uncle, *inter Europæ Gentes*, among the nations of *Europe*. Upon my word, the boy ſet the paſſage in a different light to what perhaps I ſhould have ſeen it in ; and poſterity muſt conſider our great patriot as the patriot of all countries, foes or friends, when they underſtand, from this ſentence (as it cannot be well conſtrued otherwiſe) *that he reſtored the ancient honour and authority* [*not only of his own, but*] *of* each their ſeveral reſpective countries *to all the nations*,

tions of Europe. Had, indeed, the little word *ſuæ* here happened to have ſlipt in . . . *Patriæ* ſuæ *antiquum Honorem & Auctoritatem*, &c. it would have given the ſentence that meaning which the author doubtleſs intended it ſhould convey.

Cives Londinenſes, uno Conſenſu,
huic Ponti inſcribi voluerunt Nomen
GULIELMI PITT.

It cannot be ſufficiently lamented, that the inſcription throughout is ſo intirely devoid of the genuine marks of juſt and claſſical compoſition. I have pointed out the egregious ignorance of the author, in this kind of writing, in his very firſt line, *in veſtibulo*, as it were ; and he has ſhewn no leſs ignorance in the concluſion. *Cives Londinenſes* . . . What a pity it is, that he had not made uſe of that magnificent range of capitals, P. A. C. C. F. L. Q. L. as before recommended ! but how ſhocking is it, that the ignorant has not had reading enough to know, that the letters C. L. (nothing more than C. L.) were more full, more expreſſive, or more intelligible, and more *inſcriptive* by themſelves, than with the uſeleſs addition of *ives ondinenſes !*

The common reader will hardly imagine that I ſhould be able to ſpy out any miſtake in the laſt line, *Gulielmi Pitt* ; but I hope to prove, to the ſatisfaction of every body, at leaſt of every *antiquary*, that the author is wrong in both the *chriſtian* and *ſurname* of this gentleman. Firſt then, it is well known, that the word *Gulielmi* was never uſed in inſcriptions, except upon the barbarous modern medals, or coins, of king *William* III. I wonder the author did not write it, *Williami*, which is certainly as good *Latin* for *William*, as this ſtrange *Gulielmi* ; at leaſt, he might have *barbaro-latinized* it into *Wilhelmi*, or (as the chaſte *Roman* alphabet abhorred a VV or W) called it *Vilhelmi*. But, if it muſt be ſomething like *Gulielmi*, is it not notorious, that it ſhould be ſpelt Guil*elmi* and not Guli*elmi*, as it is vulgarly and ignorantly written ?

But to come to the name *Pitt* . . . . . O what a glorious opportunity was here let ſlip of naturalizing an *Engliſh* name into the *Latin* tongue, by a *latinization* of it . . . . *Pitt ! Pitt !* a LOW *Engliſh* word ! Sink, ditch, bog, quagmire, would ſound equally noble. But if, inſtead of this, it had been written *Foſſa*, how grandly would that have ſounded ! And, ſurely, every admirer of antique learning will agree with me, that *Foſſa !* Guil*elmi Foſſæ !* . . . would have made the illuſtrious name of the *Foſſas* adored and remembered to all poſterity.

As to the objection, which will poſſibly be raiſed, that poſterity may perhaps apprehend the word *Foſſa* to mean *Ditch* inſtead of *Pitt*, that can have no force at all, as they will eaſily find, that though *Will Pitt* was at the head of the miniſtry at

this

this prefent time, there was no fuch perfon joined with him in the adminiftration, as *Will Ditch*. It is true, indeed, that the city formerly joined *two* names together in their prefentation of their freedom and gold boxes: It might therefore be a matter of fome wonder, that they did not think fit to couple them on the prefent occafion, and at the fame time that they immortalized Guil*elmus Foffa*, they did not pay the fame honours to *Henricus Bilfonus Crus*.

And now I have touched upon the fubject of converting *Englifh* proper names into *Latin*, I fhall beg leave to enlarge upon it a little further, and to fhew its peculiar elegance and propriety. We cannot but be fenfible, that moft of our *Englifh* names, which have any meaning at all, are borrowed from the loweft, and fometimes the moft ridiculous, as well as offenfive objects. Thus, for inftance, what can be more fhocking to a delicate ear, than Mangey, Rag, Belcher, Gorge, Grub, Trollop, Nanny, Huffey, &c. &c. &c. Not to mention fome others, that border very nearly on indecency. Many, again, take their appellation from the loweft tradefmen and mechanics; fuch as Smith, Mafon, Gardener, Packer, Dyer, Turner, Taylor, Cook, Cooper, Carter, Draper, Glover, Butcher, Plumber, Painter, Carpenter, &c. Almoft all kinds of beafts, birds, and fifhes, are alfo to be found among us; as Buck, Stag, Hart, Hind, Fox, Hare, Bull, Bullock, Lamb;—Duck,

Drake, Gosling, Crow, Hawk, Kite, Heron, Crane, Parrot, Partridge, Cock, Woodcock ;—Sprat, Herring, Crab, Whiting, Salmon, &c. The four quarters of the wind, East, West, North, and South, are also frequently used as surnames ; and almost all the colours of the rainbow are appropriated to the same purposes ; as Green, Scarlet, Grey, Brown, Black, Blackall, Blackmore, White, Whitehead, Redhead, &c. Even the different parts of our habitations furnish us with no inconsiderable number of names : We have House, Garden, Court, Wall, Hall, Kitchen, Garret, Stair, Chambers, Wood, Stone, Lock, Key, Street, Lane, &c. We have also Fields, Meadows, Hills, Rivers, Lakes, Ponds, Pools, Dykes, Hedges, &c. in abundance. Some parts of the body likewise serve for the same end ; as Head, Scull, Leg, Foot, Trotter, &c. But why need I dwell any longer on this subject ? There are Rich and Poor, Sharp and Blunt, Young and Eld, Long and Short, Small and Great, Walker and Rider, Swift, Hastings, and On-slow ; with a variety of other names taken from the most common actions of our lives.

Let us then suppose, that these names, or the most vulgar and disagreeable of them, were to be changed into *Latin* : It would perhaps be objected, that the words in either language would still bear the same import ; yet it must be allowed, that the sound being altered, the ear is not so immediately

mediately ſhocked, or the mind ſo directly ſtruck with the vulgarneſs or indelicacy of their meaning. For inſtance, though the name *Belcher* ſhould of right belong to nobody but a *Dutchman*, the *Latin* word *Eructator* greatly alleviates the filthineſs of its meaning by the magnificence of its ſound; at leaſt, it would not be inferior to the title of that emperor, who laid a tax on a certain natural evacuation, and was thence, by his flatterers, ſtiled *Urinator*. Beſides, there are a great many *Engliſh* names, that nearly reſemble thoſe of the moſt illuſtrious families and offices in old *Rome*: Thus the *Smiths*, by a very fair alluſion, might be ſtiled FABRICII, the *Gardeners* HORTENSII, the *Taylors* SARTORII, the *Drapers* TOGATI, the *Maſons* ÆDILES, *&c. &c. &c.* So, in other inſtances, *Long* would be readily converted into LONGINUS, as *Short* would be CURTIUS, *Great* or *Greathead* might be called MAXIMUS, or CAPITO MAXIMUS; *Young* (eſpecially the reverend ſatiriſt of that name) would not be improperly ſtiled JUVENALIS, as *Eld* or *Oldham* might fairly make SENECA: *Swift* or *Haſtings* is FESTINUS, and *On-ſlow* directly anſwers to LENTULUS. So alſo among the colours, *White* may be either ALBIUS or CANDIDUS, as *Black* or *Blackall* may at once aſſume the title of the emperor NIGER: And pray what is FUSCUS, to whom *Horace* addreſſes one of his odes, but downright *Brown*? Suppoſe, therefore, a gentleman of the name of *Wenman* or *Warton*, would he not be proud to be called after CICERO, who received that name on account of a *wen* or *wart* growing on the ſide of his face? And the *Italian* muſician, whom the courteſy of the galleries have, in a manner, naturalized by the appellation of *Noſy*, would, I believe, very readily exchange it for that of the poet NASO; whom we may conclude to have been ſo called for the very ſame reaſon, if we conſider his ſuppoſed intimacy with a certain lady of the firſt faſhion in his time.

But the utility of this proceeding is ſtill further evident from the practice of other nations in affairs of this kind. The *French*, perhaps conſcious of the lightneſs and futility of their own language, always make uſe of this manner of writing on their public monuments; and their famous *Academy of Inſcriptions*, &c. was eſtabliſhed for ſcarce any other purpoſe, than to find out proper *Latin* words for the names of thoſe illuſtrious perſonages, who are, by theſe means, to be immortalized. Thus, on a medal ſtruck in memory of their famous poet *Racine*, that word ſignifying a *Root*, they have called him *Radix*; on another, in honour of the two *Corneilles*, father and ſon, they have been contented, by a ſlight mutation, to ſtile them *Cornelii Pat.* et *Fil.* i. e. *Pater* et *Filius*; but, I am informed, they are preparing another alſo for the *ſon* of the latter, on which is to be inſcribed

ſcribed the claſſical name of CORNELIUS NEPOS . . . *Nepos*, in their language, ſignifying the *Petit-Fils* or *Grandſon*.

The *Dutch* (who have always preſerved a true taſte for compoſitions of this kind, as well as for the fineſt branch of criticiſm, that of emending letters) are very accurate in the tranſlations of their excellent *Dutch* names into *Latin*. One inſtance may ſuffice for all. In the church of *Rotterdam*, on the monument of that famous burgomaſter (the firſt projector of ſtock-jobbing) **Mynheer Van Hugger-Mugger Higgledy-Piggledy Helter-Skelter**, he is conciſely ſtiled, in the moſt elegant latinity . . . *Omnium Gatherum*.

Having then theſe great examples before our eyes, what ſhould hinder this nation, which, though ſlow at invention, is every ready at improvement, from making itſelf equally remarkable for its taſte in ſimilar undertakings. A noble opportunity offers itſelf in the public monument ſhortly to be erected; and, if the inſcription concerning a city bridge muſt be in *Latin*, the inſcription on this monument will undoubtedly be in the ſame language; at leaſt it ought to be ſo, if for no other reaſon, than that the name of *Wolf* will admit to be *latinized* into *Lupus*.

But to return from this digreſſion . . . As I have found ſo much fault with the preſent form of the *city inſcription*, I may be aſked, perhaps, what other would I ſubſtitute in its ſtead? To this I anſwer . . . . If we would conſult elegance, clearneſs, ſtrength, and brevity of expreſſion, if we would regard the uſual practice in theſe caſes, it ſhould certainly run ſomewhat in the following manner.

NON. VIII. MENS.
A. U. C. MM.C.LXXIX.
T. CHITTEIO PR.
PONT.
AP. A. C. C. F. L. Q. L. CONSTR.
LAP. P. P.

What can be more plain and intelligible than this? What can look nobler and more ſignificant than this? An antiquarian could hang over it with rapture for hours, nay years together, and find out the beauty of every ſingle capital. But, as the author of the prolix and wordy *city inſcription* will doubtleſs be puzzled to get at its meaning, I will condeſcend to become a decypherer to his ignorance.

NON. VIII. MENS. *Nonis Octavi Menſis*, on the nones of the eighth month, that is, *October* 31.

If we look, indeed, into the *Roman* calendar, as adapted to ours, at the end of the dictionaries, we ſhall find it differently ſet down; but, alas! the editors have never conſidered the *alteration of the ſtyle*.

A. U.

A. U. C. MM.C.LXXIX. *Anno Urbis Conditæ*, in the year from the firſt building of the city, 2179.

The date of this æra is modeſtly ſet down from authentic records; but there are traces of its foundation much earlier; though it does not appear, either from *Stow*'s *Survey*, or *Maitland*'s *Hiſtory of London*, that the mayors were called *lords*, or that any of the citizens were *knighted*, till a long while after this period.

T. CHITTEIO PR. *Thomâ Chitteio Prætore*, *Thomas Chitty* being mayor.

Though no one can be better affected to his majeſty than myſelf; yet I thought it unneceſſary, in a city inſcription, to mention the time of his *beginning to reign*, eſpecially if no expreſſion can be found than *regnum jam ineunte*. It is ſufficient to remark the preciſe date by the manner I have done; from the year of the firſt building of the city: But if this ſhould be uncertain, authentic records will fully prove it, by informing poſterity in what year *Thomas Chitty* was mayor; and, as to *Georgio Tertio Regnum jam ineunte*, it might as well have been ſaid *Thomâ Chitty Mayoraltum jam exeunte*, *Thomas Chitty* juſt going out of his mayoralty.

PONT. A. P. A. C. C. F. L. Q. L. CONSTR. LAP. P. P. *Pontis a Prætore*, *Aldermannis*, &c. (as explained before) *conſtruendi Lapis primus ponebatur*,

batur, of a bridge to be built by the mayor, aldermen, &c. the firſt ſtone was laid . . . This is clear, ſhort, and ſignificant . . . But, you will ſay, as a compliment to Mr. *Pitt* is neceſſary, how is that to be expreſſed ? Why in the ſame conciſe and intelligible manner.

GUIL. FOSSÆ.
PATR. PATRIÆ D. D. D.

Is there any occaſion to explain theſe letters ? *Guilelmo Foſſæ Patri Patriæ Datur, Dicatur, Dedicatur*, dedicated to *William Pitt*, the father of his country.

It is now high time to have done with this dry and unintereſting ſubject; for ſo it may appear to all, who are not converſant in antiquity: And though I could eaſily have confirmed my remarks by numerous quotations from ancient and modern authors and critics, yet I chuſe rather to leave it to the true virtuoſo to determine, whether my criticiſms are juſt or groundleſs. I ſhall only obſerve further, that, as the inſcription, which has given riſe to this little work, is ſaid to have been engraven on *pure tin*, I think, with more propriety, it might have been upon *pure lead*.

POSTSCRIPT.

POSTSCRIPT.

My publiſher having informed me, that this pamphlet was refuſed a place in the Daily Advertiſer, *I ſent my amanuenſis to* Jenour over the door, *to know the reaſon; but the fellow having been accuſtomed only to ſet down ſo many words, without knowing, or even enquiring after, their meaning . . . conſequently having very little practice of memory . . . he quite forgot what was ſaid to him. I muſt therefore deſire* Jenour over the door *will be pleaſed to acquaint my publiſher, why the ſame favour ſhould not be ſhewn by him to* my *learned labours, as to other works of genius and literature; eſpecially as* Jenour over the door *could not have read a line of my work, as the advertiſement was ſent him before it was publiſhed.*

A veritable

A veritable Coppie of the Inſcripcione founde by me Martin Marforius, in the Barge belongynge to the ryghte worſchippfull Companie of Stationers; ſeid to be penned by that notable Penman and profounde Scholler icleppd Johan. R—b—ngTonie, Armiger, Commun. Concilij. Frater, Bibliopol. Archiepiſc. Cantuarienſ. & Court-aſſiſtant-mannus Stationariorum, Lond.

THIS

BARG[e] wAs buiLt

1766.

henry woodFaLL maſter

domIne dirGe nos

On Mr. Yorke's *taking a Patent of Precedence in* 1764.

YORKE's great humility, I own,
At firſt may ſeem a ſtretcher;
He takes a patent from the crown,
To ſit ——— below Sir Fletcher.

Epigram on a Counſellor's having his Hat ſtolen in Weſtminſter-Hall.

SHould'ſt thou to juſtice, honeſt thief, be led,
Swear that you ſtole his hat who had no head.
That plea alone all danger ſhall remove,
Nor judge, nor jury can the damage prove.

Inſcription

Inſcription found upon a Stone ploughed up in a Field in Devonſhire, *that was formerly a Lake.*

WHEN e'er this ſtone, now hid beneath the lake,
The horſe ſhall trample, or the plough ſhall break;
Then, oh, my country! ſhalt thou groan diſtreſt,
Tears fill thine eyes, and ſorrow chill thy breaſt;
Thy ſtreets with violence of woe ſhall ſound
Loud as the billows burſting on the ground;
Then o'er thy fields ſhall ſcarlet reptiles ſtray,
And murthers and pollutions mark their way;
Shall glutton on the induſtrious peaſant's ſoil,
Live without care, and fatten without toil.

A Scottiſh thane ſhall triumph in this land,
And Engliſh ſubjects die at his command;
Judges and juſtices revere his nod,
Obey his mandates, and deſpiſe their God.
The *Moon* * enrag'd, the affrighted *Bear* † ſhall dread,
Lilies ‡ triumphant o'er the vale ſhall ſpread,
And traiterous m——s hide their guilty head.

* The Turkiſh creſcent. † The Ruſſians.
§ France.

Extempore by a POETICAL JUNTO, *on hearing a certain impertinent Addrefs in the News-Papers.*

THOU effence of dock, of valerian and fage,
At once the difgrace and the peft of this age,
The worft that we wifh thee for all thy damn'd crimes,
Is to take thy own phyfic and read thy own rhimes.

Anfwer to the JUNTO.

THEIR wifh muft be in form revers'd,
To fuit the doctor's crimes;
For, if he takes his phyfic firft,
He'll never read his rhimes.

Dr. H——'s Reply to the JUNTO's *Epigram.*

YE defperate junto, ye great, or ye fmall,
Who combat dukes, doctors, the devil and all!
Whether gentlemen, fcribblers, or poets in jail,
Your impertinent curfes fhall never prevail:
I'll take neither *fage*, *dock*, nor *balfam of honey*;
Do you take the phyfic, and I'll take the money.

ANTI-JUNTO.

EPIGRAM,

By DAVID GARRICK, *Esq;*

Written soon after Dr. HILL's *Farce called* THE ROUTE *was acted.*

FOR physic and farces,
His equal there scarce is;
His farces are physic,
His physic a farce is.

To Dr. Hill *upon his Petition of the Letter* I *to Mr.* Garrick. *By the same.*

IF 'tis true, as you say, that I've injur'd a letter,
I'll change my note soon, and I hope for the better;
May the just right of *letters*, as well as of *men*,
Hereafter be fixed by the tongue and the pen;
Most devoutly I wish that they both have their due,
And that *I* may be never mistaken for *U*.

Epitaph on Jerry Sneak *the Taylor.*

READER, within this turf-rais'd grave
There lies the body of a knave;
Nor deem it strange, this stone should tell,
That while he liv'd, he liv'd in *hell*;

Now

Now death has rid him of that evil,
He's gone *in earneſt* to the *devil.*

On the grave-ſtone, upon which is inſcribed the above epitaph, is figured a cluſter of angels looking down from the clouds, that are meant to repreſent heaven, with arms extended as if about to receive the taylor; which circumſtance, together with the inſcription, gave riſe to the four following lines, that were written extempore underneath it:

Sad verſe to read! but charming ſight to ſee!
How *ill* the *ſculptor* and the *bard* agree:
To different men, what different arts are giv'n;
One ſings of *hell*, the other pictures *heav'n!*

To the EDITOR.

THE following is the moſt exact copy I could procure of the Latin inſcription upon the column intended very ſoon to be erected in the centre of the area, before a very grand houſe, now building on a pleaſant ſpot not far from town. It is ſuppoſed to have been written by the celebrated Monſ. de Bouganville, profeſſor in the academy of inſcriptions and belles lettres at Paris, the ſame who writ the Latin epitaph on the marble monument, ſent over to Quebec, for the Baron de Dieſkau.

In

In Memoriam
Nob, Dom. Vice Com. H———
In hâc Viciniâ olim defuncti
Ob dimidiam Rei familiaris partem
fibi legatam,
(Uxore et fratris filio defuncti nobilis
etiam fuperftitibus)
Et nullam aliam ob Gratiam de illo
bene merenti,
Nifi quod ægroto in extremâ Valetudine
affiduè affuit,
Atque in ipfius mortis Articulo
Teftamentum fupremum
compofuit,
Ædificium hoc ex lateribus conftructum,
Viatorum Admiratis,
Vicinorum Invidia,
Ut Monumentum fidelis amicitiæ
Et Domicilium fibi met ipfi accommodatum,
A poffeffore præfenti,
Attornato Artis fuæ haud imperito,
Extrema licet Senectute,
Erigitur.
Idus Jul. An. Sal. 1768.
Accede, Viator, contemplare, et fi
poteris, imitare.

To a certain Magiſtrate on the Dedication of a Tower to him in the Iſle of Thanet.

CURSED by the friends of liberty reſtored,
By Tories praiſed, by Jacobites adored;
What elſe remained to ſtigmatize thy cauſe?
Nought—but expiring H—d's laſt applauſe.

Inſcription for the Villa of a decay'd Satesman on the Sea-Coaſt.

OLD and abandon'd by each venal friend,
Here H**** form'd the pious reſolution,
To ſmuggle ſome few years, and ſtrive to mend
A broken character, and conſtitution.
On this congenial ſpot he fix'd his choice,
(Earl Goodwin trembled for his neighb'ring ſand)
Here ſea gulls ſcream, and cormorants rejoice,
And mariners, tho' ſhipwreck'd, dread to land.
Here reigns the bluſt'ring North and blighting Eaſt;
No tree is heard to whiſper, bird to ſing,
Yet nature cannot furniſh out the feaſt:
Art he invokes new horrors ſtill to bring.
Now mould'ring fanes and battlements ariſe,
Arches, and turrets nodding to their fall,
Unpeopled palaces delude his eyes,
And mimic deſolation covers all:

" Ah!

" Ah ! (ſaid the ſighing peer) had B**e been true,
" Nor —'s, —'s, —'s friendſhip vain,
" Far other ſcenes than theſe had crown'd our view,
" And realiz'd the ruins that we feign.
" Purg'd by the ſword, and beautify'd by fire
" Then had we ſeen proud London's hated walls ;
" Owls might have hooted in St. Peter's choir,
" And *Foxes* ſtunk, and litter'd in St. Paul's."

The TIMES. 1768.

——————*Omnes congruunt*
Unum cognoris, omnes noris. TER.

FAME's mouth is ſteep, and he who dares aſ-
cend,
Will find his toils a thouſand foes attend :
Hence, G——m, much 'tis wonder'd, in theſe days,
How you acquire ſuch univerſal praiſe.
Mild, kind, and juſt, who, from your earlieſt youth,
Have ſpoke the *truth*, and nothing but the *truth !*
Tell them, by meekneſs taught—while lives a Bute,
While B—n S—e is M——d's ſubſtitute ;
While B——n, by nobleſt motives warm'd,
Applauds the deeds by *loyal* Scots perform'd ;
While H——d, honeſt to his lateſt hour,
To H——y's praiſe inſcribes the marble tower ;
While N—n pleads ; while W—b our juries claim,
You, though well-meaning, have but *ſecond* fame.

IMITATION. ANACR. Od. 46.

To J. W. *Esq;*

WOULD you wiſh to ſerve the ſtate,
Would you ſtrive with honours due,
That a court confeſs you great,
You, my friend, wrong ſchemes purſue.

Wiſdom that I know is your's,
Brighteſt talents too you boaſt;
But where gold extends its curſe,
All intrinſic merit's loſt.

'Tis the quantum that you pay,
For the corporation bought:
'Tis how ductile you obey,
By the grand dictator taught *.

Curs'd be he, the wretch of yore,
Who, from womb of parent earth,
Firſt produc'd the tempting ore,
Poiſon to all moral worth!

This domeſtic peace deſtroys,
This diſſolves all human ties;
Urg'd by this, a brother's joys
Are a brother's ſacrifice.

* Cet admirable maitre des muets, quand il leur donne ſes premieres leçons, forme avec ſes mains dans leurs organes la diſpoſition, qui eſt neceſſaire pour prononcer chaque lettre.

LAMY.

This,

This, where in the raptur'd ſoul
  Love ſhould boaſt his pureſt fire,
Does each gen'rous thought controul,
  Bids profeſſion's vow expire.

This (and let bold honour mourn,
  Hearing the recorded tale)
This bade P— a villain turn,
  This confines a W—s in jail.

Newport, Iſle of Wight,
    Sept. 12.

Epiſtle to John Wilkes, *Eſq; in Confinement.*

WHILE ev'ry truly Engliſh breaſt
  Swells with regret and rage poſſeſs'd,
    And mourns, O Wilkes, thy doom!
I rather joy, who hope to view
Thy ſteady ſoul her plan purſue,
  And equal ancient Rome.

See M——-—d, impotent of ſoul,
In pale and ſilent malice ſcowl,
  And yield to Y—s the blow!
Vain all their rage! thy noble heart
Invulnerable ſcorns the dart,
  Nor heeds the feeble foe.

Thus faithful to his country's good,
Unmov'd the menac'd Roman ſtood
  At all the Punic rage;

Bravely he met the death he dar'd,
Nor fear'd the cruel pains prepar'd,
Their malice to aſſuage.

Nor leſs the malice of thy foes
I deem, O man of many woes!
And much-enduring mind!
Nor leſs ſhall be thy fame: I ſee
Thy reſcu'd country ſmile on thee,
And glory gleam behind.

But ſhould a venal ſenate fear
To check oppreſſion's proud career,
Nor vindicate thy wrong,
Let hope, with conſcience to attend,
Be thy inſeparable friend,
And ſpeed the hours along.

Then let no penſive thought be thine,
Nor let thy patriot heart repine,
But be *theſe things* thy ſport;
For know—that time ſhall ſet thee free,
Unthank'd, relentleſs m——y,
Unthank'd a thoughtleſs court.

Oxford, June 30, 1768.

The

The whole present Dispute in Law and Politics.

TO contradict Wilkes, now M—— replies,
'Twixt *tenour* and *purport* no difference lies:
They both in one meaning appear to entwine,
Like tendrils that twist round the stem of a vine,
Tho' the one suits your purpose, the other suits mine.

To M—— cries Wilkes, I pray you, my lord,
Give its own honest meaning to each proper word:
Suppose, you should make a proposal to B—,
To bring in his C— (tho' we hope he can't do't)
The *purport* means only, his kinsman to bring
Thro' Scotland to England, and here make him—:
But the *tenour* implies, and with very good reason,
The unmaking another; and that's, you know, treason.

The LION *in the* TOILS. *A political Fable.*
By Mr. KENRICK.

Ex ungue leonem.

COMMITTED by the hand of power
To close confinement in the Tower,
Where many a dangerous beast we know
Is lodg'd for royal raree-show;
A lion, in a leopard's skin,
His spots without, his heart within,

Held forth to privilege his paw,
And claim'd protection of the law.

Alarm'd! the foreſt ſtare a-while!
The aſſes bray! the foxes ſmile!
And tygers tam'd, untry'd, condemn
Their brother brute too wild for them.
The ſages of the law conſult
The nature of his crimes occult,
While, wavering 'twixt the wrong and right,
They let him looſe, and hope his flight;
'Till, baſely hurt in bloody fray,
To diſtant lands he's lur'd away.

Let juſtice bring him now to ſhame:
The abſent ever are to blame.
Accus'd he ſtands of horrid crimes,
Strange to theſe loyal, pious times!
Againſt his king—a biſhop nods—
Nay, more, he ſcratch'd againſt the gods.
Behold the impious traitor's claw,
Known, and obnoxious to the law.

The lion heard, and, with diſdain,
Returning to his native plain,
Demands the records juſt and true,
The fine and puniſhment his due.
Appall'd deluded juſtice ſtands,
Her balance trembling in her hands,
Nor holds uprais'd th' avenging blade
Without the rancorous lynx's aid.

Again the ſnare of power is ſpread,
Incloſing his devoted head;
Again is urg'd the ſhame and ſin
Of ſpots upon a leopard's ſkin;
When lo! he caſts his wanton ſpoils,
And proves a lion in the toils.

HARRY *and* NAN.

An ELEGY, *in the Manner of* TIBULLUS.

I.

CAN Apollo reſiſt, or a poet refuſe,
When Harry and Nancy ſolicit the muſe;
A ſtateſman, who makes the whole nation his care,
And a nymph, who is almoſt as chaſte as ſhe's fair.

II.

Dear ſpouſy had led ſuch a damnable life,
He determin'd to keep any whore but his wife:
So Harry's affairs, like thoſe of the ſtate,
Have been pretty well handled and tickled of late.

III.

From fourteen to forty our provident Nan
Had devoted her life to the ſtudy of man,
And thought it a natural change of her ſtation,
From riding St. George, to ride over a nation.

IV.

Secret ſervice had waſted the national wealth,
But now——'tis the price of the miniſter's health:

An

An expence which the treaſury well may afford ;
She who ſerves him in bed, ſhould be paid at the
board.

V.

So lucky was Harry, that nothing could mend
His choice of a miſtreſs, but that of a friend ;
A friend ſo obliging, and yet ſo ſincere,
With pleaſure in one eye, in t'other a tear.

VI.

My friend holds the candle—the lovers debate,
And among them, God knows how they ſettle the
ſtate ;
Was there ever a nation ſo govern'd before,
By a jockey and gambler,—a p—p and a wh——?

A SONG.

WHILE a thouſand fine projects are plann'd
ev'ry day,
Old England to white-waſh, and make her look
gay,
The exorbitant price of proviſions forgot,
And ſtarving, I fear, is the poor people's lot.
Derry down, &c.

Tho' the markets are ſtor'd with good mutton and
beef,
To the tradeſman no help, to the poor no relief ;
By curs'd foreſtallers the rates are ſo high,
That none but a Jew or a Dutchman can buy.

Whilſt

Whilſt the ſtreets to enlarge, our good citizens
ſcheme,
And on pulling down houſes continually dream;
Theſe clever projectors, their wiſdom ſo great,
Forget, while they labour, poor wretches muſt eat.

While the purſe-proud directors, with riches o'er-
grown,
Are raiſing up mountains of timber and ſtone,
The poor ſcarce a bit of belly-timber can find,
To patch up their bodies and keep out the wind.

While our eaſtern baſhaws are amaſſing great
treaſure,
And making, and unmaking nabobs at their plea-
ſure;
While theſe wealthy engroſſers their millions tell
o'er,
The want of a dinner ten thouſand deplore.

As the right of their conqueſts are now in debate,
By the money obtain'd, and the blood of the ſtate,
If the nation is wrong'd, and no recompence made,
Demoliſh their charter, and give a free trade.

While the epicure alderman's cramming his belly,
And feaſting on pheaſants, on ven'ſon, and jelly,
While turtles and turbots his tables beſpread,
A poor family dines on a morſel of bread.

While guttling committees and companies meet,
To eat and to drink, and to drink and to eat;

Full

Full bellies regard not the poor man's diſtreſs;
Then what hopes of relief? And what means of redreſs?

Ye lords of the court, and great dons of the city,
On the poor people's wants and diſtreſſes take pity;
And when for the good of the nation you treat,
Contrive that the poor may have ſomething to eat.

The Particulars of a happy Government.

BLEST is that government where greedy knaves
Are ever plotting to make ſubjects ſlaves;
Where parliaments, intended to controul
Bad miniſters, themſelves fill up the roll;
Where all the money current thro' the land
Is yearly paid into the treaſurer's hand;
Where lords and gentlemen for places pray,
As ſtarving paupers do for pariſh pay;
Where politicks in dirty jobs conſiſt,
And office-clerks acquire juſt what they liſt;
Where ſelf all public duty diſannuls,
And wealth denotes baſe hearts and baſer ſkulls;
Where courts of law relax or ſtretch their power
As premier means to pardon or devour;
Where rapes, ſeduction, all unnotic'd paſs,
And ev'ry vicious peer may ſeize his laſs;

Where

Where murders ſleep unpuniſh'd, 'till the day
Which ſtateſmen's works of darkneſs will diſplay;
Where titles are beſtow'd to create tools,
And honeſt men are counted downright fools.

On the D. of B——'s *Arrival in* Ireland. 1768.

I.

SOFTLY ſweet in *Lydian* meaſure,
Let the flute reſound our pleaſure;
Stop the noiſe of rattling drums:
For the *Great* PEACEMAKER comes.

II.

Let no din of frightful war
With dread alarms his fancy ſcare;
Nor let the thund'ring cannons roar,
To ſpeak his welcome to the ſhore.

III.

You vile, you venal, ſlaviſh band,
In uſeleſs pageantry that ſtand,
Begone! he likes not your parade;
He hates a *martial* cavalcade.

IV.

But let the gently lulling lute
In mildeſt ſtrains the chief ſalute:
And let the thrum of light guittar
With grateful trifling pleaſe his ear.

V. Ye

V.

Ye matrons, twine the *olive* wreath,
Whofe valiant friends thro' him ftill breathe:
Ye maids, who have not loft a fpoufe,
Adorn with *thiftle* ev'ry houfe.

VI.

Ye ladies fair, fhew your regards,
And ftrew the ftreets with heaps of *cards*,
Be PAM with glad amazement dumb;
His fervant and his patron's come.

VII.

Ye fons of ALMA, tune your lays,
And fing your *worthy* fav'rite's praife,
Extol the heroes of his *name*,
Whofe valour won immortal fame.

VIII.

Chiefs, who the fword for FREEDOM drew,
Alike to *prince* and *people* true;
Nor barter'd fhame for fordid pelf;
Nor made the *public* yield to *felf*.

IX.

Laft in the glorious record be
The MARTYR for fweet LIBERTY;
Who for *religion* nobly bled,
And for his *virtue* loft his HEAD.

X. In

X.

In theſe bright patterns of renown,
Trace *worth* continual handed down:
Then ſay, what virtue of a *man*
Adorns *this worthy?*—if you can.

XI.

Deſcribe his dangers on the main,
Or on the great NEW-MARKET plain;
His wounds of *honour* in the *face*,
Or ſtripes his *back* got at a *race*.

XII.

Diſplay, to the admiring nations,
His wond'rous ſkill in *negotiations;*
Or, what more near engage his heart,
The tricks of the *ſtock-jobbing* art.

XIII.

The loſſes tell, which haughty SPAIN
Sorely lamented once *in vain;*
Soon he with *gen'rous eaſe* reſtor'd
The earnings of the BRITISH *ſword*

XIV.

Deſcribe the fall of GALLIC pride,
Her arms o'erthrown on ev'ry ſide;
And, that ſo high her creſt's now rais'd,
Be *this great* DUKE by *hirelings* prais'd.

Ireland, Sept. 6, 1768.

A Sailor's

A Sailor's Defcription of the Mafquerade:

As played before the King of Denmark *to a crouded, motley audience in the* Hay-market.

LITTLE Moll, faith, and I from Wapping
came up,
To fee the fine fhew and the folks;
But for fear of miftakes we thought beft for to fup;
For thefe courtiers have comical jokes.

When firft we came in, I was 'maz'd to behold,
Night at once was all chang'd into day:
The folks feem'd to roll like a vaft fea of gold,
And the gall'ry ftuft'd full like a play.

Little Moll dropp'd a-ftern, being afraid to make
fail,
'Till I at her helm took a fpell;
When whip in a trice, fhe fteer'd up within hail
Of the devil, juft landed from hell.

Lord blefs me, fays fhe, Ben! where have we got?
This company's too good for *we!*
Sure at home he was cold, and's come here to be
hot,
For fuch devils I never did fee!

The devil! ne'er mind—heave a-head, my dear
girl,
And I'll fhew you the KING of the crew;

Each

Each duke, ev'ry duchefs—each lady and earl,
And when I bump—do you court'fy *do!*

Like a *tragedy queen*, when Moll faw the king,
Plump *on her bare knees fhe fell down:*
But, by Neptune, I foon made her rife with a fpring,
And fwore fhe knew nought of the town.

We parted—and I, faith, who like to be fmart,
Clapp'd on board of a fhepherdefs fweet,
Who, with no other crook than her eyes, hook'd my heart,
As faft as if preft in the Fleet.

She pull'd me about (till parch'd was my mouth)
At the rate of ten knots by the log:
But I foon found this king was no tar—but a youth
For he Burgundy gave us as grog.

This gay little fhepherdefs, faith, was fo fmart,
She tow'd me from pillar to poft,
Some call'd me a lubber, unfit for my part,
And wreck'd on the mafquerade coaft.

Mandarins and nabobs were as plenty as *rice*,
Jews, Negroes, Banyans, and what not;
There were characters purchas'd at every price,
Unlefs the raw, bra, letter'd *Scot*.

In this ocean of pleafure, egad, there were tars,
Who ne'er paft the Buoy of the Nore;
There were foldiers, like Hymen, who knew not of wars,
And *domino* fools by the fcore.

There were pilgrims and quakers, blacks, witches, and nuns,
Minervas without fenfe or tongue,
Who falter'd and lifp'd out fome feminine puns:
"Do you know me?"—was all faid or fung.

Grave conjurors too, who ne'er conjur'd before,
And Harlequins heavy as drofs;
Mild *Night* too, who long fhone the fun of this fhore,
But fet in the fair Mrs. Rofs *.

Old wives were at once to dull gen'rals turn'd;
And *Tancred* in forrowful ftrain,
Wept PHILIP's wrongs — and then inftantly burn'd,
For Diana from lewd Drury-lane.

There was fupper they faid—we got nothing to eat;
Here a fort, there a town, here St. Paul:

* Behold in character of *Night*,
All clad in dark array,
Fanny appears!—the thought how right!—
Fanny has had her *Day*.

But all cramm'd, as at *ſhort allowance* of meat,
Gorging garriſons, gardens, and all.
By ſtrange kitchen alchymy every diſh
Seem'd tranſmuted for Epicure Mammon:
There was fiſhified fleſh, and fleſhified fiſh;
A calf's head ſeem'd a fine jole of ſalmon.
When I thought I took one thing another I got;
The French cook ſo well knew his trade,
That ev'ry thing look'd like what it was not,
And the diſhes were all MASQUERADE.
There were none loſt their wit, there were ſome loſt ſome ſweat,
In ſhort 'twas all Hebrew to me;
So my anchor I trip'd, with my kind little Bet,
And paid Moll *with a top-ſail* at ſea.

PARODY on CATO, Act II. Scene II.

On Occaſion of the Middleſex *Election in* December, 1768, *when the Candidates were* John Glynn, *Eſq;* (who was elected) *and Sir* W. B. Proctor.

Enter MURPHY.

Murphy.

WILLIAM ſends health to *John.*

John.

Could he ſend it
To my poor ſlaughter'd friends, it would be welcome.
Are not your orders to inſult the people?

Murphy.

My bufinefs is with you, Sir: *William* fees
The ftraits to which he's driven; but as he knows
Hibernian ftrength, is anxious for your life.

John.

My life is grafted on the public weal:
Wou'd he fave *me*, Sir, bid him fpare the *county*:
Tell your employer this, and tell him, *John*
Difdains a life which *he* has power to offer.

Murphy.

All Britain's minifters combine for *William*;
Her much-lov'd patriot's to a prifon doom'd,
Who late at *Brentford* robb'd him of his triumph.
Why will not *John*, then, be this *William*'s friend?

John.

Thofe very reafons thou haft urged, forbid it.

Murphy.

My orders, Sir, are to expoftulate,
And reafon with you, as from friend to friend:
Think on the bludgeons hov'ring o'er your head,
And threat'ning every hour to fall upon it:—
Still may you ftand high in the county's favour,
Which will rejoice and caft it's eyes on you,
Againft the next election

John.

Murphy, no more:
My foul difdains fo bafe a compromife.

5 *Murphy.*

Murphy.

William is well acquainted with your virtues,
And therefore ſets this value on your life:
Let him but have the honour of your friendſhip,
And name your terms.

John.

Bid him diſband his gangs, then
Reſtore the county to it's liberty,
Submit his actions to the public cenſure,
And ſtand the judgment of a *Britiſh* S—e—
Bid him do this, and know me for his friend.

Murphy.

The county, Sir, talks loudly of your wiſdom—

John.

Nay more;—tho' I wou'd never be employ'd
To clear the guilty, and to varniſh crimes;
Myſelf will mount the huſtings in his favour,
And ſtrive to gain his pardon from the people.

Murphy.

A ſtile like this becomes a candidate,
Who knows——

John.

——A ſtile like this becomes a *Briton.*

Murphy.

What is a *Briton*, that is *William*'s foe?

John.

Greater than *William*;—he's a friend to virtue.

Murphy,

Confider, Sir, that you're at *Brentford* now,
At the fnug table of your little prieft :
You don't now thunder down at *Weftminfter*,
With ev'ry patriot mouth to fecond you.

John.

Let him confider that who drove us hither;
His mob it was that made my friends difperfe,
And clear'd the huftings.—Alas! thy dazzled eye
Beholds this man in a falfe glaring light,
Which ftars and titles only throw upon him :
Didft thou but view him right, thou'dft fee him black
With twice ten thoufand complicated crimes,
That ftrike my foul with horror but to name 'em.
I know thou look'ft on me, as on a wretch
Befet with ills, and covered with misfortunes;
But by the gods I fwear, all *England*'s honours
Should never bribe me to be like that *William*.

Murphy.

Do you then fend this anfwer back to *William*,
For all his gen'rous cares, and proffer'd friendfhip?

John.

His cares for me are infolent and vain :
Prefumptuous man! the public are my friends.
Wou'd *William* fhew the greatnefs of his foul,

Bid

Bid him protect the widow and the orphan,
Made wretched by the curfed rage of party;
And make good ufe of all his ruffian gangs,
By ſhelt'ring men much better than himſelf:
So ſhall the poll henceforward ſmoothly run,
And honour end what murder has begun.

SCENE III.

FREEHOLDERS.

O *John!* we thank thee.
The mighty genius of old *Albion*'s iſle
Speaks in thy voice,—thy ſoul breathes liberty.
The *Thane* will ſhrink to hear the words thou utter'ſt,
And purge Bareges' waters, drank in vain.

M.

The MIDDLESEX ELECTION.

A BALLAD *on the ſame Occaſion.*

To the Tune of "Chevy Chace."

GOD proſper long our noble king,
And eke his ſubjects too;
And grant ſuch deeds as now I ſing
We never more may rue.
In ſeventeen hundred ſixty-eight,
All on a ſummer's day,

 Grim

Grim death did on our member wait,
And took him clean away.

O then a writ was iſſued *out*,
To chuſe a member *in*,
And ſoon began a mighty rout,
For *Proctor* and for *Glynn*.

When as the day advanced nigh,
Each party did its beſt ;
And *Horne* (who ſcorns to tell a lie)
Turn'd P——r's cauſe to jeſt.

Some worthy wights, the Lord knows who,
Of *Iriſh* ſtrength aſſur'd,
Provided many a gallant crew,
True men, I'll pawn my word.

Such crowds to Brentford town did hie,
As fill'd the place outright ;
While thouſands knew not where to lie,
And ſo—ſat up all night.

At length the fatal morning came,
O had it ne'er arriv'd !
For many a wight crawl'd home quite lame,
Full glad that he ſurviv'd.

Soon as the riſing ſun had clear'd
The gloomy ſhades of night,
All on the huſtings they appear'd—
O 'twas a glorious ſight !

With

With ribbon and with ftar befpread,
  (Given by the good old king)
Sir W——m hung his languid head,
  And look'd—*like any thing*.

The ferjeant held his head upright,
  For confcious ftill was he,
That thofe who do the deed that's right,
  Have real caufe for glee.

Mr. O'M——y too was there,
  Hight councellor at law—
His bus'nefs was to ftrut and ftare,
  And *find* or *make* a flaw.

Count Gambler look'd as who fhould fay,
  " I'll bet ye fix to one
" That Beauchamp Proctor gets the day,"
  —" I take *it*, damme."—" Done."

Whilft buftling ftill from place to place,
  Old *Brentford*'s prieft was feen,
Who for this meal faid many a grace,
  And fervent pray'r, I ween.

And ftill to heighten all they could
  This mighty gallant fhow,
Clofe by the huftings numbers ftood,
  Like—*Soldiers all a-row*.

The clock told two, up flew the hat,
  (A fignal for each wounder)

And

And ſoon the freeholders lay *flat*
As ever lay a *flounder*.

Then eyes and ſkulls, and arms and legs,
Were darken'd, fractur'd, broke;
And thoſe who could not keep their pegs,
Fell down—to mend the joke.

And many a ribbon flew about,
For *favours* then were common,
And hundreds of the rabble rout
Were dizen'd out like yeomen.

What they did more, let other bards
In other guiſe declare;
For, truth to ſay, they play'd their cards,
To make all England ſtare.

Now God preſerve our noble king,
And grant henceforth, for aye,
No future poet e'er may ſing
The deeds of ſuch a day!

On the Inveſtiture of Cardinal De Bernis, *with a Blue Ribbon at* Verſailles.

THE exaltation of de Bernis, who was naturally of a very amorous conſtitution, and ſeemed to have no other recommendation than his perſon, and art to pleaſe the fair ſex, provoked the

nobility

nobility and gentry beyond all moderation: ſo that when he was inveſted with the order of the Holy Ghoſt, in the chapel of Verſailles, there was, during the ceremony, a ſcroll of paper thrown out of the gallery among the knights, on which was wrote a French parody, on the hymn called Veni Creator, and is thus tranſlated:

Thou holy ſpirit, power divine,
  Do thou for France's glory deign
On this new miniſter to ſhine,
  And lighten up his clouded brain.

Of twelve unlearn'd thou heretofore
  Didſt raiſe up miracles to thee;
Renew thoſe miracles once more,
  By giving ſenſe to poor Bernis.

His boſom with thy flames poſſeſs;
  On him the love of heaven pour,
That he may kiſs the ladies leſs,
  And leaſt of all——La Pompadour.

Bernis inveſted with the rank of a miniſter, and decked out with a blue ribbon, could not, doubtleſs, but appear, more agreeable in the eyes of his protectreſs; and ſhe, never eaſy, day and night, out of his company, looked upon his athletic conſtitution, and conſummate knowledge in the art of love, to be ſuch ſuperior talents, as made him extremely capable of unravelling the moſt knotty,

and

and conducting the moſt arduous affairs of ſtate; imagining with great reaſon, that in the courſe of an adminiſtration, which ſhe alone had put into his hands, he would certainly take no ſtep without firſt conſulting her.

EPIGRAM.

O BUTE! if, inſtead of contempt, and of
odium,
You'd wiſh to obtain univerſal elogium,
From your breaſt to your gullet transfer the blue
ſtring,
Our hearts are all your's at the very firſt ſwing.

The following curious Paper was publiſhed in one of the public Prints in March, 1763, *and is ſuppoſed to be wrote by an Alderman of* London.

To the EDITOR.

—— *Cretâ an carbone notandi* Hor.

THE following columns contain nothing more than two ſeparate liſts of the celebrated perſonages, who have at any time been honoured with abuſe by the *Auditor* or *North-Briton*. Theſe liſts, I know, muſt neceſſarily be imperfect, becauſe they are taken down merely upon memory; and becauſe ſuch keen ſatiriſts cannot ſo groſly have miſpent their time, as to have

have laſhed ſo few people; yet I have been the leſs curious to render theſe liſts compleat, becauſe I know that the writers in queſtion are ſuch ſtirring ſpirits, that they will each be continually ſwelling their ſeveral catalogues, for which reaſon I have contented myſelf with leaving certain vacant ſpaces, for the inſertion of ſuch names already diſtinguiſhed as I muſt without doubt, have omitted, or to be filled up, as time ſhall ſerve, and the Auditor or North-Briton ſhall hereafter pleaſe to direct.

Let us, however, do juſtice to the candour, as well as acrimony, of our political writers. They deal in panegyrick, as well as ſatire. If they throw dirt with the ſcavenger's ſhovel, they alſo lay on praiſe with a trowel. Every modern controverſial writer in politicks ſits down with encomium on the right and obloquy on the left, like Jupiter between the tubs of good and evil; or, to lower my ſimile, like brother PAMPHLET in the *Upholſterer*, with white-waſh in one hand and black-ball in the other. All their characters, or rather caricatures, may be conſidered as the *rough draughts* of the maſters in the modern ſchool of crayons, who ſometimes draw in chalk, but moſt commonly in charcoal. It was my firſt intention to have given both the chalk and charcoal portraits of each of the great maſters in queſtion;

queſtion; but I ſoon reflected that I might ſave that trouble by deſiring your readers to take it for a general rule, that ſuch as are blackened in the North Briton, are, by act of grace, *white-waſhed* in the Auditor, and ſo *vice verſâ*. Every great character, like a poſt or a wainſcot, is deſtined to be painted in different colours, at leaſt twice over; and in this various light we may at pleaſure conſider the two following columns either as the two principal pillars of the temple of ſlander, or the two tables in the temple of fame. As we are now however in the very middle of Lent, I would have the noble lords and gentlemen, whoſe names appear in theſe liſts, to regard the peruſal of them as an act of humiliation and mortification; I adviſe them to remember that they have been *told their own* by the great writers under whoſe awful names they are here arranged.

It muſt be premiſed, as our fixed opinion, that *the* Auditor is by far the moſt reſpectable character, and the moſt polite writer of the two. The North Briton ſounded the *nether trump of fame* at the very firſt onſet, and furiouſly charged the Scots and the miniſtry at once. The Auditor ſet out with profeſſions of moderation and impartiality. He did not ſeek for defamation, but *it lay in his way, and he found it.*

He

He has indeed been as ſcurrilous as his neighbours, yet has he had the grace to inveigh againſt ſcurrility; which ſhews that he hath the *milk of human kindneſs* in his nature, though perhaps that milk may, by too long keeping, have turned ſour in his breaſt Mark his candid declarations in his firſt number! "The malevolent are not to "expect to be gratified with *ſlander*, the illiberal "with *ſcurrility*, or the inconſiderate with *buffoonery*. Ingredients like theſe can have no ad-"miſſion into a paper, which is undertaken upon "principles laudable in themſelves; which is in-"tended to reconcile the minds of men to their "own good, and to one another; to refute or "laugh out of countenance all party diſtinctions; "to extinguiſh national prejudices, and to re-"commend that ſpirit of concord, which alone "can make us a ſucceſsful and preſerve us an "happy people. In ſhort it is *intended* in the "conduct of this plan, to try whether it is not "*poſſible* to talk *politics*, with temper; to deli-"neaet characters with *decency*; to treat of fac-"tions with *good humour*; and to love our "country, without hating individuals." Here are mild words; and yet in the ſecond number he ſerves up no leſs than ſix or ſeven individuals, ſome of them no inconſiderable perſonages neither; and yet even this trifling inconſiſtency may

may be accounted for, if we recollect that the auditor himſelf begins his ninth number with this reflection: " It is a curſe entailed upon the re-
" tainers to deſpairing faction, that they are not
" only *miſerable men* and *wretched writers*, but
" they muſt be *lyars* into the bargain ; they
" muſt *forge crimes* to affright the people, they
" muſt ſcatter abroad the words of prevarication,
" &c."

AUDITOR.	NORTH-BRITON.
Duke of Cumberland	P. D. of W.
Duke of Newcaſtle	Duke of Bedford
Duke of Devonſhire	
Earl Temple	Earl of Bute
	Earl of Loudon
	Earl of Litchfield
	Earl of Talbot
	Earl of Talbot's *Horſe*
Lord Barrington	Lord Mansfield
	Lord Eglington
Rt. Hon. Mr. Pitt	Rt. Hon. Mr. Fox
Rt. Hon. Mr. Legge	Rt.Hon.Mr.G.Grenville
Lord Mayor of London	Rt. Hon. Mr. Rigby
Sir James Hodges, Knt. *Town Clerk of the City of London*	Hon. Horace Walpole

AUDITOR.	NORTH-BRITON.
The King of Pruſſia	Sir John Philips, Bart.
Author of the Addreſs to the Cocoa-Tree	Sir Francis Daſhwood, Bart.
Thomas Nuthall, Attorney	Samuel Touchet
Mr. Beardmore, ditto	Samuel Martin
Charles Churchill	Samuel Johnſon
Charles Say	John Home
Charles Macklin, *alias* Mac-lochlin	David Mallet, *alias* Malloch
Dr. Shebbeare	Arthur Murphy
John Wilkes	Dr. Burton
David Garrick	William Hogarth
The Toaſt Maſter at Guildford	The Poet-Laureat
Col. Lamb, Fiſhmonger } Officers in the Militia.	
Capt. Lamb, Auctioneer }	
Mr. Hoyle	
Mr. Pond	
Mr. Arthur	
Counſellor Jones	

AUDITOR.	NORTH-BRITON.
The Monitor	The Briton
The Whigs	The Tories
The Minority	The Majority
Againſt	
War	Peace

The above liſts not only ſhew, who have been the butts of ſatire to each writer, but may alſo, with due attention to the turnings and windings in the court calendar, ſerve as unerring guide-poſts to point out ſuch as ſeem to be in the high road to abuſe from either paper. Being made acquainted with the colour of the heroes of both parties, we know that if a great officer of the court ſhould be turned out, or, to uſe the more courtly phraſe, *reſign*, the Auditor will immediately tear out the white leaf wherein he ſo lately ſang his praiſes, and, like another *Peachum*, ſet his name down in his *black book*, and call on him to exerciſe the full powers of the chriſtian virtue of *reſignation*. We know too, that if a noble member of one houſe ſhould call forth an able commoner to lead the buſineſs of the other, the North Briton will immediately open his deep mouth on that leader, and *maul* a manager with as great alacrity as Mr. *Fitz-*

patrick.

patrick. But as rules and precepts are never clearly enforced, unlefs illuftrated by example, I will fubmit a fmall *peep into futurity* to your rea ders ; and as I have, in fome places above, rather made extraordinary diftinctions in favour of the Auditor, I fhall here pay my particular compliments to the North Briton. We have already feen whom that writer has *abufed* (craving his pardon for the grofsnefs of the expreffion) ; and the Auditor's lift of fcandal (craving his pardon alfo) is a pretty exact catalogue of thofe whom the North Briton has *praifed*. I fhall now therefore, take upon me to predict, with as much fagacity as Partridge or even Bickerftaff, whom he WILL *praife*, whom he *will* abufe, and whom he *may poffibly* praife or abufe : and for the fulfilling thefe my predictions I refer to time, or even appeal to the *fecond fight* of the North Briton himfelf. Some that are turned out, I know he will take every opportunity to *praife*, and that clafs I fhall diftinguifh by *Chalk* ; fome that are put in, I know he cannot refift the temptation of abufing, and that clafs I fhall diftinguifh by CHARCOAL. But there are another clafs, of a dubious, indeterminate *twilight* character, whofe conduct will not fuffer us to fpeak precifely of the *colour* of their intentions ; a kind of heterogeneous or amphibious animals, hermaphrodites or otters in politicks, neither *in* nor *out*, *pro* or *con*, *court* nor *country*, *whig* nor *tory*, *Scot* nor *Engliſh*; who are, like Sir Anthony Branville, *in a ſtate of fluctuation*, and hang like Mahomet's coffin, in ſuſpence; who ſeem ready to veer and turn, like approved weather-cocks, with every guſt of politics; who ſtand, between *ay* and *no*, like the aſs of the ſchoolmen between two bundles of hay; or, like prince Volſcius in love,—hip hop, hip hop, one boot on, the other boot off. Theſe ſtateſmen of the neuter gender we can place in neither liſt, and yet they ſeem to bid fair for a place in both. Where then can we ſtation theſe lovers of *the golden* mean, but in the middle? In the middle, therefore, upon ſtilts between both, one foot on one liſt, the other foot on the other liſt, I have placed one right honourable gentleman, as the grand archetype of political ſcepticiſm. Far be it from me to arraign ſuch commendable prudence and moderation! But as the North Briton is not ſuch an admirer of impartiality, I have reaſon to think, that he will not long permit this gentleman to remain in a ſtate of indifferency; he will not be contented to ſay of him ALBUS *an* ATER *homo ſit*, *neſcio*; but having once brought himſelf to imagine, that he has diſcovered the gentleman's *bias*, he will ſoon be induced to favour us with

a portrait

a portrait of ſo diſtinguiſhed a perſonage either in chalk or in charcoal.

——A PEEP into FUTURITY.——

From the NORTH-BRITON.

CHALK.	CHARCOAL.

The Right Hon. Charles Townſhend.

Duke of Grafton	Ld Mayor of London
Duke of Portland	Earl of Powis
Thomas Prowſe, Eſq;	Lord Groſvenor
Edward Popham, Eſq;	Lord Strange
	Sir Arm. Wodehouſe
	Sir Cha. Mordaunt
	Welbore Ellis
	James Oſwald
	Bamber Gaſcoyne
	Paul Whitehead.

Written Extempore by a young Gentleman, from a Morning View on a Mountain in the South of Wales, a few Weeks ſince.

I.

HOW awful the morning breaks over yon
hill,
Not a whiſper is heard on the plain,
Save the murmuring ſweetneſs of yonder clear rill,
By the mountains re-ecchoed again.

II.

See Phœbus, how roſy he opens the day;
See his beams how they ſport in the ſtream;
Obſerve how contented that hind takes his way,
And tackles his beaſts to the team.

III.

From his ſtraw-cover'd cot, juſt roſe for the day,
See contentment and health in his face;
The ſmiles of thoſe bantlings his labours repay,
The effects of a wholeſome embrace.

IV.

What a crowd of ſweet pratlers! how healthy
they look!
Yet their tann'd little buffs are all ſeen;
Obſerve how they wantonly paddle in the brook,
And race till they dry on the green.

V.

V.

Had I on the ſide of yon mountain a cot,
With a moderate competence bleſt,
I'd take a good wife, thank Heaven for my lot,
And conſider the world as a jeſt.

The following is an explanatory Note of a Paſſage in Mr. Churchill's Candidate, *never before printed, where he ſpeaks of* Medmenham Abbey.

——" Whilſt womanhood, in habit of a nun,
" At Medmenham lies, by *backward* monks undone,
" A nation's reckoning, like an alehouſe ſcore,
" Whilſt *Paul* the aged chalks behind the door,
" Compell'd to hire a foe to caſt it up,
" D——— ſhall pour, from a communion cup,
" Libations to the goddeſs without eyes,
" And hob or nob in cyder or exciſe."

MEdmenham, or as it is pronounced Mednam-Abbey, is a very large houſe on the banks of the Thames, near Marlow in Buckinghamſhire. It was formerly a convent of Ciſtertian monks. The ſituation is remarkably fine. Beautiful hanging woods, ſoft meadows, a chryſtal ſtream, and a grove of venerable old elms near the houſe, with the retiredneſs of the manſion itſelf, made it as ſweet a retreat, as the moſt poetical imagination could create. Sir F—— D———, Sir T——s S———, *P—l* W———d, Mr. Wilkes, and other gentlemen to the number of twelve, rented the abbey, and often retired there in the ſummer. Among other amuſements, they had ſometimes a mock celebration of the more ridiculous rites of the foreign religious orders among the Roman Catholics; of the Franciſcans in particular, for the gentlemen had taken that title from the founder, Sir F—— D———. *Paul*, the aged, was ſecretary and ſteward to the order. Mr. Wilkes had not been at the abbey for many months before the publication of this poem in 1764.

No prophane eye has dared to penetrate into the Engliſh Eleuſinian myſteries of the *Chapter-Room*, where the monks aſſembled on all ſolemn occaſions, the more ſecret rites were performed, and libations poured forth in much pomp to the *Bona Dea*. I ſhall only venture to relate what many mortal eyes have ſeen, and *ſit mihi fas audita loqui.*

Over the grand entrance was the famous inſcription on Rabelais's Abbey of THELEME, *Fay ce que voudras*. At the end of the paſſage over the door was, *Aude, hoſpes, contemnere opes*. At one end of the refectory was, Harpocrates, the Egyptian god of ſilence, at the other, the goddeſs defs Angerona, that the fame duty might be enjoined to both fexes.

The garden, the grove, the orchard, the neighbouring woods, all fpoke the loves and frailties of the *younger* monks, who feemed at leaft to have *finned naturally*. You faw in one place—*Ici pâma de joie des mortels le plus heureux.* — In another very imperfectly—*Mourut un amant fur le fein de fa dame.*—In a third—*En cet endroit mille baifers de flamme furent donnés, & mille autres rendus.* Againft a fine old oak was

Hic fatyrum naïas victorem victa fubegit.

At the entrance of a cave was the Venus, ftooping to pull a thorn out of her foot. The ftatue turned from you, and juft over the *two nether hills of fnow*, were thefe lines of Virgil,

Hic locus eft, partes ubi fe via findit in ambas:
Hac iter Elyzium nobis: at læva malorum
Exercet pœnas, et ad impia Tartara mittit.

On the infide of the cave over a moffy couch, was the following exhortation.

Ite, agite, O juvenes; pariter fudate medullis
Omnibus inter vos; non murmura veftra columbæ,
Brachia non hederæ, non vincant ofcula conchæ.

The favourite doctrine of the abbey is certainly not *penitence*; for in the center of the orchard

was

was a grotefque figure, *and in his hand a reed* STOOD *flaming, tipt with fire,* to ufe Milton's expreffion, and you might trace out

PENI TENTO
non
PENI TENTI.

On the pedeftal was a whimfical reprefentation of Trophonius's cave, from whence all creatures were faid to come out melancholy. Among that ftrange, difmal group, you might however remark a *cock* crowing and a Carmelite laughing. The words *Gallum gallinaceum et facerdotem gratis* were only legible *.

Near the abbey was a fmall, neat temple, erected to Cloacine, with the infcription, *This chapel of eafe was founded in the year* 1760. Facing the entrance in the infide,

Æquè pauperibus prodeft, locupletibus æquè,
Æquè neglectum pueris fenibufque nocebit.

The curious and entertaining defcription of Weft Wycombe church, publifhed in the firft part of the New Foundling Hofpital for Wit, page 42, will enable the reader to give a fhrewd guefs at the *goddefs without eyes*, to whom Sir F——

* Omne animal poft coitum trifte eft, præter gallum gallinaceum, et facerdotem gratis fornicantem.

D——

D——— not only poured libations from a communion-cup, but actually built a temple in his gardens at West Wycombe.

The five following Pieces are said to be written by Mr. W—s.

The TEMPLE *of the* MUSES.

To the Countess TEMPLE.

THE muses and graces to Phœbus complain'd;
" That no more on the earth a Sappho remain'd,
" That their empire of wit was now at an end,
" And on beauty alone the sex must depend;
" To the men he had giv'n all his fancy and fire;
" Art of healing to Armstrong, as well as his
" lyre."
When Apollo reply'd; " To make you amends,
" In one fair you shall see wit and virtue good
" friends;
" The Grecian's high spirit and sweetness I'll join
" With a true Roman virtue, to make it divine:
" Your pride and my boast, thus form'd would
" you know,
" You must visit the earthly elyzium of STOW."

To a Lady, who ſung in too low a Voice.

WHEN beauteous Laura's gentle voice
Divides the yielding air,
Fix'd on her lips, the fault'ring ſounds
Exceſs of joy declare.

There ling'ring round the roſy gate,
They view their fragrant cell,
Unwilling to depart that mouth,
Where all the graces dwell.

Some tuneful accents ſtrike the ſenſe
With ſoft imperfect ſound,
While thouſand others die within,
In their own honey drown'd.

Yet thro' this cloud, diſtinct and clear,
Sweet ſenſe directs its dart;
And while it ſeems to ſhun the ear,
Strikes full upon the heart.

To LAURA *on New Year's Day.*

REVOLVING years add, Laura, to your charms,
And bolder throbs my pulſe to love's alarms;
Yet ſhall thoſe heavenly charms at laſt decay,
And this my ſprightly pulſe forget to play:
Then wiſely let me all my hours employ;
Too ſwift they fly, but be they wing'd with joy.

May

May wit and beauty their bleſt pow'rs unite,
Wit rule the day, and beauty rule the night;
The pleaſing chace may I thro' life purſue,
All day with *Daphnis*, and all night with *you*.

To Miſs W—— *on her Birth-Day*, Auguſt 16, 1767.

Wrote in France.

AGAIN I tune the vocal lay
On dear Maria's natal day;
This happy day I'll not deplore
My exile from my native ſhore;
No tear of mine to-day ſhall flow
For injur'd England's cruel woe;
For impious wounds to freedom given,
The firſt moſt ſacred gift of heaven.
The muſe with joy ſhall prune her wing,
Maria's ripen'd graces ſing,
And at ſeventeen, with truth ſhall own,
The bud of beauty's fairly blown:
Softneſs and ſweeteſt innocence
Here ſhed their gentle influence;
Fair modeſty comes in their train
To grace her ſiſter virtue's reign;
Then to give ſpirit, taſte, and eaſe,
The ſov'reign art, the art to pleaſe,
Good humour'd wit, and fancy gay,
To-morrow chearful as to-day,

The

The ſun-ſhine of a mind ſerene,
Where all is peace within, are ſeen.
What can the grateful muſe aſk more?
The gods have laviſh'd all their ſtore,
Maria ſhines their darling care,
Still keep her heaven from every ſnare;
May ſtill unſpotted be her fame,
May ſhe remain thro' life the ſame,
Unchang'd in all—except in name.

To Miſs W—— *on her Birth-Day.* Auguſt 16, 1768. *Wrote in Priſon.*

HOW ſhall the muſe in priſon ſing!
How prune her drooping ruffl'd wing!
Maria is the potent ſpell
Ev'n in theſe walls all grief to quell,
To chear the heart, rapture inſpire,
And wake to notes of joy the lyre,
The tribute verſe again to pay,
On this auſpicious feſtive day.
When doom'd to quit the patriot band,
And exil'd from my native land,
Maria was my ſure relief,
Her preſence baniſh'd every grief;
Pleaſure came ſmiling in her train,
And chas'd the family of pain.

Let

Let lovers every charm admire,
The eaſy ſhape, the heav'nly fire
That from thoſe modeſt-beaming eyes,
The captive heart at once ſurprize;
A father's is another part,
I praiſe the virtues of the heart;
And wit ſo elegant and free,
Attemper'd ſweet with modeſty;
Yet may kind heaven a lover ſend,
Of ſenſe, of honour, and a friend;
Thoſe virtues always to protect,
Thoſe beauties—never to neglect.

A Copy of VERSES.

By the Right Honourable the Earl of CARLISLE, *on his Schoolfellows at* Eton.

IN youth, 'tis ſaid, you eaſily may ſcan,
Strong ſtamp'd, the outlines of the future man;
This maxim true, how bright will St. John ſhine,
Form'd by the hand of all the tuneful Nine!
If not to careleſs indolence a prey,
How will whole nations liſten to his lay!

Say, will Fitzwilliams ever want a heart
Cheerful, his ready bleſſings to impart?
Will not another's woe his boſom ſhare,
The widow's ſorrow, and the orphan's prayer?

Who aids the old, who ſoothes the mother's cry,
Who wipes the tear from off the virgin's eye?
Who feeds the hungry? who aſſiſts the lame?
All, all, re-echo with Fitzwilliam's name.
Thou know'ſt I hate to flatter, yet in thee,
No fault, my friend, no ſingle ſpeck I ſee.

Nor, if alike my former maxims true,
Shall e'er ill nature tinge thy heart, Buccleugh;
Shall deep remorſe thy honeſt boſom tear,
Diſdainful anger, or corroding care;
Shall e'er ambition diſſipate that ſmile,
Diſturb that heart, ſo free from every guile:
Sooner to Bute ſhall Temple bend his knee,
And * or ** pious chriſtians be.

How will my Fox, alone, thy ſtrength of parts,
Shake the loud ſenate, animate the hearts
Of fearful ſtateſmen? while around you ſtand
Both peers and commons liſtening your command;
While Tully's ſenſe its weight to you affords,
His nervous ſweetneſs ſhall adorn your words:
What praiſe to Pitt, to Townſhend e'er was due,
In future times, my Fox, ſhall wait on you.

Mild as the dew that whitens yonder plain,
Legge ſhines ſereneſt 'midſt your youthful train;
He whom the ſearch of Fame with rapture moves,
Diſdains the pedant, tho' the muſe he loves;
By nature form'd with modeſty to pleaſe,
And join'd with wiſdom unaffected eaſe.

Will

Will e'er Ophaly, confciouſly unjuſt,
Revoke his promiſe, or betray his truſt?
What tho' perhaps with warmer zeal he'd hear
The ecchoing horn, the ſportman's hearty cheer,
Than god-like Homer's elevated ſong;
Loud as the torrent, as the billows ſtrong,
Caſt o'er this fault a friendly veil, you'll find
A friendly, ſocial, and ingenuous mind.

Witneſs, ye Naiads, and ye guardian powers,
Who ſit ſublime on Henry's lofty towers;
Witneſs if e'er I ſaw thy open brow,
Sunk in deſpair, or ſadden'd into woe,
Well natur'd Stavordale——the taſk is thine
Foremoſt in pleaſure's feſtive band to ſhine:
Say, wilt thou paſs alone the midnight hour,
Studious the depth of Plato to explore?
To lighter ſubjects ſhall thy ſoul give way,
Nor heed what grave philoſophers ſhall ſay?
The god of mirth ſhall lift thee in his train,
A cheerful vot'ry, and the foe of pain.

Whether I Storer ſing in hours of joy,
When every look beſpeaks the inward boy;
Or when no more mirth wantons in his breaſt,
And all the man appears in him confeſt;
In mirth, in ſadneſs, ſing him how I will,
Senſe and good-nature muſt attend him ſtill.

To the Earl of CARLISLE, *on the preceding* POEM.

MY lord, your verfes, penn'd with fo much eafe,
The fair, the young, and ev'n the critics pleafe;
Such folid fenfe, and grace, and judgment meet,
We add the epithet of Strong to Sweet.
That fome are peers by ftars and ftrings we find;
You, by intrinfic noblenefs of mind;
Fair Fancy's manly ftrokes your lines adorn;
We truly may pronounce you, poet born:
And if in youth your genius we may fcan,
How will it glow, and brighten in the man!
True fings the bard, that one well-natur'd deed,
Does all defert in fciences exceed:
And if, my lord, from what you write, we guefs,
Yourfelf thofe virtues, which you paint, poffefs:
The fenfe of St. John, Fox, and Legge's your due,
The fweetnefs of unblameable Buccleugh;
Ophaly's honour, Stavordale's defert,
Storer's good-nature, and Fitzwilliam's heart.

An EPITAPH *on the late Right Hon.* Thomas Winnington, *Efq. By Sir* Charles Hanbury Williams.

NEAR his paternal feat, here buried lies,
The grave, the gay, the witty, and the wife.

Form'd for all parts, in all alike he ſhin'd,
Variouſly great! a genius unconfin'd!
In converſe bright, judicious in debate,
In private amiable, and in public great:
With all the ſtateſman's knowledge, prudence, art,
With friendſhip's open, undeſigning heart.
The friend and heir here join their duty: One
Erects the buſto, one inſcribes the ſtone.
Not that they hope from theſe his fame ſhould live,
That claims a longer date than they can give;
Falſe to their truſts, the mould'ring buſts decay,
And, ſoon effac'd, inſcriptions wear away:
But Engliſh annals ſhall their place ſupply;
And, while they live, his name can never die.

The GRAND CATHOLICON:

Being a genuine Family Receipt. *Written in* 1753.

TO form a miniſter, the ingredients
Are, a head fruitful of expedients,
Each ſuited to the preſent minute
(No harm if nothing elſe be in it):
The mind, though much perplex'd and harraſs'd,
The count'nance muſt be unembarraſs'd:
High promiſes for all occaſions:
A ſet of treaſons, plots, invaſions:
Bullies, to ward off each diſaſter:
Much impudence to brave his maſter:

 The

The talents of a treaty-maker;
The ſole diſpoſal of th' exchequer:
Of right and wrong no real feeling;
Yet in the names of both much dealing.
In ſhort, this man muſt be a mixture
Of broker, ſycophant, and trickſter;
Who well can pack his cards, and tell 'em,
And knows as much as Mr. Pelham.

On HEALTH. *By the late Lord* HERVEY.

THO' life itſelf 's not worth a thought,
Yet, whilſt I live, could health be bought;
Whate'er brib'd ſenators receive,
Or back again in taxes give;
Whatever force or fraud obtains,
What Pruſſia from Sileſia gains,
Or Hanover from England drains;
Whate'er the Auſtrian wars have coſt,
Or Hung'ry's queen diſburſs'd or loſt;
What France has paid to ſhape her crown,
Or we, like fools, to keep it on;
All that the Indies have ſupply'd
To beggar'd Spain, to feed the pride
Of that Italian fury-dame,
Who keeps all Europe in a flame,
For her two brats, thoſe princely things,
Whom God made fools, and ſhe'd make kings:

In

In ſhort, to ſum up all, whate'er
Or pride, or avarice, makes its care,
Did I poſſeſs it, I'd reſign,
To make this richer treaſure mine.

On a late INCIDENT *.

Jam ſatis Terris Nivis atque diræ
Grandinis miſit Pater. HOR.

THREE eminent men of the law
  Lately travell'd on Sunday together,
Thro' roads that were cover'd with ſnow,
  Not regarding the day or the weather:

At length they got into a pit
  (How diſmal the tale to be told!)
Where they and their horſes——*to wit*,
  Had like to have periſh'd with cold.

Tho' they often before, none can doubt,
  Had waded thro' thick and thro' thin,

* *Theſe lines were written on ſeeing the following article in the public prints:*

York, Jan. 20, 1767. We hear they have a prodigious quantity of ſnow upon the Wolds; and that on Sunday the 11th inſtant, as three gentlemen, eminent in the profeſſion of the law, were travelling from Pocklington to Hugget, they all three ſtuck faſt in a ſnow-drift together, from which they were extricated with great difficulty.

Yet the more now they try'd to get out,
The deeper, alas! they ſunk in.

O fortune! now lend 'em thine aid,
Or how can'ſt thou anſwer thy charge?
Thou haſt Coke upon Littleton laid,
And pull'd down the *Statutes at large.*

The goddeſs was moved with their cries,
And determin'd to ſave all their lives;
Then quick to their ſuccour ſhe flies,
To the joy of their clients and wives.

Ye lawyers, remember their doom,
And be warn'd at the fall of theſe men;
I hope you will never preſume
To travel on Sundays again.

G. W—L—Y.

A Motto for the Hon. Charles Yorke, *an orator of the long Robe*——Spero meliora.

A Noble ambition this motto reveals.
It tells you—the orator hopes for the ſeals!

BON MOT *of a certain witty* LORD.

HIS Lordſhip being informed, that a lady, lately divorced, would probably be married to the E. of *upper* O—y, ſaid it is time ſhe was *upper* O—y, for ſhe had been *under* O—y long enough.

A CON-

A CONUNDRUM.

WHY is the Duke of G—— a proper person to be Chancellor of Cambridge?

Because he loves——PARSONS.

The SCHOOL of RHETORICK.

NEAR *London Bridge* once ſtood a gate,
Belinus gave it name,
Whence the green *Nereids* oyſters bring,
A place of public fame.

Here *Eloquence* has fixt her ſeat;
The nymphs here learn by heart
In *mode* and *figure* ſtill to ſpeak
By modern rules of art.

To each fair *oratreſs* this ſchool
Its *rhet'ric* ſtrong affords;
They double and redouble tropes
With finger, fiſt, and words.

Both *nerves* and *ſtrength*, and *flow of ſpeech*
With beauties ever new,
Adorn the language of theſe nymphs,
Who give to all their *due*.

O happy ſeat of happy nymphs!
For many ages known:

To thee each *roſtrum*'s forc'd to yield,
  Each *forum* in the town.

Let other *academics* boaſt
  What *titles* elſe they pleaſe:
Thou ſhalt be call'd *the Gate of Tongues*,
  Of tongues that never ceaſe. T. P.

On a Gentleman who miſtook a Kept Miſtreſs *for a* Lady of Faſhion.

SIX tedious months young *Damon* ſigh'd,
  In vain his am'rous tale;
He ſu'd, implor'd, *Chlo* ſtill deny'd,
  No efforts could prevail.

At length he try'd the pow'r of gold——
  She ſoon to chide forgot;
The fair-one was no longer cold,
  But prov'd——*alas! too hot.*

VERSES *addreſs'd to ſome Ladies of* Hampſtead.

CONSTANT gameſters! every day,
  Ev'ry night, employ'd at play,
Squandring wealth and time away;
Never happy but at cards,
You ſhall meet with juſt rewards,
(For neglect of family,
Truſted to a ſervant's eye,

And

And domeſtick bus'neſs, care
Of each valuable fair.)
Bane of quiet, peace and joy,
Every comfort you deſtroy,
Whilſt your thinking friends bemoan,
Waſte and riot left at home:
Childrens ruin, huſbands curſe,
Prelude to an empty purſe;
No man leaves to ſuch a wife
More than bare ſupport for life:
Have recourſe to common ſenſe,
Reform, or take the conſequence.

On the Run of ROMEO *and* JULIET.

WELL—what to night? ſays angry Ned,
As up from bed he rouſes:
Romeo again!—and ſhakes his head,
Ah! pox on both your houſes.

Notes on Mr. Churchill'*s Fragment of a Dedication to the B—— of* G———.

In the Manner of Mr. WILKES.

THERE is nothing in the poet's works more highly finiſhed than this fragment. A moſt happy vein of irony runs through the whole, and the grave Cervantes maſk of humour never once falls off.

off. Tho' we have only a part of what was intended, yet the episcopal hero shines so much in the different lights of a pious prelate, a profound critic, an exemplary clergyman, and a meek divine, that we are at a loss which we ought the most to admire.

The benevolence of the bishop only remains unsung: I mean, his benevolence to man. As to the other due benevolence of which St. Paul speaks, it ought in strictness to be considered as a part of justice, or family duty to good Mrs. W——. I need not tell so great a scholar as her husband, that Horace calls it *uxorius amnis*. I will only add my wishes, in the words of this dedication, that, as the bishop and his wife are most uniformly join'd, it may continue *regularly flowing from that wholesome source his*——mind.

I ask no favour, not one note I crave.
In the Candidate he says,
Nor soul-gall'd *bishop* damn me with a note.

- - - - - - - My mortal journey done.

The last act of his life was an act of humanity and friendship. Mr. Wilkes under the despotick administration of the Thane's deputies had the honour

of

of being an exile. Mr. Churchill came to France on a visit to a friend, and died of a miliary fever at Boulogne on the 4th of November, 1764. The goodness of his heart and the firmness of his philosophy were in full lustre during the whole time of a very severe illness, nor were the amazing faculties of his mind in the least impaired till a few moments before his death.

An inscription, in the close stile of the antients, engraven on a sepulchral urn of alabaster, gives us his true character, as a friend, a poet, and a patriot.

CAROLO CHURCHILL,
Amico jucundo,
Poetæ acri,
Civi optimè de patria merito,
P.
Johannes Wilkes, 1765.

In spirit I'm right proud, nor can endure
The mention of a bribe.

The reverend emissary of lord H——, who, waited on the poet soon after the advertisement of Ayliffe's Ghost by C. Churchill, can best explain this passage. The untimely death of the author deprived us of that elegy; but his lordship was convinced

convinced at laſt, that every man has NOT his price.

Let thy own offspring all thy fortunes ſhare.

The irony here is beſt explained by a paſſage in the duelliſt,

> No huſband, tho' he's truly wed ;
> Tho' on his knees a child is bred,
> No father :——

> ——By miſtaken kings
> Titles are oft miſplac'd.

The ſame ſpirit of diſcernment, and attention to reward all true merit, which advanced the immaculate ——— to be ſecretary of ſtate, and the brave —— to be ſteward of the houſhold, gave Mr. ——— the peerage. An univerſal odium had long purſued his name. Many breaches of private faith had left him not the leaſt ſhare of confidence with any friend ; and repeated violations of public truſt had ruined him in the opinion of mankind, when it pleaſed —— the —— to ſign a patent, commanding us always to call him the right honourable lord ———.

> Thy open front, thy love-commanding eye,
> Where fifty Cupids, as in ambuſh lie.

I

I never could form an adequate idea of what Virgil calls the *lætos oculis honores*, the *lumen purpureum*, till I was bleſſed with a ſight of W—— W———, lord b—— of G———. His fine eye carries us even beyond what a Pagan poet could poſſibly conceive, for it beams forth all the meakneſs and forbearance, all the mildneſs and benevolence of that goſpel which is engraven on his heart. The beauty and ſymmetry of features in his face are indeed admirable, but beauty and ſymmetry are by no means confined to his face. His whole figure excells the moſt perfect Grecian forms, and in my opinion is a ſuperior compoſition to the Belvidere Apollo. The harmony of the ſoul too ſeems exactly anſwerable to that of the body. Among all the arts of ancient Egypt, which the b—— ſo much admires, I moſt regret that the art of embalming in a manner to preſerve every the minuteſt feature, is now totally loſt. The W——— ſet of features might otherwiſe have convinced our children's children, that the moſt heavenly fire of the eye, and true dignity of aſpect, may be tempered with grace and ſweetneſs. Our poſterity in that caſe would have exclaimed as we do now; *how meek, how gentle, how forbearing, was this primitive chriſtian?*

Oh! what a grace is ſeated on that brow!

This

This lofs is the more to be lamented, becaufe the heir to his fortunes is unhappily not the heir to his graces. It is generally allowed, that the boy does not in the leaft refemble him, but feems to be of quite another mould, or *Potter*'s earth.

After the b—— of G———, though at a great diftance, comes F— lord H——d, moft happy in that kind of look, which fteals the heart at firft glance, though the foul ftill fits at fquat, and peeps not from it's hole.

If I was forced to name a third human face divine, after all beauty and harmony have been nearly exhaufted by the other two, it fhould be that of Mr. M——. I do not however infift upon this, becaufe I know good judges differ as to him; and Mr. Quin once, pointing to M——, whifpered a friend; *Sir, if that fellow is not a villain, God Almighty does not write a legible hand.*

Thofe fheep, which never heard their fhepherd's voice,
Which did not know, yet wou'd not learn the way;
Which ftray'd themfelves, yet griev'd that I fhou'd ftray;

Inftead of the two laft lines, thefe were in the firft MSS.

Which

Which accents of rebuke could never bear,
Nor would have heeded Christ, had Christ been
there.

Much did I wish, tho' little cou'd I hope
A friend in him, who was the friend of Pope.

I shall give only one instance of the b——'s friendship for Mr. Pope. The judicious public applied to the duke of Chandos the character of *Timon*, in Pope's poetical epistle to the earl of Burlington. Mr. Pope denied that he meant any allusion to his grace, and published a formal justification of himself in a prose letter to the same earl. He says, "a report, which, in regard to that "noble person, was impertinent; in regard to me, "villainous——his humanity feels a concern for "the injury done to me"——Warburton's edition, vol. VIII. p. 194. This injury is however done him after his death, and this villainy is charged on him, by his friend, the b——p. After these lines,

Another age shall see the golden ear
Imbrown the slope, and nod on the parterre,
Deep harvests bury all his pride has plann'd,
And laughing Ceres re-assume the land,

follows this note: "Had the poet lived but three "years longer, he had seen this *prophecy* ful-
"filled,"

" filled," vol. III. p. 288. This can only allude to the prefent ftate of Cannons, the duke of Chandos's feat near Edgware.

Are thefe a chriftian b——'s ideas of friendfhip? The total difregard of truth, which Pope has fhewn on this occafion, admits of no apology; but it ill became a friend to prove to the world, that the poet had folemnly afferted a falfhood. The four lines are, we are told, a *prophecy* of the fate of Cannons; and we receive this information from a man, who is appointed by the author himfelf, to explain and illuftrate his works. The character of *Timon* is in every part that of the duke of Chandos, except a trifling circumftance or two purpofely difguifed. The veil Pope ufed was too thin and flimfy. Even in his defence we fee his guilt. He fays, "I had no great caufe to wonder, that a "character belonging to twenty fhould be applied "to one; fince, by that means, nineteen would "efcape the ridicule." Is not this a plain confeffion, that the character was applicable to the duke, fince it belonged to all the twenty? A man, who makes free with truth, will generally, fooner or later, be detected. The public at the very time defpifed the meannefs of the poet, and will now equally condemn the bafenefs of fuch a friend.

Pope

Pope however deferved only fuch a friend, as this W———, from his treachery and breach of faith to Lord Bolingbroke in regard to the Letters on the Idea of a Patriot King. His three moft remarkable friends were Swift, Bolingbroke, and in the decline of life, the B—— of G———. W——— has taken much pains to prove that the two former, though men of genius, were very worthlefs characters, but has only inadvertently fhewn that the laft is the moft worthlefs of the three, without being a man of genius.

The b—— has remarked, that the moft facred of all private ties are friendfhip and gratitude. The force of his friendfhip we have feen in refpect to Mr. Pope. The ftrength of gratitude Mr. Pitt found in his bifhop to equal what the Duke of Newcaftle experienced in the greateft part of the bench, very apt, in their own phrafe, to forget their maker.

Might like himfelf teach his adopted fon.
'Gainft all the world to quote a W———.

The poet does not mean his adopted fon, mafter W———, but the fenfe is, he might teach me as an adopted fon, &c.

Mr. Edwards in the Canons of Criticifm has given us feveral inftances from the notes on Shake-

 fpeare,

ſpeare, that the b—— has adhered to W—— againſt all the world. I ſhall add only one from the commentator on Pope.

> Ev'n in a biſhop I can ſpy deſert;
> Secker is decent, Rundle has a heart.

The note is, "Theſe words are *another* inſtance of "the malignity of the public judgment. The poet "thought, and not without reaſon, that they con-"veyed a very high idea of the worthy perſon to "whom they are applied; to be decent (or to be-"come every ſtation of life in which a man is "placed) being the nobleſt encomium on his wiſ-"dom and virtue." Pope, Warburton's edition, vol. 4. p. 323. To be barely decent is however very penurious praiſe, and in this paſſage is almoſt an inſult; for it is remarkable, that Secker's being only decent, is followed, or rather contraſted, with the high compliment to Rundle of having a heart. The true meaning is evident from another paſſage of this very author,

> Virtue ſhe finds too painful an endeavour,
> Content to dwell in decencies for ever.
>
> Vol. 3. p. 205.

The poet muſt have enjoyed to a high degree his taſte for ridicule with a pedant, who believed that he was complimenting when he was ſneering.

The

The b—— of Oxford did not at that time thank Pope for the praiſe of being barely decent; and after all, decency is too often like gravity, a mere outward form to conceal ſome inward defects of the mind.

I may now aſk whether thoſe words, or, as the b—— ought to have ſaid, the remarks on thoſe words, are an inſtance of the malignity of the public judgment, or of the folly of one private judgment.

The other inſtance of the malignity of the public judgment, to which the b—— alludes, is the cenſure which he ſays has been paſſed on the following lines,

> Let humble Allen, with an aukward ſhame,
> Do good by ſtealth, and bluſh to find it fame.

I muſt confeſs that I never heard theſe lines cenſured. I have heard them commended. The public indeed paſſed a ſlight reproof on an alteration made by Pope in the firſt line, at Mr. Allen's deſire. The b—— has not noticed it among the variations. In the old edition it ſtood, *Let low born Allen*, which agreed better with the *aukward ſhame.* The epithet humble, by no means ſuited the man, who could not diſguiſe that quaker-pride, which is the moſt diſguſting thing in the world, and ridiculouſly aſſumes the name of humility.

And Potter trembles even in his grave.

Thomas Potter Eſq; of Ridgmont in Bedfordſhire. He was ſon of a late archbiſhop of Canterbury, but far from being himſelf a bigot. He was even ſuſpected to be well inclined towards ſeveral miſtaken men, who differ from the Church of England. It is however certain he never went ſo far as to join in communion with any of the ſectaries. He had great abilities for parliament, and was no leſs amiable in private life. The livelineſs of his wit ſometimes indeed carried him too far, and even revealed religion did not always eſcape his ridicule; but we ought to remember Martin Luther's apology for himſelf; *Conſider I was bred a Monk.* It is to be preſumed, that he kept at leaſt a ſtrict guard over his tongue when he was with good Mr. Allen, or with the b—— of G—— and his lady, at leaſt in the latter period of his life. In the former, if we believe the poet, neither he nor the b—— were very exemplary. In the third book of the Dueliſt it is ſaid that the b——

liv'd with ſinners,
Herded with infidels for dinners;
With ſuch an emphaſis and grace
Blaſphem'd, that Power kept not pace.

The b—— ſeems by this to have out-ſtripped the layman in the race of infidelity, if the picture is not rather overcharged.

This gentleman's many accompliſhments and acquired talents, with a high admiration of their two characters. recommended him to the friendſhip of the poſtmaſter of Bath, and his epiſcopa nephew. His fine natural parts introduced him to the intimacy of the niece, no incompetent judge. Yet this excellent lady could not help ſometimes lamenting that Tom was vaſtly wild,

——then calls her child,
And ſwears that *Tom* was vaſtly wild.

Duelliſt, Book III.

I the rather mention this circumſtance that poſterity may not be miſled. Some have imagined from this paſſage that the child was chriſtened *Thomas*. It is a miſtake; he was not named after his father, but after his uncle, Mr. Allen. We have church authority for this. The baptiſmal regiſter informs us, that we ought to call the boy, *Ralph*, *Ralph*.

With all the confcious pride of innocence,
Methinks I hear him in his own defence,
Bear witnefs to himfelf, whilft all men knew,
By gofpel rules, his witnefs to be true.

This alludes to what paffed in the —— of —— on the 15th of November 1763. The b—— of ——— made a complaint againft Mr. W—— of a b—— of p——, that the name of ——— had been put by him to a variety of notes in a wicked poem, called, An Effay on Woman. It is faid that thefe notes were of an erudition fo deep and fo uncommon, that the learned —— might have been fufpected of being the author, but at the fame time of fo ludicrous a caft, it was highly improbable a grave divine could employ his time in that way. This matter is now fully cleared up, for the b—— rifing in his place, and with the utmoft folemnity laying his hand on his heart, declared, that he did not write *any one* of thofe notes, and called *his* God to witnefs the truth of the affertion. He obtained in this inftance full credit to what he affirmed. What a pity it is that to vindicate his reputation he did not at the fame time deny the notes on Shakefpeare and Pope?

The

The chriſtian zeal of the b—— did not end with his own vindication. It flamed forth with becoming fury againſt the poem itſelf, which he declared was worthy of the devil; then after a ſhort pauſe added—*no, I beg the devil's pardon, for he is incapable of writing it.*—He would not venture even there a little ſatire, but as a well-bred Frenchman, with a *pardonnez-moi* to temper it. He is fearful of offending, equally prudent and polite, and keeps a very good look-out into futurity. He remembers the caution of the wary Spaniard, who always ſaid, my good lord the devil, that he might in all events be in favour *below*. A few years ago the b—— publiſhed a treatiſe upon Grace, or the Office and Operations of the Holy Spirit. In the preface he ſays, *I have a maſter above, and I have one below.* Lord B—— has been his maſter above. Is the perſon whoſe pardon he begged his maſter below?

Pitied himſelf, in turn had pitied you.

——Seriouſly, my Lord of G—— is to be pitied.

Pope, Warburton's edition, vol. 4. 197.

But you, my Lord, renounced attorneyſhip.

The commentator of Pope has been careful to give us not only all the blots in the foul copy of the poet, but moſt of the variations in the printed editions. One however, which is remarkable, he has omitted. In the firſt book of the Dunciad we read according to the b——'s edition,

What can I now? my Fletcher caſt aſide,
Take up the bible, once my better guide.

Vol. 5. p. 101.

But no notice is taken of the former editions publiſhed by Pope himſelf, in ſeveral of which we read;

But what can I? my Flaccus caſt aſide,
Take up the *attorney's* (once my better) *guide*,

with this note, "In alluſion to his firſt profeſſion "of an attorney." The b—— could not bear to copy theſe words, which are ſpoken by Cibber, the hero of the Dunciad, who was no dunce. Did he fear they would rather lead the reader to one of the *low-born, cell-bred, ſelfiſh, ſervile, band*, to a *reverend Flamen in his lightened dreſs*, formerly an attorney?

Dunciad, b. 2. vol. 354.

The

The name and profeſſion of attorney my lord did indeed renounce; the wrangling and cavilling, the ſubterfuges and mean arts of vile attornies (as Pope calls them vol. 3. p. 247) may be found in all his controverſial writings. He can however at a pinch ſtill do buſineſs for himſelf as an attorney, and in the idea of the world, Mr. Allen's Will does honour to the proficiency he made in his former trade.

Doctor, Dean, Biſhop, Gloſter, and my Lord.

It is always difficult to mount the firſt ſtep of the ladder of preferment; this ſimple title of *doctor* would not for above thirteen years take to the name of W———. In 1741 Pope ſays, I have received ſome chagrin at the delay of your degree at Oxon. vol. 9. p. 341. There was indeed no ſmall delay from the univerſity. At laſt in 1754 the degree of doctor in divinity was conferred on him by the archbiſhop of Canterbury.

The b—k of G——— paid the petticoat obligations which a princeſs had to Mr. and Mrs. Allen during her reſidence at Prior Park.

Poetical

Poetical Defcription of a GREAT FUNERAL.

By a late celebrated BARD.

[Never before printed.]

I.

A Tale I will tell you with great indignation,
A reproach it muft bring on the whole English nation;
Our good old ——'s funeral a raree fhow made,
While the d—— for the fight hath largely been paid.
Derry down.

II.

Old Peter was ne'er made a joke of before,
Tho' a rendezvous oft for each politick whore,
But before this grand farce the d—— feized the keys,
And for prophanation he took double fees;
Derry down.

III.

Without paying toll he fwore none fhou'd be there,
And left they fhou'd fculk he forbid publick pray'r;
The keys of the vaults and odd places took,
And threaten'd the fervants, bell, candle, and book.
Derry down.

Now

VI.

Now the chapter conven'd, old —— took the chair,
And the maſk laid aſide with a true prieſtly air;
On this happy occaſion my friends 'tis my will,
We ſtrive in convention our pockets to fill.
Derry down.

V.

His health in a bumper went chearfully round,
And each wiſh'd, he declar'd, to ſee the k——c——'d,
And moſt fervently pray'd, ſhou'd heaven him call,
It might be (tho' late) yet while they had a ſtall.
Derry down.

VI.

To Buſineſs now cries the m——'d old P——,
Ways and means are the things for which we met here,
Riſe B—— P——, and the reſt in your turns,
We will fix it this night and admit no adjourns;
Derry down.

VII.

But then ſaid the d— e'er this matter we ſettle,
Here F——'s the key, go fetch t'other bottle,
Nay

Nay frown not good F—— becauſe I bid you,
I would have ſent T——— but he'd have ſtole
two.
Derry down.

VIII.

Then each roſy Pr——d got up from his chair
And touching the matter his mind did declare;
But one by the mammon being tickl'd full ſore,
Thought it fit the proceſſion ſhou'd pay at the
door.
Derry down.

IX.

At length they reſolv'd and in minute book ſcroll'd,
Three ſcaffolds to build—be the C——'s cajol'd;
But one for the ſervants his L———p allow'd,
Which favour being told, the honeſt blocks
bow'd.
Derry down.

X.

Then carpenters vile with their hammering rend
The roof of St. P—— and the dead do offend,
For Sir Iſaac cried out, What a pox do ye there?
For God's ſake—ye're mad—ſee you've ſhatter'd
my ſphere:
Derry down.

Old

XI.

Old —— ſhook his head and ſaid, ſure t'was prophane
For a man of his parts to take God's name in vain,
And bid him of ſuch naughty words to beware,
Lye down in his place—try the circle to ſquare.
Derry down.

XII.

Each V—— ſoon follow'd the B——'s example
And boldly on decency ventur'd to trample,
Like the chapter in filling their pockets combine,
One ſells ham and rolls, t'other porter and wine.
Derry down.

XIII.

Eight ſtrikes—the bell tolls—and the ſhow doth begin,
And half crowns and twelvers fly thick to get in,
Such crowding and bribing, yourſelf wou'd have ſwore
'Twas paradiſe gate and the ſaint at the door.
Derry down.

XIV.

Arrived, Harry's chapel at length they aſcend,
And —— haſtens the ſervice to end;

Duſt

Duſt to duſt cries the D—— —ſlap the corps was
interr'd,
And the muſick ſtruck up—Long live George
the Third.

Derry down.

AN INSCRIPTION.

Written in 1749, *by the late Right Honourable* CHARLES TOWNSHEND, *on Lady* C——— *wiſhing to be buried in his Shrubbery at* Adderbury *in* Oxfordſhire.

Within this monument doth lie
What's left of Cælia's gallantry.

STRANGER, whoe'er thou art, beſtow
One ſigh in tribute ere you go;
But if thy breaſt did ever prove
The rapture of ſucceſsful love,
Around her tomb the myrtle plant,
And berry'd ſhrubs, which ring-doves haunt;
The ſpreading cypreſs, and below
Bid lumps of arbor vitæ grow;
Th' uxorious plant that leans to find
Some female neighbour of its kind,
With beech to tell the plighted flame,
And ſavine to conceal the ſhame;

3 That

That ev'ry tree and every flow'r
May join to form the am'rous bow'r;
Wherein at close of summer's heat,
The lovers of the green shall meet,
While Cælia's shade propitious hears
Their sanguine vows, their jealous fears;
Well pleas'd to consecrate her grove
To Venus and the rites of love.

Earl Delawarr's *Farewell to the Maids of Honor, on his being promoted to his late Father's Troop, and resigning the Place of Vice Chamberlain to the Queen.*

YE maids, who Britain's court bedeck,
Miss Wrottesly, Beauclerk, Keck,
Miss Meadows and Boscawen!
A dismal tale I have to tell;
This is to bid you all farewel:
Farewel! for I am going.

I leave you, girls; indeed 'tis true,
Altho' to be esteem'd by you
Has ever been my pride:
'Tis often done at court, you know;
I leave my dearest friends, and go
Over to t'other side.

No

No longer ſhall we laugh and chat
In th' outer room on this and that,
Until the queen ſhall call:
Our gracious king has call'd me now;
Nay holds a ſtick up too, I vow,
And ſo God bleſs you all!

They tell me that one word a day
From him is worth the whole you ſay,
Fair ladies, in a year:
A word from him I highly prize:
But who can leave your beauteous eyes
Without one tender tear?

No longer ſhall I now be ſeen
Handing along our matchleſs queen,
So generous, good, and kind;
While one by one each ſmiling laſs,
Firſt drops a curtſey as we paſs,
Then trips along behind.

Adieu, my much-lov'd golden key!
No longer to be worn by me,
Adorn'd with ribband blue;
Which late I heard look'd ill and pale—
I thought it but an idle tale,
But now believe 'twas true.

Farewell,

Farewell, my good Lord Harcourt, too!
What can, alas, your lordſhip do
Alone among the maids?
You ſoon muſt ſome aſſiſtance aſk;
You'll have a very arduous taſk,
Unleſs you call for aid.

Great is the charge you have in care:
Indeed, my pretty maidens fair,
His ſituation's nice:
As Chamberlain we ſhall expect
That he, ſole guardian, ſhall protect
Six maids, without a vice.

Epigram on the NEW PAVEMENT.

THE new Scottiſh pavement is worthy of praiſe,
We're indebted to Scotland for *mending our ways*;
But, what we can never forgive 'em, ſome ſay,
Is, that they have taken our *poſts* all away.

On the DUCHESS *of* RUTLAND.

By the EARL *of* CHESTERFIELD.

WHAT do ſcholars, and bards, and aſtronomers wiſe,
Mean by ſtuffing our heads with nonſenſe and lies,
By telling us Venus muſt always appear
In a car, or a ſhell, or a twinkling ſtar,
Drawn by ſparrows, or ſwans, or dolphins, or doves,
Attended in form by the graces and loves:
That ambroſia and nectar is all ſhe will taſte,
And her paſſport to hearts on a belt round her waiſt;
Without all this buſtle I ſaw the bright dame;
To ſupper laſt night to P——y's ſhe came
In a good warm ſedan; no fine open car;
Two chairmen her doves, and a flambeau her ſtar:
No nectar ſhe drank, no ambroſia ſhe eat;
Her cup was plain claret, a chicken her meat:
Nor wanted a ceſtus her boſom to grace,
For Rutland, that night, had lent her her face.

On

On the Banifhment of CICERO.

Written by the Duke of Wharton, *and firft printed when* Atterbury, *Bifhop of* Rochefter, *was banifhed in* 1724.

I.

AS o'er the fwelling ocean's tide
An exile Tully rode,
The bulwark of the Roman ftate,
In act, in thought, a god;
The facred genius of majeftic Rome
Defcends, and thus laments her patriot's doom.

II.

Farewell! renown'd in arts, farewell!
Thus conquer'd by thy foe,
Of honours, and of friends depriv'd,
In exile muft thou go:
Yet go content; thy look, thy will fedate,
Thy foul fuperior to the fhocks of fate.

III.

Thy wifdom was thy only guilt,
Thy virtue thy offence,
With god-like zeal thou didft efpoufe
Thy country's juft defence:

No ſordid hopes could charm thy ſteady ſoul,
No fears, nor guilty numbers could controul.

IV.

What tho' the nobleſt patriots ſtood
  Firm to thy ſacred cauſe,
What tho' thou could'ſt diſplay the force
  Of rhet'rick and of laws;
No eloquence, no reaſon could repel
Th' united ſtrength of Clodius and of hell.

V.

Thy mighty ruin to effect
  What plots have been deviſ'd!
What arts! what perjuries been uſ'd!
  What laws and rites deſpiſ'd!
How many fools and knaves by bribes allur'd,
And witneſſes by hopes and threats ſecur'd!

VI.

And yet they act their dark deceit
  Veil'd with a nice diſguiſe,
And form a ſpecious ſhew of right
  From treachery and lies;
With arbitrary power the people awe,
And coin unjuſt oppreſſion into law.

VII.

VII.

Let Clodius now in grandeur reign,
Let him exert his pow'r,
A ſhort-liv'd monſter in the land,
The monarch of an hour;
Let pageant fools adore their wooden god,
And act againſt their ſenſes at his nod.

VIII.

Pierc'd by an untimely hand
To earth ſhall he deſcend,
Tho' now with gaudy honours cloath'd,
Inglorious in his end.
Bleſt be the man who does his pow'r defy,
And dares or truly ſpeak, or bravely die.

Stanzas by Lord CAPEL. *Written when he was a priſoner in the* Tower, *during* Cromwell's *uſurpation.*

I.

BEAT on, proud billows; Boreas, blow;
Swell, curled waves, high as Jove's roof;
Your incivilities do plainly ſhew,
That innocence is tempeſt proof.

Tho' furly Nereus frowns, my thoughts are calm:
Then ftrike, affliction, for thy wounds are balm.

II.

That which the world mifcalls a jail,
A private clofet is to me;
Whilft a good confcience is my bail,
And innocence my liberty:
Locks, bars, and folitude, together met,
Make me no pris'ner, but an anchoret.

III.

Here fin, for want of food, muft ftarve,
Where tempting objects are not feen;
And thefe ftrong walls do only ferve
To keep rogues out, and keep me in.
Malice is now grown charitable, fure;
I'm not committed, but I'm kept fecure.

IV.

And whilft I wifh to be retir'd,
Into this private room I'm turn'd;
As if their wifdom had confpir'd
The falamander fhould be burn'd.
Or, like thofe fophifts who would drown a fifh,
I am condemn'd to fuffer what I wifh.

V.

V.

The Cynic hugs his poverty,
  The pelican her wildernefs;
And 'tis the Indian's pride to be
  Naked on frozen Caucafus.
Contentment feels no fmart; ftoics, we fee,
Make torments eafy by their apathy.

VI.

I'm in this cabinet lock'd up,
  Like fome high prized margarite;
Or like fome great mogul or pope,
  I'm cloifter'd up from public fight.
Retir'dnefs is a part of majefty,
And thus, proud fultan, I'm as great as thee.

VII.

Thefe manacles upon mine arm
  I as my miftrefs' favours wear;
And for to keep mine ancles warm,
  I have fome iron fhackles there.
Thefe walls are but my garifon; this cell,
Which men call jail, doth prove my citadel.

VIII.

Thus he that ftruck at Jafon's life,
  Thinking to make his purpofe fure,

By a malicious friendly knife
  Did only wound him to his cure.
Malice, we ſee, wants wit, for what is meant
Miſchief, oft times proves favour by th' event.

IX.

Although I cannot ſee my king,
  Neither in perſon, nor in coin;
Yet contemplation is a thing
  That renders what I have not mine.
My king from me no adamant can part,
Whom I do wear engraven in my heart.

X.

Have you not heard the nightingale,
  A pris'ner cloſe kept in a cage,
How ſhe doth chant her wonted tale
  In that her narrow hermitage.
Ev'n that her melody doth plainly prove,
Her boughs are trees, her cage a pleaſant grove.

XI.

My ſoul is free as is th' ambient air,
  Which doth my outward parts include;
Whilſt loyal thoughts do ſtill repair
  To company my ſolitude.

What

What tho' they do with chains my body bind,
My king can only captivate my mind.

XII.

I am that bird which they combine
Thus to deprive of liberty;
And tho' my corpſe they can confine,
Yet maugre that my ſoul is free.
Tho' I'm mew'd up, yet I can chirp and ſing,
Diſgrace to rebels, glory to my king.

In ſome copies of this poem the following ſtanza is inſerted between the ſeventh and eighth:

When once my prince affliction hath,
Proſperity doth treaſon ſeem;
And for to ſmooth ſo rough a path,
I can learn patience from him.
But now to ſuffer ſhews a legal part;
When kings want eaſe, ſubjects muſt learn to ſmart.

But this ſtanza utterly deſtroys the uniformity of the poem, and is inconſiſtent with every other part of it. The deſign of the whole is, to repreſent as benefits what had by his enemies been intended as puniſhments, and to ſhew, that "malice wants wit to effect its purpoſe:" but this ſtanza contains

contains an acknowledgment, that malice has effected its purpose upon him; that he suffers; and that it is fit he should suffer. For this reason, and because it is not in all copies, it is omitted in this, either as composed by the author, and afterwards rejected, or as interpolated by some other.

Verses by Sir WALTER RALEIGH.

GO soul, the body's guest,
Upon a thankless arrant,
Fear not to touch the best,
The truth shall be thy warrant.
Go, since I needs must dye,
And give them all the lye.

Go, tell the court it glowse
And shines like painted wood;
Go, tell the church it showes
What's good, does no good.
If court and church replye,
Give court and church the lye.

Tell potentates they live
Actinge, but oh! their actions
Not lov'd unless they give!
Not strong, but by their factions.

If

If potentates replye,
Give potentates the lye.

Tell me not of high condition,
That rule affairs of ſtate,
Their purpoſe is ambition;
Their practice only hate.
And if they do replye,
Then give them all the lye.

Tell thoſe that brave it moſte,
They begge more by ſpendinge;
Who, in their greateſt coſte,
Seek nothing but commendinge.
And if they make replye,
Spare not to give the lye.

Tell zeal it lacks devotion;
Tell love it is but luſte;
Tell time it is but motion;
Tell fleſh it is but duſte.
And wiſh them not replye,
For thou muſt give the lye.

Tell age it daily waſteth;
Tell honour how it alters;
Tell beautye that it blaſteth;
Tell favour that ſhe falters.

And

And as they do replye,
Give every one the lye.

Tell wit how much it wrangles
In fickle points of niceneſs;
Tell wiſdom ſhe entangles
Herſelf in over-wiſeneſs.
And if they do replye,
Then give them both the lye.

Tell phyſick of her boldneſs;
Tell ſkill it is pretenſion;
Tell charity of coldneſs;
Tell law it is contention.
And if they yield replye,
Then give them ſtill the lye.

Tell fortune of her blindneſs;
Tell nature of decay;
Tell friendſhip of unkindneſs;
Tell juſtice of delay.
And if they do replye,
Then give them all the lye.

Tell artes they have no ſoundneſs,
But vary by eſteeminge;
Tell ſkollers lack profoundneſs,
And ſtand too much on ſeeminge.

If

If artes and ſkollers replye,
Give artes and ſkollers the lye.

Tell faith its fled the cittye;
Tell how the country errethe;
Tell manhood ſhakes of pytie;
Tell virtue leaſt preferreth.
And if they do replye,
Spare not to give the lye.

So when thou haſt, as I
Commanded thee, done blabbing;
Althoughe to give the lye
Deſerves no leſs than ſtabbing.
Yet ſtab at thee who will,
No ſtab the ſoul can kill.

A PARODY *on the Foregoing.*
Written in 1764.

GO, truth, unwelcome gueſt!
Upon a thankleſs errant;
Fear not to touch the beſt,
For truth is a ſafe warrant.
Go, ſince thou needs muſt die,
And give them all the lie.

Go

Go, tell the Tory faction,
  Now in their noontide hour,
England won't bear an action
  Of an arbitrary power.
If Tories should reply,
Give Tories all the lie.

Go, tell th' ennobl'd Thief,
  While cares oppress him most,
He ne'er shall taste relief
  From guilt——from Ayliffe's ghost.
And if the Thief reply,
Then give the Thief the lie.

Go, tell the Scottish Thane,
  Rais'd high by r—— lust,
That lust shall prove his bane,
  And lay him in the dust.
And should the Thane reply,
Then say, Proud Thane, you lie.

Go, tell the immortal Pitt,
  Author of England's glory,
He shall recorded sit
  Foremost in future story.
* * * * * * * * * * * * *
* * * * * * * * * * * * *
* * * *Cætera desunt.*

The

The DIAMOND.

A FABLE.

LONG on Golconda's ſhore a diamond lay
Neglected, rough, conceal'd in common clay:
By every paſſenger deſpis'd and ſcorn'd,
The latent jewel thus in ſecret mourn'd,
" Why am I thus to ſordid earth confin'd,
" Why ſcorn'd and trod upon by every hind?
" Were theſe bright qualities, this glitterring " hue,
" And dazzling luſtre, never meant for view?
" Wrapt in eternal ſhade if I remain,
" Theſe ſhining virtues were beſtow'd in vain."
As thus the long-neglected gem diſplay'd
Its worth and wrongs, a ſkilful artiſt ſtray'd
By chance that way, and ſaw with curious eye,
Tho' much obſcur'd, th' unvalu'd treaſure lie.
He ground with care, he poliſh'd it with art,
And call'd forth all its rays from every part;
And now young Delia's neck ordain'd to grace,
It adds new charms to beauty's faireſt face.

And

The mind of man neglected and untaught,
Is this rough diamond in the mine unwrought;
Till education lend her art, unknown
The brighteſt talents lie, a common ſtone;
By her fair hand when faſhion'd, the new mind
Riſes with luſtre, poliſh'd and refin'd.

The FARMER.

O Happy he! happieſt of mortal men!
Who far remov'd from ſlavery as from pride,
Fears no man's frown, nor cringing waits to catch
The gracious nothing of a great man's nod:
Where the lac'd beggar buſtles for a bribe,
The purchaſe of his honour; where deceit,
And fraud, and circumvention, dreſt in ſmiles,
Hold ſhameful commerce, and beneath the maſk
Of friendſhip and ſincerity, betray.
Him, nor the ſtately manſion's gilded pride,
Rich with whate'er the imitative arts,
Painting or ſculpture, yield to charm the eye;
Nor ſhining heaps of maſſy plate, unwrought
With curious, coſtly workmanſhip, allure.

Tempted

Tempted nor with the pride nor pomp of power,
Nor pageants of ambition, nor the mines
Of grafping av'rice, nor the poifon'd fweets
Of pamper'd luxury, he plants his foot
With firmnefs on his old paternal fields,
And ftands unfhaken. There fweet profpects rife
Of meadows fmiling in their flow'ry pride,
Green hills and dales, and cottages embower'd,
The fcenes of innocence, and calm delight.
There the wild melody of warbling birds,
And cool refrefhing groves, and murmuring fprings,
Invite to facred thought, and lift the mind
From low purfuits, to meditate the God!

On Good Humour. Written at Eton *School,* 1729.

TELL me, ye fons of Phœbus, what is this
Which all admire, but few, too few poffefs?
A virtue 'tis to ancient maids unknown,
And prudes, who fpy all faults except their own.
Lov'd and defended by the brave and wife,
Tho' knaves abufe it, and like fools defpife.

Say, Wyndham, if 'tis poſſible to tell,
What is the thing in which you moſt excell?
Hard is the queſtion, for in all you pleaſe,
Yet ſure good-nature is your nobleſt praiſe;
Secur'd by this your parts no envy move,
For none can envy him, whom all muſt love.
This magic pow'r can make e'en folly pleaſe,
This to Pitt's genius adds a brighter grace,
And ſweetens ev'ry charm in Cælia's face.

LYTTELTON.

LUCIAN'S *Greek Epigram.*

Inſcribed on a Column erected in a Piece of Land, that had been often bought and ſold; Imitated.

I Whom thou ſee'ſt begirt with towering oaks,
Was once the property of John o'Nokes;
On him proſperity no longer ſmiles,
And now I feed the flocks of John o'Stiles.
My former maſter call'd me by his name,
My preſent owner fondly does the ſame;
While I, alike unworthy of their cares,
Quick paſs to captors, purchaſers, or heirs.
Let no one henceforth take me for his own,
For Fortune! Fortune! I am thine alone.

A De-

A Defcription of Spring in London.

NOW new-made filks the mercer's window fhows,
And his fpruce 'prentice wears his Sunday cloaths,
His annual fuit with niceft tafte renew'd,
The reigning cut and colour ftill purfu'd.
The barrow now, with oranges a fcore,
Driven by at once a gamefter and a whore,
No longer gulls the ftripling of his pence,
Who learns that poverty is nurfe to fenfe.
Much-injur'd trader whom the law purfues,
The law which wink'd, and beckon'd to the Jews,
Why fhould the beadle drive thee from the ftreet?
To fell is always a pretence to cheat.
" Large ftewing oyfters" in a deepening groan,
No more refounds, nor " muffels" fhriller tone;
Seven days to labour now is held no crime,
And Moll " new mackrel" fcreams in fermon-time.
In-ruddy bunches raddifhes are fpread,
And Nan with choice-pickt fallads loads her head;
Now in the fuperb window Chriftmas green,
The bays and holly, are no longer feen,

But ſprigs of garden-mint in phials grow,
And gather'd laylocks periſh as they blow.
The truant ſchool-boy now at eve we meet,
Fatigu'd and ſweating thro' the crowded ſtreet,
His ſhoes embrown'd at once with duſt and clay,
With white-thorn loaded, which he takes for
May;
Round his flapp'd hat in rings the cowſlips twine,
Or in cleft oſiers form a golden line.
On milk-pail rear'd the borrow'd ſalvers glare,
Topp'd with a tankard, which two porters bear,
Reeking, they ſlowly toil o'er rugged ſtones,
And joyleſs beldames dance with aking bones:
More blithe the powder'd tye-wig'd ſons of ſoot
Trip to the ſhovel with a ſhoeleſs foot.
In gay Vaux-hall now ſaunter beaux and belles,
And happier cits reſort to Sadler's-wells.

On HAPPINESS.

O Happineſs, where's thy reſort?
Amidſt the ſplendor of a court!
Or doſt thou more delight to dwell
With humble hermit in his cell,
In ſearch of truth? or doſt thou rove
Thro' Plato's academic grove?

Or

Or elſe, with Epicurus gay,
Laugh at the farces mortals play?
Or with the Graces, doſt thou lead
The ſportive dance along the mead?
Or in Bellona's bloody car,
Exult amidſt the ſcenes of war?
No more I'll ſearch, no more I'll mind thee,
Fair fugitive;———I cannot find thee!

The Conqueror and the Old Woman. A FABLE.

A Perſian monarch, one of thoſe
Whoſe great ambition knew no bound;
Some Cyrus, or Darius we'll ſuppoſe,
In whom no other vice was found,
If we dare name ambition ſo,
For ſome doubt whether it be vice or no;
I have not time at preſent to confute,
So grant the queſtion rather than diſpute.
This Sophi far and wide his conqueſts ſpread;
Full thirty crowns, or more,
Were pil'd on his anointed head,
And yet the weight with eaſe he bore;
For 'twas his great and chief delight
To break the yoke his vanquiſh'd ſubjects wore,
And make their burden light.

Attentive to the voice of the diſtreſs'd,
Juſtice and virtue flouriſh'd in his reign;
When from the confines of his vaſt domain
A good old woman who had been oppreſs'd,
Came to the footſtool of his throne
To have her grievances redreſs'd;
And thus in piteous tragic tone
His majeſty addreſs'd:
" Encourag'd by your fame, I come from far;
" Sir, you're our king by right of war;
" By right of ſubject I for juſtice ſue;
" I claim it; and you'll grant it; 'tis my due.
" My daughter raviſh'd, and my houſe deſtroy'd,
" And all by one whom you employ'd
" To act the king in place of you."
" I doubt not but all this is true,"
The conſcious prince replied;
" But ſo far off, what can I do?
" To make my people happy is my pride;
" And yet I cannot every where reſide.
" The ſun, which all the world ſurrounds,
" Shines and enlivens but to certain bounds;
" The reſt are dark and cold."
" That's argued ill, if I may be ſo bold,"
Return'd the matron to the ſovereign,
" 'Twas weak to graſp at what you cannot hold,
" And conquer more than you can govern."
While

While o'er the ſea of life we take our trip,
  Kings are by heaven commiſſion'd to command;
Captains, not owners of the ſhip,
  'Tis theirs to ſteer the people ſafe to land;
And when the bark with prudence they convey,
We row with pleaſure, and with pride obey.

The Courtier's CREED. *Written in the Year* 1731; *and never before printed.*

I Believe in K. G. II. the greateſt captain and the wiſeſt monarch between heaven and earth; and in Sir R. Walpole his only miniſter, our lord; who was begotten by B—— the a——y, born of Mrs. Walpole of Houghton, accuſed of corruption; was convicted, expelled, and impriſoned; he went down into Norfolk the third year; he came up again, got into the adminiſtration, and now ſits at the head of the Treaſury, from whence he ſhall pay all thoſe who vote as they are bid.

I believe in Horace's treaties, the *ſanctity* of the biſhops, the *independency* of the lords, the *integrity*

integrity of the commons; and I look for reſtitution from the Spaniards, diſcharge of the public debts, and peace everlaſting.

AMEN.

The Art of Coquetry. By Mrs. CHARLOTTE LENOX.

YE lovely maids! whoſe yet unpractis'd hearts
Ne'er felt the force of love's reſiſtleſs darts;
Who juſtly ſet a value on your charms,
Pow'r all your wiſh, but beauty all your arms;
Who o'er mankind would fain exert your ſway,
And teach the lordly tyrant to obey;
Attend my rules, to you alone addreſt,
Deep let them ſink in every female breaſt.
The queen of love herſelf my boſom fires,
Aſſiſts my numbers, and my thoughts inſpires;
Me ſhe inſtructed in each ſecret art,
How to enſlave and keep each vanquiſh'd heart;
The ſigh that heaves by ſtealth, the ſtarting tear,
The melting languiſh, the obliging fear,

Half-

Half-utter'd wiſhes, broken, kind replies,
And all the ſilent eloquence of eyes;
To teach the fair by various wiles to move
The ſoften'd ſoul, and lead the heart to love.
Proud of her charms, and conſcious of her face,
The haughty beauty calls forth every grace,
With fierce defiance throws the killing dart;
By force ſhe wins, by force ſhe keeps the heart.
The witty fair a nobler game purſues,
Aims at the head, but the rapt ſoul ſubdues.
The languid nymph enſlaves with ſofter art,
With ſweet neglect ſhe ſteals into the heart,
Slowly ſhe moves her ſwimming eyes around,
Conceals the ſhaft, but meditates the wound;
Her gentle languiſhments the gazers move,
Her voice is muſic, and her looks are love:
To few tho' nature may theſe gifts impart,
What ſhe with-holds, the wiſe can win from art.
Then let your airs be ſuited to her face,
Nor to a languiſh tack a ſprightly grace.
The ſhort round face, briſk eyes, and auburn hair,
Muſt ſmiling joy in every motion wear,
The quick unſettled glance muſt deal around,
Hide all deſign, and ſeem by chance to wound.

Dark

Dark rolling eyes a languifh may affume,
Thefe the foft looks and melting air become:
The penfive head upon the hand reclin'd,
As if fome fweet diforder fill'd the mind;
Let the heav'd breaft a ftruggling figh reftrain,
And feem to ftop the falling tear with pain.
The youth, who all the foft diftrefs believes,
Soon wants the kind compaffion that he gives;
But beauty, wit, and youth may fometimes fail,
Nor always o'er the ftubborn foul prevail;
Then let the fair one have recourfe to art;
Who cannot ftorm, may undermine the heart.
Firft form your artful looks with ftudious care,
From mild to grave, from tender to fevere;
Oft on the carelefs youth your glances dart,
A tender meaning let each glance impart.
Whene'er he meets your looks, with modeft pride,
And foft confufion turn your eyes afide;
Let a foft figh fteal out, as if by chance,
Then cautious turn, and fteal another glance.
Caught by thefe arts, with pride and hope elate,
The deftin'd victim rufhes on his fate:
Pleaf'd, his imagin'd victory purfues,
And the kind maid with foft attention views;
Contemplates now her fhape, her air, her face,
And thinks each feature wears an added grace;

Till

Till gratitude, which firſt his boſom proves,
By ſlow degrees ſublim'd, at length he loves
'Tis harder ſtill to fix, than gain a heart;
What's won by beauty, muſt be kept by art.
Too kind a treatment the bleſt lover cloys,
And oft deſpair the growing flame deſtroys:
Sometimes with ſmiles receive him, ſometimes tears,
And wiſely balance both his hopes and fears.
Perhaps he mourns his ill-requited pains,
Condemns your ſway, and ſtrives to break his chains;
Behaves as if he now your ſcorn defy'd,
And thinks at leaſt he ſhall alarm your pride:
But with indifference view the ſeemed change,
And let your eyes to ſeek new conqueſts range;
While his torn breaſt with jealous fury burns,
He hopes, deſpairs, adores, and hates by turns;
With anguiſh now repents the weak deceit,
And powerful paſſion bears him to your feet.
Strive not the jealous lover to perplex,
Ill ſuits ſuſpicion with that haughty ſex;
Raſhly they judge, and always think the worſt,
And love is often baniſh'd by diſtruſt:
To theſe an open free behaviour wear,
Awful diſguiſe, and ſeem at leaſt ſincere;

Whenc'er

Whene'er you meet, affect a glad ſurprize,
And give a melting ſoftneſs to your eyes:
By ſome unguarded word your love reveal,
And anxiouſly the riſing bluſh conceal.
By arts like theſe the jealous you deceive,
Then moſt deluded when they moſt believe.
But while in all you ſeek to raiſe deſire,
Beware the fatal paſſion you inſpire;
Each ſoft intruding wiſh in time reprove,
And guard againſt the ſweet invader love.
Not for the tender were theſe rules deſign'd,
Who in their faces ſhow their yielding mind:
Whoſe eyes a native languiſhment can wear,
Whoſe ſmiles are artleſs, and whoſe bluſh ſincere;
But for the nymph who liberty can prize,
And vindicate the triumph of her eyes:
Who o'er mankind a haughty rule maintains,
Whoſe wit can manage what her beauty gains:
Such by theſe arts their empire may improve,
And unſubdu'd controul the world by love.

On

On the Death of YORICK, *the Reverend Mr.* STERNE, *Author of Triſtram Shandy,* &c.

WITH wit and genuine humour to diſpel,
From the deſponding boſom, gloomy care,
And bid the guſhing tear, at the ſad tale
Of hapleſs love or filial grief, to flow
From the full ſympathiſing heart, were thine
Theſe pow'rs, O Sterne ! But now thy fate demand
(No plumage nodding o'er the emblazon'd hearſe,
Proclaiming honours, where no virtue ſhone)
But the ſad tribute of the heart-felt ſigh.
What, tho' no taper caſt its deadly ray,
Or the full choir ſing requiems o'er the tomb,
The humbler grief of friendſhip is not mute.
And poor Maria, with her faithful kid,
Her auburn treſſes careleſsly entwin'd
With olive foliage, at the cloſe of day
Shall chant her plaintive veſpers at thy grave.
Thy ſhade too, gentle monk, 'mid awful night
Shall pour libations from its friendly eye;
For erſt his ſweet benevolence beſtow'd
Its generous pity, and bedew'd with tears
The ſod, which reſted on the aged breaſt.

Epitaph

Epitaph on Mr. QUIN. *By Mr.* GARRICK.

THAT tongue, which ſet the table on a
roar,
And charm'd the public ear, is heard no more!
Clos'd are thoſe eyes, the harbingers of wit,
Which ſpoke, before the tongue, what Shake-
ſpeare writ.
Cold are thoſe hands, which, living, were ſtretch'd
forth,
At friendſhip's call, to ſuccour modeſt worth.
Here lies James Quin! deign, reader, to be
taught,
(Whate'er thy ſtrength of body, force of thought,
In nature's happieſt mould however caſt)
To this complexion thou muſt come at laſt.

On the Friendſhip of two young Ladies, 1730.

HAIL, beauteous pair, whom friendſhip
binds
In ſofteſt, yet in ſtrongeſt ties;
Soft as the temper of your minds,
Strong as the luſtre of your eyes:

So

So Venus's doves in couples fly,
And friendly ſteer their equal courſe;
Whoſe feathers Cupid's ſhafts ſupply,
And wing them with reſiſtleſs force.

Thus as you move love's tender flame,
Like that of friendſhip, paler burns;
Both our divided paſſion claim,
And friends and rivals prove by turns.

Then eaſe yourſelves and bleſs mankind,
Friendſhip ſo curſt no more purſue:
In wedlock's roſy bow'r you'll find
The joys of love and friendſhip too.

A MAN *in* LOVE.

L'Homme qui ne ſe trouve point & ne ſe trouvera jamais.

By Lady Mary Wortley Montague.

THE man who feels the dear diſeaſe
Forgets himſelf, neglects to pleaſe:
The crowd avoids, and ſeeks the groves,
And much he thinks when much he loves;

Treſs'd

Prefs'd with alternate hope and fear,
Sighs in her abfence, fighs when fhe is near.
The gay, the fond, the fair, the young,
Thofe trifles pafs unfeen along;
To him a pert, infipid throng.
But moft he fhuns the vain coquet;
Contemns her falfe affected wit:
The minftrels found, the flowing bowl
Opprefs and hurt the am'rous foul;
'Tis folitude alone can pleafe,
And give fome intervals of eafe:
He feeds the foft diftemper there,
And fondly courts the diftant fair;
To balls the filent fhade prefers,
And hates all other charms but hers.
When thus your abfent fwain can do,
Molly, you may believe him true.

An INSCRIPTION.

Written upon one of the Tubs in Ham *Walks*, September MDCCLX.

DARK was the fky with many a cloud,
The fearful lightnings flafh'd around,
Low to the blaft the foreft bow'd,
And bellowing thunders rock'd the ground;

Faft

Faſt fell the rains upon my head,
And weak and weary were my feet,
When, lo! this hoſpitable ſhed
At length ſupplied a kind retreat.

That in fair memory's faithful page
The bard's eſcape may flouriſh long,
Yet ſhuddering from the tempeſt's rage,
He dedicates the votive ſong.

For ever ſacred be the earth
From whence the tree its vigour drew!
The hour that gave the ſeedling birth!
The foreſt where the ſcyon grew!

Long honour'd may his aſhes reſt,
Who firſt the tender ſhoot did rear!
Bleſt be his name!——But doubly bleſt
The friendly hand that plac'd it here!

O ne'er may war, or wind, or wave,
This pleaſurable ſcene deform,
But time ſtill ſpare the ſeat which gave
The poet ſhelter from the ſtorm.

A SONG. *By a Noble Lord.*

RESOLV'D, as her poet, of Cælia to ſing,
For ideas of beauty I ſearch'd thro' the ſpring;
To flowers ſoft blooming compar'd the ſweet maid;
But flowers, tho' blooming, at ev'ning may fade.

Of ſun-ſhine and breezes I next thought to write,
Of the breezes ſo ſoft, and the ſun-ſhine ſo bright;
But theſe with my fair no reſemblance will hold,
For the ſun ſets at night, and the breezes grow cold.

The clouds of mild ev'ning array'd in pale blue,
While the ſun-beams behind them peep'd glittering thro',
Tho' to rival her charms they can never ariſe,
Yet, methought, they look'd ſomething like Cælia's ſweet eyes.

Theſe beauties are tranſient, but Cælia's will laſt,
When ſpring, and when ſummer, and autumn are paſt;

For ſenſe and good humour no ſeaſon diſarms,
And the ſoul of my Cælia enlivens her charms.

At length, on a fruit-tree a bloſſom I found,
Which beauty diſplayed, and ſhed fragrance around,
I then thought the muſes had ſmil'd on my pray'r,
This bloſſom, I cry'd, will reſemble my fair!

Theſe colours ſo gay, and united ſo well,
This delicate texture and raviſhing ſmell,
Be her perſon's ſweet emblem! but where ſhall I find
In nature a beauty that equals her mind!

This bloſſom ſo pleaſing, at ſummer's gay call,
Muſt languiſh at firſt, and muſt afterwards fall,
But behind it the fruit, its ſucceſſor, ſhall riſe,
By nature diſrob'd of its beauteous diſguiſe.

So Cælia, when youth, that gay bloſſom, is o'er,
By her virtues improv'd ſhall engage me the more,
Shall recall ev'ry beauty that brighten'd her prime,
When her merit is ripen'd by love and by time.

JOHN, *the* ENGLISH *Footman.* *A Tale.*

THE chiming bells from ev'ry ſteeple
Proclaim'd to well-diſpoſed people,
That they muſt be repairing ſoon
To ſervice of the afternoon:
That is—it now was almoſt three;
My lord, ſtill at his morning tea,
(For it was Sunday, and you know
What then good folks of faſhion do)
My lady holds engag'd in chat,
In blaming this, reforming that:
" Since, my dear lord, at your command,
" I took the management in hand,
" You know, 'twas always my endeavour,
" Your houſe ſhould be polite and clever.
" How well your dignity it ſuits
" To have diſcharg'd your Engliſh brutes!
" I think, there now remains but one—
" And he, becauſe your tenant's ſon!
" Muſt we be plagu'd with ſuch a ſot
" In complaiſance to farmer Trot?"
My lord replies,—" Trot pays his rent,
" And can make votes to parliament:
" And often ſends us chines and turkies;
" And John, too, capable of work is.

—" Send

—" Send him to work then in your ſtable—
" Oh! ſuch a wretch to wait at table!
" Indeed, my dear, it gives me pain,
" To ſee him ſhock the *Gens de bien*
" With toes turn'd in, and awkward mien!
" So this I do inſiſt upon,
" That he immediately be gone!"
" Since 'tis your pleaſure, go he muſt—
" Yet to aſſign ſome cauſe—were juſt—
" At leaſt what plauſible may ſeem——
" And that's conſiſtent with my ſcheme.
" In the militia we will ſwear him;
" I'll write to Fielding not to ſpare him:
" Theſe purpoſes will anſwer double,
" Firſt, in diſcharging you of trouble,
" And in procuring me the merit
" Of acting with a gen'rous ſpirit:
" My lord (they ſay) don't even ſpare,
" His own domeſtics from the war,
" How ardent for the public weal!
" Example rare of noble zeal!
" But, let us ſound him firſt, to know
" Whether the rogue's inclin'd to go;
" If you, my dear, approve the meaſure,"—
" Yes—call him up"——My lord, your pleaſure.
" John, thou'rt a fellow tall and luſty,
" Of heart right ſound, and courage truſty;

" Can you yourfelf in humour bring
" To ferve your country and your king,
" And ftrait fome juftice go before,
" In the militia to be fwore?"
Militia!—what is that, my lord?
I do not underftand the word—
" Why, John, it means the French (ah, hang 'em!)
" Soundly whene'er you meet to bang 'em"—
Is that the cafe?—with all my heart—
I'll do my beft to play my part—
John ftrait retires with awkward airs,
And meets the valet on the ftairs,
Whom he accofts with one falute
Of rightly pois'd, elaftic foot,
Which fent Monfieur a headlong falling,
And left him at the bottom fprawling.
My lord's Frifeur he next attacks
With frequent cuffs, and Englifh thwacks:
And while he drefs'd my lady's tête
John curl'd his locks and comb'd his pate.
Then hurrying in the kitchen goes,
And baftes the cook, and tweaks his nofe;
" Vat be de matter, villian, rogue,
" Me kill you, thou one Englifh dog!"
Soho, quoth John, Monfieur Ragou,
Since you thus froth and fputter fo,
I muft apply my drudger too; }

I

If that won't do—you ſhall, unpity'd,
Be ſent to Garrick to be ſpitted!
Janton he next attacks, and throws
Over her head at once her cloaths:
(And (ſad diſaſter!) found—to ſhock one,
That poor Janton had no ſmock on!)
Who hurries ſtrait to Ma'moiſelle
Enrag'd her loud complaints to tell,
Who interfering in the rout;
" Fine vark indeed dis, Maitre Trotte!
" I'll do your bus'neſs ſtrait," ſhe cries,
And up ſtairs to my lady flies,
And ſcarce, quite out of breath, could ſay,
" *Eh! quelles barbares, quelles ſots Anglois!*
" Trot has been making ſuch a riot!"
The ſcoundrel Trot? lord, lady cry out—
Your Valet—Cook—and Friſeur bang'd!
—Send him to Fielding to be hang'd!
" And in the ſight of the poſtilion
" O'er Janton's head caſt her *cotillon*;
" And *vat vas varſe, à mon ſurpriſe,*
" *Pauvre Janton* had no *Chemiſe*"—
Go hang him without judge or jury,
Cries out my lady in a fury.
John ſummon'd now before 'em all,
With aching heart attends the call,

" *Fripon, poltron,* vile Engliſh varlet,"
My lady ſcreams, as red as ſcarlet;
While the ſoft voice of Ma'moiſelle
With poll and lap-dog join the yell.
Poor John, confus'd with wild diſmay,
Trembling, and fault'ring, ſcarce could ſay,
Only—one word—my lord, I pray.
I'm ſorry thus to have offended,
But I no harm at all intended.
Your lordſhip's orders, and my oath,
You know, my lord, oblige me both
To maul the French, to bang and beat 'em
In whatſoever place I meet 'em.
" Hold, John—you quite miſtake the matter,
" But not on this ſide of the water;
" In Flanders beat 'em if you can;
" And there you'll ſhew yourſelf a man.
" Or if they ever ſhould be found
" To land their force on Britiſh ground,
" Why then you might exert your ſallies
" To drive 'em back again to Calais.
" The French ſo ever *degagé*,
" So airy, gay, polite, and free,
" Tho' object of the vulgar ſpite,
" By long preſcription have a right
" To the protection of the great,
" Who live in affluence and ſtate:

" Whom

" Whom our domeftics, when we ftyle 'em,
" Our houfes are their fure afylum ;
" Their characters are facred there ;
" So that, if faucy fcoundrels dare
" T' infult their perfons, or to bait 'em,
" 'Tis conftru'd *Scandalum magnatum* ;
" Then breach of privilege enfues,
" With fines, imprifonments, and dues :
" Nor, till unto our wills we bend 'em,
" Can *habeas corpus's* defend 'em.
" Therefore for your prefumption, John,
" Uncafe this moment—and be gone !"

The Laughing PHILOSOPHER.

WHEN I take an attentive furvey of mankind,
From their follies and vices diverfion I find ;
Their humours, caprices, their whims and odd ways,
Senfations of mirth in me conftantly raife.
Ev'ry place is with curious, choice characters ftor'd,
Which, from morning to night, entertainment afford.

In

In each lane, in each alley, court, ſquare, row, or ſtreet,
Scenes truly Hogarthian I fail not to meet;
Scenes which would not in many a muſcle provoke,
But I, from the dulleſt can ſtrike out a joke.
In every man's motions I merriment trace,
And can laughter extract from the diſmalleſt face.
When I ſee men and women induſtriouſly ſhun
Their own thoughts, and each ev'ning to card-tables run;
When dowagers, dreſs'd up like girls of fifteen,
In the front of a ſide box are mad to be ſeen;
When a blooming young creature to threeſcore is ty'd,
That to routs and to plays ſhe in diamonds may ride;
When ladies, to ſhew their no-learning, talk Latin,
And tradeſmen their ſcabbards adorn with white ſattin;
When a poor tallow-chandler, deceas'd, lies in ſtate,
Who alive, perhaps, had not five pounds worth of plate;

When

When fat-headed aldermen ſet up for wit,
With laughter my ſides are juſt ready to ſplit:
When a pert Temple beau the fine gentleman apes,
And prentices brag of their duels and rapes;
When a young academic aſcends, with an air,
To the pulpit, and tries to attract all the fair,
And oft, in the midſt of his flow'ry diſcourſe,
Looks around to obſerve if his eyes have had force:
When travell'd young fops talk of nothing but France,
When old maids learn to ſing, and grown gentlemen dance;
When pious Ned Shuter at Whitefield's appears,
I laugh till my eyes are bedimm'd with my tears.
When women neglect their domeſtic affairs,
And puzzle their heads with political cares;
When with zeal patriotic they puddings deſpiſe,
And chatter of taxes, and loans, and ſupplies;
When thoſe who have nothing to loſe fume and fret
At the lowneſs of ſtocks and the national debt,
And rail at the court in a paſſionate ſtyle,
I hollow ſo loud, you may hear me a mile.

TEMPO-

Tempora Mutantur.

IN former days I've heard it ſaid,
'Ere Grafton was in place,
A diff'rent ſort of life he led,
And wore a different face.

His cheek with patriotiſm glow'd,
At Wildman's oft he din'd;
To liberty he plann'd the road,
And was, like juſtice, blind.

With Temple, and with Wilkes was ſeen,
The glorious cauſe wou'd drink:
But now, ſuch names create the ſpleen,
And liberty may ſink.

Is friendſhip baniſh'd from the great?
Are there no honeſt hearts?
Thrice happy is that modern ſtate,
Thus rul'd by men of parts;

A birth-day ſuit might now take place,
Wou'd ſilence all repining;
Courtiers wear honour 'ſtead of lace,
And honeſty for lining.

Patriots

Patriots might, then, walk hand in hand,
Thus arm'd tout cap-à-pee;
Diſſention, ſoon, wou'd quit the land,
And Wilkes again be free.

The WITCH: *A* FABLE.

A Witch, that from her ebon chair
Could hurl deſtruction thro' the air;
Or, at her all commanding will,
Make the tumultuous ocean ſtill;
Once, by an incantation fell,
(As the recording Druids tell)
Pluck'd the round moon, whoſe radiant light
Silver'd the ſober noon of night,
From the domain ſhe held above,
Down to a dark infernal grove.

Give me, the goddeſs cry'd, a cauſe
Why you diſturb my ſacred laws?
Look at my train—yon wand'ring hoſt!
See how the trembling ſtars are loſt!
Through the cœleſtial regions wide
Why do they range without a guide?

Chaos,

Chaos, from our confuſion, may
Hope for his old deteſted ſway.

I'm, ſays the Witch, ſeverely croſt,
Know that my favourite Squirrel's loſt.
Search—for I'll have creation torn,
If he's not found before the morn.

Soon as the impious charge was given,
From the tremendous ſtores of heaven
Jove, with a bolt, revengeful!—red!
Struck the deteſted monſter dead.

If there are ſlaves to pity blind,
With power enough to plague mankind,
That for their own nefarious ends,
Tread upon freedom and her friends,
Let them beware the Witch's fate!
When their preſumption's at the height
Jove will his angry powers aſſume,
And the curs'd miſcreants meet their doom.

J. CUNNINGHAM.

Her R—— H—— the P. D. of W.

Lines

Lines to Mr. WILKES. *By* Robert Lloyd *of* Weftminfter, *written juſt before his Death; and not printed in his Works.*

WHAT tho' oppreffion, with her defperate tools
Of bold mean knaves, and weak complying fools,
Send it abroad; yet, Wilkes, thy honour'd name,
Built on the folid bafe of patriot fame,
Shall in truth's page to lateft years defcend,
And babes unborn fhall hail thee England's friend;
A juft reward fhall future times beftow,
And pay thofe honours which the prefent owe.

The REVIEW. *Written in the Year* 1719; *and never before printed.*

I.

SERENE the morn, the feafon fine,
Great G—— advancing on the plain,
To view his hoft, and concubine,
The goodly bleffings of his reign;

CHORUS.

CHORUS.

The trumpets ſound,
The courſers bound,
The field all blaz'd with arms;
His Trojans true,
Their tacticks ſhew,
And Helen ſhews her charms.

II.

The gods of war, and love, by turns,
Preſide upon his phiz;
One while you think for war he burns,
Another while for Miſs.

III.

You think, when he ſurveys his men,
He'd waſte the world for fame;
And that he'd people it again,
When he ſurveys the dame.

IV.

But all is farce, and nothing more,
This am'rous martial wight
Age won't allow t'enjoy his whore,
Nor courage let him fight.

The

An ODE *upon the present Period of Time,*
*By the Author of the Ode to Lord C——m.**

IN times like these, when party rage
  Quickens the feeble pulse of age,
    And fires the youthful breast;
When confidence, that social chain,
Which link'd the faith of man to man,
    Shrinks from the gen'rous test;

When ev'ry organ, spring, and wheel,
Destin'd to move the public weal,
    For good and noble ends;
Forgetful of that great design,
Act, counteract, distract, combine,
    As power recommends;

O whither shall the muse retreat
To seek that safe-establish'd seat,
    Where freedom spreads her wing?
Where can she breathe her honest fire,
When public virtue tunes her lyre,
    When Grenville bids her sing?

* See the first part of the New Foundling Hospital for Wit, page 118.

Yet, ere ſhe leaves this ſtormy ſcene,
To fly to proſpects more ſerene,
To ſeats ſtill calm and gay;
To you, her genius, refuge, friend,
(Titles by flatt'ry unobtain'd)
She ſends a parting lay.

There is a ſeaſon, men agree,
Fixt by the laws of deſtiny,
To nations, as to man;
In this precarious, bounded ſpace
They meet their triumph or diſgrace,
As rulers act and plan.

Let us, my friend, our thoughts convey,
To ſeaſons of the brighteſt day,
Times of auſpicious date;
When Britons eaſy and content,
Felt, in the hand of government,
The ſafety of the ſtate.

Experience then, mature in years,
Train'd from the cradle to affairs,
Sat active at the helm;
Practis'd to break the caſual wave,
Too cautious wantonly to brave
Storms, that would riſk the realm.

Juſtice,

Juſtice, too prudent to believe,
And mercy, panting to relieve,
In all his actions ſprung:
The laws their ſettled courſe maintain'd,
The prince belov'd and loving reign'd,
The people toil'd and ſung.

Whatever India's treaſure yields
From mines or aromatic fields,
Rich commerce made his own;
His virtues made his friends revere,
His powers taught his foes to fear,
He's great, the more he's known.

Gods! what a golden ſcene was this,
Of public fame, of private bliſs!
——But hold, deluſive fire——
The morning view is gone and paſt,
The bright meridian's overcaſt,
The downy hours retire.——

Subject to ev'ry natural ill
That ſprings from impious, lawleſs will,
From paſſion, and polution;
To day, the nation's glory flies,
To-morrow, health and virtue dies,
And then——'tis diſſolution.——

The legal ſword, and equal ſcale
Of juſtice, unprotected, fail,
The martial word is given;
Wiſdom, in vain, may drop a tear,
And piety addreſs her prayer
For interpoſing heaven.

In vain pale virgins, in deſpair,
To freedom's altar may repair,
That wonted ſeat of reſt:
There ruffians have uſurp'd her name,
And men, intruſted with her fame,
Alike have ſtabb'd her breaſt.

The tumult ſpreads——rank, honour, birth,
Are levell'd with their native earth,
Each man, as Cæſar's great——
Farewell allegiance to the throne,
And duty due to kings alone,
Farewell the plumes of ſtate!

Where can Britannia find a friend?
The great profeſs, the good commend,
But can't avert her doom:
The faithful B—df—ds all proclaim
" Friendſhip and charity the ſame,
" And both commence at home."

Muſt

Muſt ſhe at G—ft—n's feet repine,
Or ſue to G—ft—on's concubine,
With flattery, bribes, or tears?
Bribes, like the magic of champaign,
Can ſteal the feeling ſoul from pain,
And ſoothe the wound of cares.

But theſe, however well deſign'd,
Like opiums to the fev'riſh mind,
Inſnare it to endure:
Waking again, it raves and burns,
Each agonizing pain returns,
Till nature works the cure.

Come then, my Grenville, come away,
'Tis criminal to loſe a day,
With talents bright as thine:
Let indolence, on beds of flowers,
Conſume the weary, lagging hours,
Action's thy nobler line.

Like Quintus, at his country's call,
Haſte to avert a nation's fall,
Thy abſence ſigns its fate:
Felt by the ſenate's loud applauſe,
Thy manly truths ſhall plead its cauſe,
Thy counſels make it great.

Haſte to correct theſe upſtart things,
Theſe modern counſellors of k—gs,
Who toy with ſtate, and pow'r;
Expoſe the lines they draw, and break,
Blow down the baſeleſs plans they make,
Like play-things of an hour.

This gen'rous courſe of glory run,
Fame ſhall record thy triumph won,
The muſe her tribute pay:
Britannia to her ſons ſhall tell,
"That, anxious for the public weal,
"Grenville ne'er loſt a day."

A Converſation between the two Heads upon Temple Bar; on Occaſion of the Merchants Addreſs, March, 1769.

SAYS Townly to Fletcher, What cauſes this rout?
Pray what are the people of London about?
Such noiſe I ne'er heard—'tis a ſhame and diſgrace——
No man can be eaſy or ſafe in his place.

I'll

I'll tell you, ſays Fletcher, if rightly I gueſs,
The merchants are met with their loyal addreſs;
My eyes are not clear, you may fairly ſuppoſe;
But it ſmells pretty ſtrong—I can truſt to my noſe.——
Quoth Townley, gude troth, tho' my eyes are but dim,
You are certainly right, for there's Eddy B—m;
And, as I'm alive, there's our favourite Charley,
And aſs-men, and mule-men, and W——s, and H—l—y.
" What! H—l--y, that liv'd in the city's great " houſe,
" Who made all the mob once as ſtill as a mouſe?"
" Yes, H—l--y, the man—(good lord, how " the folks hoot!)
" The man that ſeiz'd petticoat, gibbet, and " boot."
" But who's he before, on the woundy fine horſe?
" He's as ſtiff as his majeſty at Charing-croſs."
" Why he, ſir, tho' ſtately and bluſt'ring in " look,
" Strip off his fine gear, and he's only a—Cook."
" And who are all thoſe whom the mob treat " uncivil?
" Why Dutchmen, and Scotchmen, and Jews— " and the devil."

" Jews, Dutchmen, and Scotchmen, prefent an
" addrefs ?"
" Yes."——The devil was right then—he cou'd
do no lefs.
An addrefs in thefe times !—it is much, very
much——
An Englifh addrefs carried up by the Dutch !—
'Tis nat'ral for Scotchmen, I know, to rebel ;
To be loyal-—'tis ftrange !——but 'tis all very
well—
This incenfe of brimftone fome nofes may fuit ;
Tho' Britons diflike it, it likes my Lord B——e.
The Macs have all fteadily join'd in the work,
All the Macs in the city, excepting Mac Quirk—
But fee how the mob there are breaking their
pates——
'Tis time that we ftop them, fo fhut up the gates ;
For if they go on with addreffes and letters,
We muft fhortly refign——and make room for
our betters.

TEMPLE-BAR.

A DIA-

A DIALOGUE *at* St. James's Gate *on the ſame Occaſion; between a Noble Lord and the Mob*

Lord. OH! Engliſhmen, Engliſhmen, can't you be quiet,
For your wives and your childrens ſake do not riot;
The duty I owe to my k—— and to you,
Makes me beg you'll diſperſe, leſt the cauſe you ſhould rue.
You've inſulted the crown, and for theſe honeſt cits,
You've ſcar'd the poor gentlemen out of their wits.
When they muſter'd at 'Change they were decent and clean,
But are now ſo bedaub'd they're not fit to be ſeen.
I am ſent by the k—— to entreat you'll diſperſe;
And hark ye, you fellow there, drive off that hearſe.
If you don't go away all the guards will be ſent,
'Tis a deſp'rate ſtep, and I dread the event.
I ſuppoſe you're ſet on by ſome raſcal or other,
And have had money given you to make all this pother.

Mob.

Mob. The caufe by your lordfhip is falfely afcrib'd,
For tho' we are poor, yet we fcorn to be brib'd,
Befide we declare, were we ever fo willing,
We don't know a man who would give us a fhilling.

Lord. Now I vow and declare, tho' I hate all this ftrife,
Yet the people of England I love as my life.
I would down on my knees in the dirt and the mire,
If it would but induce you, my friends, to retire.

Mob. My lord, with fubmiffion, we muft interpofe,
'Twere a terrible pity to dirt thefe fine cloaths.

Lord. My cloaths I don't mind, and as for the dirt,
I value it not, 'tis the fafhion at court.
I know you're all loyal, I wifh I could ferve you,
From the danger that threatens, I fain would preferve you:
So I beg you'll difperfe, and go home to your wives,
Nor foolifhly ftay at the rifk of your lives:
If recourfe muft be had to the milit'ry power,
I dread the event of a fingle half-hour.

If

If ſuch tumults as theſe were in France or in Spain,
Five hundred by this time had ſurely been ſlain;
But the k— loves you all with ſuch ardent affection,
He would lay down his life for the people's protection.

Mob. Oh God bleſs the k—, he's the beſt of mankind,
We wiſh thoſe about him were all of his mind,
No guards would be wanting to keep us in awe,
As we honour his name, and we reverence the law.
Let elections be free, and whoever we chuſe,
His ſeat in the houſe, you ſhould never refuſe.
And if great men were honeſt the poor would be quiet,
So yourſelves you may thank for this buſtle and riot.

F I N I S.

A List of BOOKS *and* PAMPHLETS *printed for* J. ALMON, *opposite* Burlington-house, *in* Piccadilly.

In the Press,

CAMDEN's Britannia, 2 vols. folio.

Chambers' Dictionary and Supplement, 3 vols. folio.

Debates in the House of Commons, from 1746 to 1748, 3 vols, octavo.

Just Published,

A New Baronetage of England; with all the Arms engraved, 3 vols. 10 s. 6 d.

An Extinct Peerage of England, 3 s. 6 d.

The Pocket Herald; or a compleat View of the present Peerage of the Three Kingdoms, with all the Arms engraved, 2 vols. 7 s.

⁂ The above three Books being printed in an uniform Size and Manner, the whole six vols. may be had, neatly bound, Price One Guinea.

The New Foundling Hospital for Wit. Part I. with a curious Frontispiece, 2 s. 6 d.

The Second Part of the same Work, 2 s. 6 d.

The Third Part of the same Work, containing several original Pieces, 2 s. 6 d.

Lyric Consolations, with a fine Frontispiece, 3 s.

Makarony Fables. By the same Author, 2 s. 6 d.

A Companion for a Leisure Hour, 2 s. 6 d.

Memoirs of Corsica, by Frederic, Son of Theodore, late King of Corsica, 3 s.

The Original French of the above Work, 3 s.

An Introduction to the History of England, by John Wilkes, Esq; 2 s. 6 d.

Three Interesting Tracts, by the Same, 2 s. 6 d.

Every Man his own Brewer, 3 s. bound.

Debates in the House of Commons, from 1742 to 1746, 2 vols. 12 s.

A Collection of the Lords Protests, 2 vols. 12 s.

The Political Register, 2 vols. 16 s.

BOOKS *printed for* J. ALMON.

A Collection of Interefting Letters from the Public Papers, 2 vols. 10 s.

Gee on Trade, 3 s.

Hoyle's Games, 3 s.

Boyer's French Dictionary, Quarto, 18 s.

An Abridgment of the fame, in Octavo, 7 s.

Smollet's Tranflation of Don Quixote, 4 vols. 12 s.

Letters from an American in England, 2 s. 6 d.

A New Edition of Collins's Englifh Peerage, 7 vols. Octavo, 2 l. 12 s. 6 d.

The Peerage of Scotland, in one vol. Octavo, 6 s.

The Peerage of the Kingdom of Ireland, in two vols. Octavo, 12 s.

Debates in the Houfe of Commons of Ireland, during the Years 1763 and 1764, 2 vols. 12 s.

The Speeches of the Lords of Seffion in Scotland, on the late Caufe between the Duke of Hamilton and Archibald Douglas of Douglas, Efq; with an introductory Preface, giving an impartial Account of that Suit, 5 s.

The complete Grazier, or Gentleman and Farmer's Directory, 3 s.

The Royal Kalender for England, Scotland, and Ireland, 2 s. 9 d. with an Almanack, and 2 s. without.

A new Edition of the Military Regifter; or new and complete Lifts of all his Majefty's Land Forces and Marines, 2 s. 6 d.

The Hiftory of the Minority, during the Years 1762, 1763, 1764, and 1765, 4 s.

Mr. Philipps's Hiftory of the Life of Cardinal Pole. A new Edition, in 2 vols. 8vo. 10 s. bound.

Memoirs of the late Duke of Cumberland, 6 s.

The London Merchant, a Tale, 1 s.

BOOKS *printed for* J. ALMON.

Ogilby's Book of the Roads, 1 s. 6 d.

An Account of Denmark, antient and modern, 3 s.

The Foreigner's Guide through London, 2 s. 6 d.

Double Miſtake, a Comedy, acted at Covent Garden, by the Author of the School for Rakes, 1 s. 6d.

The Dramatic Time-Piece, 1 s.

POLITICAL PAMPHLETS.

Publiſhed in 1769.

Preſent State of the Nation, a new Edition, 2 s.

Appendix to the ſame, 1 s.

Conſiderations on the Dependencies of Great Britain, 2s.

A Sermon, by Mr. Horne, 1 s.

In 1768.

A Letter to the Duke of Grafton, 1 s.

Caſe of the Duke of Portland, 1 s.

Obſervations on the Power of Alienation, 1 s.

Caveat on the Part of Public Credit, 1 s.

Reflections on the Caſe of Mr. Wilkes, 1 s.

In 1767.

A Speech againſt the Suſpending and Diſpenſing Prerogative, 1 s. 6 d.

A new Edition of the Letter on Libels, Warrants, Seizure of Papers, &c. 2 s. 6 d.

Lord Somers's Security of Engliſhmen's Lives, 1 s. 6 d.

A Liſt of all the Changes ſince his preſent Majeſty's Acceſſion, 1 s.

Dr. Williamſon's Narrative, 6 d.

Letter to the Earl of Bute, 6 d.

A Letter to a Miniſter on the Subject of the Eaſt-India Dividend, 6 d.

Proteſt againſt reſcinding the India Dividend, 6 d.

Mr. Wilkes's Letter to the Duke of Grafton, 1 s.

BOOKS *printed for* J. ALMON.

In 1766.

An Appeal to the People, 1 s.

Confiderations on the Dearnefs of Corn and Provifions, 1 s. 6 d.

Obfervations on the Farmer's Three Letters, 6 d.

Political Speculations on the high Price of Labour and Dearnefs of Provifions. In two Parts, 2 s. Either Part may be had feparate, 1 s.

Enquiry into the Conduct of a late Rt. H. Commoner, 1 s. 6 d.

An Examination of his Principles, 1 s.

Short Confiderations on fome late Grants, 6 d.

A true Hiftory of a late fhort Adminiftration, 6 d.

Addrefs to the People on the frequent Changes of Minifters, 1 s. 6 d.

Parallel between the Four laft Years of Q. Anne, and the Four firft of George III. 1 s.

The Scourge, a Poem, 1 s. 6 d.

The Precipice, a Satirical Print, 1 s.

In 1765.

The Principles of the Changes in 1765, 1 s. 6 d.

The State of the Nation, with regard to its Income, Expenditure, and unfunded Debt, 1 s.

Thoughts on the Difmiffion of Officers, 1 s.

A Letter from Candor to the Public Advertifer, 1 s.

A Collection of Paffages from the Briton, North Briton, and Auditor, 1 s.

In 1764.

A Letter from Albemarle-Street to the Cocoa-Tree, 2 s.

The Budget, 1 s.

Account of the late Mr. Legge, 1 s.

The Conteft, a Poem, 1 s.

A Defence of the Minority relating to General Warrants, 1 s.

BOOKS *printed for* J. ALMON.

Reply to the Defence of the Majority, 1 s.

The Right of Appeal to Juries, 1 s.

Counter Addrefs to the Public on the Difmiffion of Gen. Conway, 1 s.

The remarkable Trials of J. P. Zenger of New-York, and W. Owen, of London, for the Publication of Libels, 1 s.

A Lift of Books and Pamphlets, on the Subjects of taxing the Britifh Colonies, and regulating their Trade.

A Review of the Controverfy between Great Britain and the Colonies, 4 s.

Conduct of the Miniftry examined, refpecting the Repeal of the Stamp Act, 3 s.

Otis's Vindication of the Colonies, 1 s.

Bland's Enquiry into the Rights of the Colonies, 1 s.

The true Sentiments of America, 2 s. 6 d.

Dickenfon's Farmers Letters, 2 s.

The Examination of Dr. Franklin, 1 s.

Authentic Account of the New-York Congrefs, 1 s.

A Defence of the Charters, by J. Drummer, 1 s. 6d.

The Rights of the Colonies afferted, by Mr. Otis of Bofton, 2 s.

Confiderations on taxing the Colonies, by Mr. Delany, 1 s. 6 d.

The Regulations of the Colonies, by Mr. Dickenfon, 1 s. 6 d.

An Account of a Conference, 1 s.

Late Occurrences in America confidered, 1 s.

The Grievances of the American Colonies examined, 1 s.

Rights of Parliament vindicated, 1 s.

An Application of Political Rules to Great Britain and America, 1 s. 6 d.

Two Protefts againft the Repeal of the Stamp Act; with Lifts of the Minority in both Houfes, 1 s.

Confiderations on Behalf of the Colonies, 1 s.

Juftice and Neceffity of taxing the Colonies, 1 s.

The Privileges of Jamaica vindicated, 2 s. 6 d.

THE NEW FOUNDLING HOSPITAL FOR WIT, PART 4 (1771)

After the first three parts appeared in 1768–9, nothing came out in 1770 – the only gap year. This may have been caused by a number of factors: Almon had heavy commitments elsewhere (he compiled eleven volumes of House of Commons debates between 1766 and 1774); he may have had trouble gathering material; and he was convicted in January 1770 of seditious libel for selling the *London Museum* which included a reprint of Junius's *Letter to the King*. Even though he was subject to an undertaking to maintain good behaviour for two years or risk losing a £500 bond, nonetheless, for the first time, Almon's name appears in the imprint to a *NFHW* title page.

The frontispiece to Part 4 shows a blindfolded watchman carrying a lantern, walking down a city street at night under a pub sign bearing the image of the Princess Dowager of Wales gazing at the boot of Bute from which dangles a bunch of grapes. The upper legend, '*A Citizen of the World*', echoes the 1762 Oliver Goldsmith title concerning the Socratic search for a wise man; '*searching for a Wise Prince*' is reminiscent of Samuel Johnson's 1759 *Rasselas*. While no source has been found for 'Oh thou Head of the Wrong Heads', the 1776 song, 'THE HEADS, or the year 1776' ('Ye wrong heads, and strong heads, attend to my strains; / Ye clear heads, and queer heads, and heads without brains …'), expresses a similar complaint. The Shakespeare quotation derives from *Romeo and Juliet* (II.ii.71–3).

Part 4 opens with David Garrick's plaintive verse following a visit to Warwick Castle which left his party starving (5). 'Nature and Garrick' (7) reminds us of his extraordinary efforts to honour the bicentenary of Shakespeare's birth (admittedly a few years late). 'Extempore, on the Death of General Wolfe' (7) suggests in one couplet that the solemn event on the Plains of Abraham in 1759 – the great soldier dying at the moment of victory – commemorated on canvas *c.* 1771 by Benjamin West (a painting which George III greatly admired), could now be used as a barb against Fox. Garrick appears again, praising his old teacher: 'On Johnson's Dictionary' (103) takes its hint from the lexicographer's remark that one Englishman accomplished a task (completing a national dictionary) which required forty French academicians to do.

Jane Austen borrowed Garrick's 'Riddle' (104) for Mr Woodhouse in *Emma*; Austenites think something racier was intended by this foundling which reappeared in Garrick's 1785 *Poetical Works*. 'The Chimney Sweeper' (153) predates William Blake's two poems on the same subject in his *Songs of Innocence and Experience* (1789/94), although the earlier poem ends more happily as the father wants his son to build chimneys rather than sweep them. John Hall-Stevenson also returns with 'Two Lyric Epistles, Or Margery the Cook Maid to the Critical Reviewers' (179).

The theme of marriage ranges from comic to tragic. Marital bliss gives way to permanent damage (in this case inflicted upon the husband) in 'Sir William Young to his Lady, on having an eye beat out' (105). 'The Lyar' (147) is a mock ballad about Jasper, a country bumpkin, who catches his wife, Dorcas, *in flagrante delicto*, but she manages to use her superior wit to convince him otherwise. 'The Beggar' (166) turns into a tragic tale of a man whose farm has failed, whose daughter has run off with a cad and whose wife has committed suicide. One reference – 'Ch—d—s' (73.10) – leads to the remarkable story of Anne, Duchess of Chandos, who worked as a chambermaid at the Pelican Inn in Newbury until she was sold by her first husband to Henry Brydges, second Duke of Chandos. She became his mistress and, after both of their spouses had died, his wife.

Readers will find some inventive, pre-Byronic rhymes: the 'Earl of Chatham' is rhymed with 'odd rat 'em' (71) and 'Durham' finds an echo in 'slur 'em' (75).

According to *The Oxford Dictionary of Phrase and Fable* (2002), 'scum of the earth' was first recorded by Arthur Wellesley, first Duke Wellington, in a dispatch dated 2 July 1813, an unflattering reference to his own men. Yet the phrase was popular in 1771, turning up no fewer than three times in Part 4 (53, 170, 172). It should be noted that another phrase – 'dregs of the people' – also recurs (169, 172) but hasn't become as popular; and the two phrases are compressed in one line: 'We can't be at once both the *dregs* and the *scum*' (170).

No other editions of Part 4 are listed on the *ESTC*.

The text for this first edition of *The New Foundling Hospital for Wit*, Part 4 (*ESTC* t139947), is reproduced from a copy held by Cambridge University Library (shelfmark Forster.d.82).

The New Foundling Hospital for Wit

Part 4 (1771)

To Mary Beth & Charles Harold Nichol (1946–2003)
Mary Elizabeth Nichol & Bill Hutchinson
Charles Adam & Marion Nichol

A Citizen of the World searching for a Wise Prince.

Alack, there lies more Peril in thine Eyes,
Than Twenty of their Swords. Shakeſpeare

THE

NEW FOUNDLING HOSPITAL FOR WIT.

BEING

A COLLECTION OF CURIOUS PIECES

IN VERSE AND PROSE,

BY

SIR C. HANBURY WILLIAMS,
EARL OF CHESTERFIELD,
---------- DELAWARR,
---------- HARDWICKE,
---------- CARLISLE,
LORDS LYTTELTON,
---------- HARVEY,
---------- CAPEL,
LADY M. W. MONTAGUE,
T. POTTER,
C. TOWNSHEND,
J. S. HALL,
J. WILKES,
D. GARRICK,
B. THORNTON,
G. COLMAN,
R. LLOYD, &c. &c.

Adorned with a curious Frontiſpiece.

PART THE FOURTH.

LONDON:

Printed for J. ALMON, in PICCADILLY.

1771.

THE

CONTENTS.

A Bon

To

[v]

Epilogue

Epiſtle

[vii]

The

THE NEW FOUNDLING HOSPITAL FOR WIT.

PART THE FOURTH.

MR. GARRICK,

INVITED AND STRONGLY PRESSED TO PASS A WEEK "EN FAMILLE" AT WARWICK CASTLE, ARRIVES, IS SHEWN THE CURIOSITIES LIKE A COMMON TRAVELLER, TREATED WITH CHOCOLATE, AND DISMISSED DIRECTLY;

UPON WHICH HE WROTE THE FOLLOWING

VERSES.

SOME ſtrollers * invited by Warwick's kind earl,
To his caſtle magnificent came,
Prepar'd to reſpect both the owner and ſeat,
And to ſhew them due honour and fame.

* One or two perſons were with Mr. Garrick.

His chambers, his kitchen, his cellars, they prais'd,
But, alas! they ſoon found to their coſt,
That if they expected to feaſt at his houſe,
They reckon'd without their great hoſt.
He ſhew'd them Guy's pot, but he gave them no ſoup,
No meat would his lordſhip allow,
Unleſs they had gnaw'd the blade bone of the boar,
Or the rib of the famous dun cow.
" But ſince you're my friends (ſays this complaiſant peer)
" I'll give you a new printed book,
" Which may to your taſtes ſome amuſement afford,
" 'Tis the hiſt'ry of Greville and Brooke."
Since your lordſhip's ſo civil, well-bred, and polite,
Pray pardon one curſe from a ſinner,
For our breakfaſt we thank you our very good lord,
But a plague on your family dinner.

AN INSCRIPTION FOR THE CASTLE GATEWAY.

When Neville, the ſtout earl of Warwick, liv'd here,
Fat oxen for breakfaſt were ſlain,
And his friends were all welcome to ſport and good cheer,
And invited again and again;
His nerves are ſo weak, and his ſpirits ſo low,
This earl, with no oxen does feed 'em,
And all of the former great doings we know,
He gives us a book—and we read 'em.

1768. D. G.

NATURE

NATURE AND GARRICK.

AS *Nature* and *Garrick* were talking one day,
It chanc'd they had words, and fell out;
Dame *Reaſon* wou'd fain have prevented a fray,
But could not, they both were ſo ſtout.
Says Garrick, I honour you, madam, 'tis true;
And with pride to your laws I ſubmit;
But Shakeſpeare paints ſtronger and better than you,
All critics of taſte will admit.
How! Shakeſpeare paint ſtronger and better than me!
Cries Nature, quite touch'd to the ſoul,
Not a word in his volumes I ever could ſee,
But what from my records he ſtole.
And thou, wicked thief—nay, the ſtory I'll tell—
Whenever I paint or I draw,
My pencils you filch, and my colours you ſteal;
For which thou ſhalt ſuffer the law.
And when on the ſtage in full luſtre you ſhine,
To me all the praiſe ſhall be giv'n:
The toil ſhall be your's, and the honour be mine;
So Nature and Garrick are even.

EXTEMPORE,

ON THE DEATH OF GENERAL WOLFE.

ALL-conq'ring cruel death, more hard than rocks,
Thou ſhould'ſt have ſpar'd the *Wolfe* and took the *Fox*.

O D E,

FOR THE INSTALLATION OF AUGUSTUS HENRY, DUKE OF GRAFTON, CHANCELLOR OF THE UNIVERSITY OF CAMBRIDGE.

BY MR. GRAY.

A I R.

HENCE! avaunt! 'tis holy ground,
Comus and his midnight crew,
And Ignorance with looks profound,
And dreaming Sloth of pallid hue!
Mad Sedition's cry prophane,
Servitude that hugs her chain,
Nor in thefe confecrated bow'rs
Let painted Flatt'ry hide her ferpent train in flow'rs.

C H O R U S.

Nor Envy bafe, nor creeping Gain,
Dare the Mufes' walk to ftain,
While bright-ey'd fcience walks around,
Hence! avaunt! 'tis holy ground.

RECI-

GRAY

TRAVESTIE.

AIR,

HENCE! avaunt! 'tis *venal* ground,
Wilkes and all his free-born crew;
Within our pale no room is found,
Ye modern *Algernons*, for you.
Mute be the bold Alcaic ſtrain
Of liberty, that ſpurns a chain,
Nor in theſe pliant courtly bow'rs
Let harſh Philippic weeds choke adulation's flow'rs.

CHORUS.

Virtue hence! with brow ſevere!
Public ſpirit come not near,
While ſervile int'reſt walks around,
Hence! avaunt! 'tis *venal* ground!

[10]

RECITATIVE.

From yonder realms of empyrean day
Burſts on my ear th' indignant lay!
There ſit the ſainted ſage, the bard divine,
The few whom Genius gave to ſhine,
Thro' ev'ry unborn age, and undiſcover'd clime:
Rapt in celeſtial tranſport they;
Yet hither oft a glance from high
They ſend of tender ſympathy,
To bleſs the place, where, on their op'ning ſoul
First the genuine ardor ſtole;
'Twas Milton ſtruck the deep-ton'd ſhell,
And as the choral warblings round him ſwell,
Meek Newton's ſelf bends from his ſtate ſublime,
And nods his hoary head, and liſtens to the rhyme.

AIR.

"Ye brown o'er-arching groves,
"That contemplation loves,
"Where willowy Camus lingers with delight,
"Oft at bluſh of dawn
"I've trod your level lawn,
"Oft woo'd the gleam of Cynthia's ſilver light,
"In cloiſters dim, far from the haunts of folly,
"With freedom by my ſide, and ſoft-ey'd melancholy."

RECI-

RECITATIVE.

From yonder realms of miniſterial day
Steals on my ear the ſoothing lay,
There mitred hirelings, dukes *divine*,
'The lead which *Fortune* made to ſhine,
Thro' ev'ry age corrupt, and unenlighten'd clime.
Warm in the royal ſunſhine they;
Yet hither oft a glance from high
They ſend of tender ſympathy,
To bleſs the place, where on their venal ſoul
The pand'ring eye of favour ſtole;
N—ſt—e beams a foſt'ring ray,
And while his midday-ſplendors play,
A hoary train of prieſts from ſtalls ſublime,
Baſk in his beams, and bleſs the golden time.

AIR.

" Ye brown o'er-arching groves,
" Which adulation loves,
" Where willowy Camus lingers with delight,
" Oft at bluſh of dawn,"
I've wiſh'd for *ſleeves of lawn*,—
Oft woo'd the gleam of *Bute*'s bright northern light,
In crowded levees, far from Virtue's haunt,
With flatt'ry on my tongue, and temporizing cant.

RECITATIVE.

But hark ! the portals ſound, and pacing forth,
With ſolemn ſteps and ſlow,
High Potentates, and dames of royal birth,
And mitred fathers in long order go ;
Great Edward, with the lilies on his brow
From haughty Gallia torn ;
And ſad Chatillon on her bridal morn,
That wept her bleeding love ; and princely Clare ;
And Anjou's heroine ; and the paler roſe,
The rival of her crown and of her woes ;
And either Henry there,
The murder'd ſaint, and the majeſtic lord
That broke the bonds of Rome.
Their tears, their little triumphs o'er,
Their human paſſions move no more,
Save charity that glows beyond the tomb.

[ACCOMPANIED.]

All that on Granta's fruitful plain
Rich ſtreams of regal bounty pour'd,
And bade their awful fanes and turrets riſe,
To hail their Fitzroy's feſtal morning come,
And thus they ſpeak in ſoft accord
The liquid language of the ſkies.

QUAR.

RECITATIVE.

But hark! the portals ſound, and pacing forth,
With ſolemn ſtep, and ſlow,
High potentates, and dames of royal birth,
And mitred *Mothers* in long order go—
Great G——, with the trophies on his brow,
From bleeding England torn—
While W——y, widow'd on her bridal morn,
Weeps for her abſent love, and B—d dim,
Falſe M———ue, and all the rav'nous crew,
That England's conſtitution ſlew,
And lopp'd each vig'rous limb.
A band accurs'd of m———l l—ds
Who forg'd for Britons—chains;
Their wiles, their damned triumphs o'er,
Their hopes to ſtand are now no more,
Deſpair alone remains.

[ACCOMPANIED.]

All that on Granta's thirſty plain
Rich ſtreams of regal bounty drank,
For whom our aweful fanes and turrets ſprung
To hail their F——y's feſtal morning come,
And ſweetly ſing on Camus' bank
The liquid lies of Flatt'ry's tongue.

QUAR-

[14]

QUARTETTO.

What is grandeur, what is pow'r!
Heavier toil! ſuperior pain!
What the bright reward of gain?
The grateful memory of the good:
Sweet is the breath of vernal ſhow'r,
The bees collected treaſure ſweet;
Sweet muſic's fall,—but ſweeter yet
The ſtill ſmall voice of gratitude!

RECITATIVE.

Foremoſt, and leaning from her golden cloud,
The venerable Margaret ſee—
Welcome, my noble ſon, ſhe cries aloud,
To this thy kindred train and me,
Pleas'd in thy lineaments to trace
A Tudor's fire, a Beauſort's grace!

AIR.

Thy lib'ral heart, thy judging eye
The flower unheeded ſhall deſcry,
And bid it round heav'n's altars ſhed
The fragrance of its bluſhing head,
Shall raiſe from earth the latent gem,
To glitter on the diadem!

RECI-

QUARTETTO.

What is grandeur, what is pow'r?
—The mead of bribes and falſehood's balm!
What is foul corruption's palm?
—The curſe of every child of grace.—
Sweet is the breath of vernal ſhow'r,
The bees collected honey ſweet—
Sweet muſic's fall; but ſweeter yet
To us, a penſion or a place.

RECITATIVE.

Foremoſt, and leaning from her golden cloud,
The goddeſs of corruption ſee—
Welcome, my wayward ſon, ſhe cries aloud,
To this thy kindred train and me,
Pleas'd in thy lineaments to trace
Thy monarch's ſmile, the premier's grace!

AIR.

Thy wily heart, thy *poaching* eye
Some wanton h—l—t ſhall deſcry,
Shalt round thy trunk her tendrils curl,
And bid her all her charms unfurl,
With *Love's bewitching tricks* enthrall,
And raiſe her—to encreaſe her fall.

RECI-

[16]

RECITATIVE.

Lo Granta waits to lead her blooming band,
Not obvious, not obtruſive ſhe;
No vulgar praiſe, no venal incenſe flings,
Nor dares with courtly tongue refin'd
Profane thy inborn royalty of mind:
She reveres herſelf and thee!
With modeſt pride, to grace thy youthful brow
The laureat wreaths that Cecil wore ſhe brings,
And to thy juſt, thy gentle hand
Submits the faſces of her ſway,
While ſpirits bleſt above and men below
Join with glad voice the loud ſymphonious lay!

GRAND CHORUS.

Through the wild waves as they roar,
With watchful eye, and dauntleſs mien,
Thy ſteady courſe of honour keep;
Nor fear the rocks, nor ſeek the ſhore,—
The ſtar of Brunſwick ſhines ſerene,
And gilds the horrors of the deep.

RECITATIVE.

Lo! Granta waits to lead her courtly band,
Nor coy, nor a recluſe is ſhe;
No praiſe ſincere, no heart-ſprung incenſe flings,
Nor dares with honeſt phraſe, and plain,
Sully the glories of thy reign—
She reveres *herſelf*—not *thee!*
With ſelfiſh pride to grace thy ſpurious pow'r,
The fading wreaths, which int'reſt wove, ſhe brings,
And to the preſſure of thy hand
The matron yields her wither'd charms,
Whilſt prebendaries, deans, and b—ps cow'r,
To bring her to thy falſe adult'rous arms.

GRAND CHORUS.

While the wild waves boil and roar,
From the threat'ning tempeſt flee,
The ſerpent courſe of traitors keep;
Cautious ſail—nor quit the ſhore;
If Brunſwick's ſtar ſhould ſet to thee,
'Twould wreck thee in the howling deep.

ANOTHER.

ANOTHER.

AIR.

HENCE! avaunt, 'tis ſacred ground,
Let pallid freedom ever fly,
Let innocence in chains be bound,
Nor e'er come truth or virtue nigh!
Oppoſition's cry prophane
Liberty that ſcorns the chain,
Nor in theſe conſecrated fields,
Let injur'd juſtice weep, that ſhe to tyrants yields.

CHORUS.

Nor dare bright truth, the patriot's friend,
The miniſter's high walk offend,
While ſtern-ey'd F—tz—y ſtalks around,
Hence! avaunt! 'tis ſacred ground.

RECITATIVE.

From yonder realms of miniſterial ſway
Burſts on my ear th'applauding lay,
There ſit the penſion'd ſage, the peer prophane,
The few whom intereſt gives to reign
O'er every unborn place, or yet unclaim'd domain.
Deep in the nation's buſineſs they,
Yet hither oft a glance from high,
They ſend of triumph and of joy,

To

To bleſs the place, where firſt, on freedom's ſoul,
He bade the Scottiſh thunder roll.
'Twas N—t—n rais'd that deep-ton'd voice,
And as diſcordant murm'rings round him roſe,
The Sp—k—r's ſelf bends from his chair on high,
And ſhakes his awful wig, and joins the courtly cry.

A I R.

Ye high o'er hanging walls
That ſure no monarch loves,
Where fain would freedom linger with delight,
Oft at the break of day
He's ſought your wearied way,
Oft by the glare of flambeaux' glitt'ring light,
In chariot cloſe, freſh from the haunts of folly,
With N-ncy by his ſide, ſworn foe to melancholy.

R E C I T A T I V E.

But hark! the door's unbarr'd, and marching forth,
With gouty ſteps and ſlow
Gen'rals and Shrieves, and peers of royal birth,
And mitred biſhops home to dinner go;
N—th, with th' Exchequer lawrels on his brow,
From haughty Gr—nv—lle torn,
And ſad F—tzp—ck on his bridal morn,
That weeps his fault too late; and proud D—nd—s;
And watchful Dy—n; and the paler B—ke,
The rival of his fortune, and his place;
And either Onſ—w there,

The

The Sp—k—r's ſon, and the majeſtic chief,
That trains the Surry bands;
Their triumphs, their addreſſes o'er,
Their county intereſt moves no more,
Save at Tha—s D-tt-n, or in O—kh—m lands.

[ACCOMPANIED.]

He that on Thame's greedy ſhore,
For ſtreams of royal bounty ſighs;
And they who wait for fickle Fortune's call,
To hail their F—tz—y's fav'rite morning come;
And thus they ſpeak in Flatt'ry's guiſe,
The liquid language of Whitehall.

QUARTETTO.

What are penſions without power,
Heavy toil, inſipid pain,
Who but would wiſh like thee to gain
The guidance of the public weal;
Sweet is D—nd—s's golden ſhow'r
Cli-e's viſionary treaſure ſweet,
Sweet H-ll—d's riſe, but ſweeter yet,
The ſtill-ſmall place of privy ſeal.

RECITATIVE.

Foremoſt, and leaning from her gilded coach,
The venerable Gert—de ſee,
Welcome, my noble friend, ſhe cries, approach
To thy new-kindred train and me,

Pleas'd

Pleas'd in thy future breed to trace
A R—ſſ—'s fire, a Wr—ttſl—y's grace.

A I R.

Thy practis'd heart, thy judging eye,
The bet unheeded ſhall deſcry,
And bid it through Newmarket ſhed
Freſh honour on thy well-known head,
Shall raiſe at White's thy drooping heart,
To glitter in a gameſter's part.

R E C I T A T I V E.

Lo! London waits to lead another band,
Not flatt'ring nor addreſſing thee;
No vulgar praiſe, no venal incenſe flings,
Nor dares with courtly tongue refin'd
Profane thy Sov'reign's royalty of mind:
She can prize herſelf and thee.
With conſcious joy to grace thy youthful brow,
The ornaments which cits oft wear ſhe brings,
Then with a juſt and equal hand,
She rids thee of thy N—ncy's ſway:
While ladies rang'd above, and boys below,
Join with glad voice the loud triumphant lay.

G R A N D C H O R U S.

Through the broad ſtreets as they roar,
With watchful eye and dauntleſs mien,
Thy ſteady conduct ne'er relax,

Nor heed their noiſe, nor fear the Tow'r:
The ſtar of S—rt ſhines ſerene,
And gilds the horrors of the axe.

SHAKESPEARE'S FEAST.

AN ODE.

I.

'TWAS at the ſolemn feaſt, for laurels won,
By WILLIAM, old JOHN SHAKE-SPEARE's ſon,
Aloft in aweful ſtate,
The May'r of STRATFORD ſate,
Rais'd on a wool-pack'd throne:
His aldermen were plac'd around,
Their brows with ſpreading antlers crown'd,
(So city ſpouſes ſhould be found)
The lovely May'reſs by his ſide
Sat like a plump High-German bride,
Not leſs for fat renown'd, than pride.
Happy, happy, happy May'r!
None but the fat,
None but the fat,
None but the fat deſerve the bouncing fair.

II.

The bard of FERNEY plac'd on high
Amid the tuneful choir,
With flying fingers touch'd the wooden lyre:

The

The notes, tho' lame, aſcend as high
As civic joys require.
The ſong began from G——K's toil,
Who left his LITCHFILD's native ſoil,
(Such were his hopes of golden ſpoil)
King RICHARD's crooked form bely'd the man:
Sublime on high-heel'd ſhoes he trod,
When firſt he courted lady ANNE
In GOODMAN'S-FIELDS, till then an unfrequented road.
As HASTINGS next round PRITCHARD's waiſt he curl'd,
Or ſhew'd, in DRUGGER's rags, an ideot to the world.
The liſt'ning crowd admire the lofty ſound,
A preſent SHAKESPEARE, loud they ſhout around:
A preſent SHAKESPEARE, loud the rafter'd halls rebound.
With prick'd up ears
His May'rſhip hears;
Aſſumes the play'r,
Affects to ſtare,
And ſhake the room about his ears.

III.

The praiſe of ven'ſon, then, the rapt enthuſiaſt ſung;
Of ven'ſon, whether old or young:
The jolly haunch in triumph comes;
Sound the trumpets; beat the drums;

Fluſh'd with a purple grace,
It ſhews its currant-jelly'd face :
Now give each feeder breath : It comes, it comes ;
Ven'ſon, ever fair and young,
Drinking joys can beſt reveal ;
Fat of ven'ſon is a treaſure,
Eating is the glutton's pleaſure :
Rich the treaſure,
Sweet the pleaſure,
Sweet as ſtuffing is with veal.

IV.

Sooth'd with the ſound, the May'r grew vain ;
Eat all his cuſtards o'er again ;
And thrice he pick'd the bones of geeſe and turkies
ſlain.
The poet ſaw his ſtomach riſe,
His watring mouth, his longing eyes ;
And while he necks and ſides defy'd,
Chang'd his note, and check'd his pride.
He choſe a TYBURN muſe
Soft pity to infuſe :
He ſung the deer-ſtealer's untimely fate
By laws ſevere, tho' good,
Swinging, ſwinging, ſwinging, ſwinging,
Swinging in too high a ſtate,
For ſpilling ſylvan blood.
Deſerted at his utmoſt need
By thoſe his former thefts had fed,

Expos'd

Expos'd, e'en near his native town,
With not a friend to cut him down.
With joylefs looks the May'r dejected fate,
Tho' ftill revolving in his foul
The various turns of fpits below;
And now and then a backward figh he ftole,
While ftreams Pactolian fought their vent, to flow.

V.

The bard of FERNEY fmil'd to fee
That fleep was in the next degree:
'Twas but a drowfy ftrain to keep,
For nurfes talk their babes afleep.
Gently dull, in hum-drum numbers,
Thus he footh'd his foul to flumbers;
Picking bones is toil and trouble,
Sillabub an empty bubble;
Never ending, ftill beginning,
Eating, ftill the fubftance miffing:
Think, if fat be worth thy winning,
Thy wife is furely worth the kiffing:
Both wife and ven'fon fee befides thee!
Take what fare thy cook provides thee!
The many rend the fkies with loud applaufe;
So fleep was crown'd, tho' FERNEY won the caufe.
The May'r, fcarce able to keep ope his eyes,
Peep'd at the food
That warm'd his blood,

And lick'd his lips, and lick'd his lips,
And lick'd his lips, (to ftir in vain he tries :)
At length, as funk in Sleep's foft arms he ftretches,
The fnorting magiftrate b——t his breeches.

VI.

Now ftrike the falt-box once again :
A louder yet, and yet a louder ftrain :—
Break the bands of fleep afunder
With noife more frequent than his poftern thunder!
Hark! hark! the horrid found
Has rais'd up his head,
Tho' as heavy as lead,
And he ftares and ftinks around!
Revenge, revenge, dread FERNEY cries,
See the critics arife!
See the volumes they rear
Only fit to curl hair,
Tho' each hop'd for an editor's prize!
Behold the fnarling band,
Each with a farthing candle in his hand!
Thofe are critical ghofts who for SHAKESPEARE were flain,
And unburied remain
On ftalls in Clare-court, Drury-lane.
Give the fun'rals due
To the wretched crew ;
Behold how they tofs their nofes on high!

Bid

Bid them ſeek CLOACINA's abode,
Congenial temples for ſuch hoſtile gods!
The company, pleas'd ſuch expedient was hit on,
The May'r ſnatch'd up CAPEL's edition to ſh--t on;
His wife the door unbarr'd,
To light him to the yard,
As H—l—y held the link that ſing'd the fam'd North Briton.
Let G——K yield our May'r the prize,
Or both divide the crown:
This, rais'd an author to the ſkies;
That, threw his critics down.

ON THE BIRTH-DAY OF SHAKESPEARE.

A CENTO.

TAKEN FROM HIS WORKS.

BY RICHARD BERENGER, ESQ.

Natura ipſa valere, et mentis viribus excitari, et quaſi quodam divino ſpiritu afflari. CICERO.

—PEACE to this meeting,
Joy and fair time, health and good wiſhes!
Now, worthy friends, the cauſe why we are met,
Is in celebration of the day that gave

Immortal Shakeſpear to this favour'd iſle,
The moſt repleniſhed ſweet work of nature,
Which from the prime creation e'er ſhe fram'd.
O thou divineſt Nature! how thyſelf thou blazon'ſt
In this thy ſon! form'd in thy prodigality,
To hold thy mirror up, and give the time
Its very form and preſſure! When he ſpeaks
Each aged ear plays truant at his tales,
And younger hearings are quite raviſhed,
So voluble is his diſcourſe—gentle
As Zephyr blowing underneath the violet,
Not wagging its ſweet head—yet as rough
(His noble blood enchaff'd) as the rude wind,
That by the top doth take the mountain pine,
And make him ſtoop to th' vale.—'Tis wonderful
That an inviſible inſtinct ſhould frame him
To royalty unlearn'd; honour untaught;
Civility not ſeen in other; knowledge
That wildly grows in him, but yields a crop
As if it had been ſown. What a piece of work!
How noble in faculty! infinite in reaſon!
A combination and a form indeed,
Where every God did ſeem to ſet his ſeal.
Heav'n has him now—yet let our idolatious fancy
Still ſanctify his relics; and this day
Stand aye diſtinguiſh'd in the kalendar,
To the laſt ſyllable of recorded time:
For if we take him but for all in all,
We ne'er ſhall look upon his like again.

ODE

ODE TO COLONEL L——.

Quis novus hic noſtris ſucceſſit ſedibus hoſpes?
Quo ſeſe ore ferens? quam forti pectore & armis!

O THOU, whom adverſe fates ordain
To rivet faſt Britannia's chain,
And bend her to controul,
Firm as Alcides tho' thou ſtand,
The curſes of an injur'd land
Shall ſhake thy guilty ſoul.

Tho' high enroll'd thy name appears
With hireling commoners and peers,
Curs'd guardians of a throne!
Tho' jockey G—ft—n who can ſpark it,
In Britain's ſenate, or Newmarket,
Adopt thee for his own.

Yet ſpite of all the venal tribe,
Tho' M——d plead, or H——d bribe,
Swift vengeance ſhall purſue;
Tho' blundering N—rt—n act his part
With Henley's * head, and Ryder's heart,
—Fit advocate for you.

* Orator Henley.

With

With ſuch abettors of his pride,
Gods! what had G—ft—n left untried,
Poſſeſs'd of ſuch a tool!
But heav'n, in pity to mankind,
That Fl—tch—r for a knave deſign'd,
Foredoom'd him to a fool.

Say, then, bepowder'd and becurl'd,
The jeſt, the play-thing of the world,
An officer, a beau!
Safe in the general contempt,
What evil genius thee could tempt
To riſe thy country's foe!

O ſlender youth, ſo nice and trim,
So neat in feature and in limb,
With wreathed roſes crown'd,
What eaſy maid with ſandy locks,
Receives thy vows, thy love, thy p——
Or is miſs ——— ſound?

Far other arts, far other charms,
Than lur'd the fair one to thy arms,
Thy dangers will require:
When patriot Glynn's learn'd voice ſhall rouze,
Or B—rke's loud thunder thro' the houſe,
With all the Britiſh fire:

Then

Then ſhalt thou wiſh, but wiſh in vain,
Thou ne'er had'ſt left dull Oxford's plain,
To ſeek a warmer ſun;
Thy courage there might daunt a proctor,
Thy wit and genius dupe a doctor,
Or bilk a brawling dun.

So when black louring clouds deform,
The angry ſkies, to meet the ſtorm
A butterfly may ſoar——
But baffled ſoon, at random hurl'd
His gilded wings in vain un url'd,
He falls to riſe no more.

Will B—df—d, doom'd to drudge thro' life,
Slave to his avarice and wiſe,
For thee his hoards diſpenſe?
Or R—gby, by his back and fiſt
Advanc'd in black corruption's liſt,
Engage in thy defence?

With double weight of braſs and lead,
Tho' vet'ran Bullface ſhake his head,
And ſweat to earn his fee,
Each flower of Billingſgate his boaſt:
—He cannot reaſon, well thou know'ſt,
But he ſhall roar for thee.

With

With pedant ſcoul and fretful look,
Now Bl—ckſ—e talks without his book,
Now Th—rl—e croaks his wrath;
As wiſe, if not ſo loud as N——s
Bewilder'd M—rt—n ſpits and ſtares—
All petulance and froth.

Say, fluent D—nning, claſſic Y—ke,
Dare ye refuſe the dirty work,
And hope ye ſtill to riſe?
Alas! not leſs your ſilence ſtung
Their cauſe, than W—rb—rn's bold tongue
Confronting all their lies.

But truſt not thou the brazen lungs
Of lawyers, placemens oily tongues—
Nor Mungo's journals quote;
Tho' Cl—re in tinſel rhet'ric ſhine
And ſophiſts all their webs refine,
To guard a lying vote.

Lo! W—ym—th, B—rr—gt—n combine
To mark the way that muſt be thine,
The blood-ſtain'd path to power—
Thou too ſhalt ſoon in thunder ſpeak,
And all pale G—ft—n's vengeance wreak
In one devoted hour.

While

While many an Allen's fall ſhall grace
Thy triumphs in the glorious chace,
Till Britain gagg'd and chain'd;
Her idle charters thrown aſide—
Admit the ſword her laws to guide
As when a Stuart reign'd.

Avert, kind heav'n! the black preſage,
Nor let us ſee a Charles's age,
In all its woes renew'd!
—Full oft at Freedom's holy ſhrine
Have Britain's ſons with zeal divine
Libations made in blood.

Yet if the rights our ſires enjoy'd
From thy free gift, muſt be deſtroy'd,
And freedom quit our ſhore—
On him that aſks in bonds to live,
And dares his country's fall ſurvive,
All thy red vengeance pour.

DARGO.

ON

ON MR. SECRETARY BRADSHAW.

ESTATE and honours !—mere caprich !
Better be fortunate than rich :
Since oft we find, or ſoon, or late,
Is verify'd what proverbs prate.

Sure 'twill be reckon'd a manœuvre,
That Bradſhaw, once ſo mean and pauvre,
Should for his life, and his two ſons,
(For ſo they ſay the patent runs)
Be veſted with a penſion clear,
Of fifteen hundred pounds a year :
For doing what ?—" Aye, there's the queſtion"—
" Fierce the aſſault, unarm'd the baſtion."

But lo ! at hand I 'ſpy another,
In dirty work his elder brother,
Who, for peruſing records duſty,
We dub a knight o'th' order Truſty,
'Quip him with ſhield and coat of mail
Of impudence, that ne'er can fail :
And humbly hope they'll ſet a price on,
The induſtry of *Jerry Dyſon*.
Who, from his being ſo deep read,
Doth much reſemble Nimming Ned,

That

That ſteals and pilfers all he can,
Tho' on a widely different plan.

Unleſs they'll add a trifle more,
It is not worth his while to pore :
His preſent ſalary ſcarce produces
Him ſpectacles for private uſes :
And if wit fail, or ſight grow dim,
A ſpectacle they'd make of him :
Therefore, the ſovereign balm to cure
Decay of ſight's—*a ſinecure!*

Whatever comes within his grapple,
He'll pocket—" as one would an apple."
It matters not, peerage or penſion,
To either he has vaſt pretenſion,
But, with ſubmiſſion, would much rather
Kiſs hands for both of them together.

No doubt they'll ſit with eaſe and grace,
Happily form'd in caſt of face
That ne'er knew bluſh—except in th' dark,
Or higher ſoar'd than to be clerk,
A clerk i'th' office where *he* now
Makes better men with homage bow.

A BON

A BON MOT,

ON A LADY'S WEDDING BEING ON THE TWENTY-FIRST OF DECEMBER.

REturn'd from the op'ra, as lately I ſat,
Indiff'rently chatting of this thing and that,
My Chloe I aſk'd how it enter'd her head,
To fix on St. Thomas, of all days to wed?
To which ſhe replied, with reaſon the ſtrongeſt,
" Tho' ſhorteſt the day is—*the night, ſir, is longeſt.*"

E P I G R A M.

WHILE *Freedom* lies bleeding, O fatal miſhap!
And Luttrell is ſitting in Jack Wilkes's lap; *
Amidſt all this rage of political pother,
The K—— ſits at eaſe in the *lap* of his mother.

* An expreſſion made uſe of by l--d C-----m in a late aſſembly.

ODE

[37]

ODE TO LORD NORTH,

ON HIS BEING APPOINTED COMMANDER IN CHIEF OF THE HOUSE OF COMMONS. 1770.

O Thou, whom placemen all adore,
Of the Exchequer chancellor,
And firſt lord of the treaſury,
How can a muſe in humble ſtrain
Pretend thy merits to explain,
Or how in numbers meaſure you!

Let G—ft—n, ſhunning public ſtrife,
Shrink in the boſom of his wife,
Scar'd at the York petition;
But thou ſhalt ſtill maintain the field,
With * heart in *two-fold* conſcience ſteel'd,
And combat oppoſition.

Bold in their front tho' Dowdeſwell ſtand,
With ſtring of motions in his hand,
Maxims of hard digeſtion!
Unanſwer'd, they ſhall periſh all,
Clogg'd with amendments in their fall,
Or choak'd by previous queſtion.

* Ille robur & æs duplex. Hor.

D Whilſt

Whilſt thou, like Falſtaff, tak'ſt the floor,
With men in *buckram* thirteen ſcore,
No cauſe you have to fear him:
The Sp—k—r too, with looks ſo big,
Waits but the motion of thy leg
To point, and call out *Hear him!*

On either hand, from left to right,
The chiefs all marſhall'd for the fight,
Preſs to partake thy glory:
There B—r—gt—n, with ſugar'd tongue,
De G—y the old, and Fox the young,
The flower of oratory;

Here P—l—mſ—n and blundering Cl—re,
And patient *Mungo every where*,
And Th-r-oe puts his caſe in;
While all amid th'oppoſing rout
The dauntleſs R-g—y, tall and ſtout,
Puſhes a modeſt face in.

E-l—t, with accents broad and ſtrong,
And J—k—ſ—n, with arms ſo long,
Still join to help the farce on;
Ellis and St—ge their voices lend,
With O—ſl—w, Wilkes's *only* friend,
That ſince has ſued the parſon.

With

With creſt erect, like Priam's ſon,
Lead but your truſty Trojans on,
Regardleſs of deſertion,
Like Swiſs they faithfully obey,
—Like Swiſs, too, they muſt have their pay,
Poſt, penſion, and reverſion.

In other fields let G—ft—n reap
A victory more ſafe and cheap,
With ſtars and garters hemm'd in;
W—m—th to anſwer Richmond's duke,
And ſober S—dw-h to rebuke,
Both Rockingham and Camden.

With Scottiſh p—rs complete ſixteen,
B—ps in meet array are ſeen,
Content—to earn promotion;
And M—sf—d, ever conſtant found,
And M—hm—t ready to propound
In *Erſe* a midnight motion.

Great polar ſtar, who now ſecure
Beams in the ſky the cynoſure
Of courtly navigation,
Oh deign to ſhed thy *influence* forth
On him whoſe needle points at *north*,
Without a *variation*.

 A CARD.

[40]

A CARD.

Norwich, Feb. 3, 1770.

CIndaretta congratulates her much loved colonel Hurlo Thrumbo, and honours him for his *bold* and *ſpirited* reflections on the *baſe-born* electors of Weſtminſter, *not worthy to enter the gates of his majeſty's palace.*

Tommy grows a fine boy; and will be big enough for an *enſign* in his *papa*'s company of *militia* in a year or two: I *brings* him to London the *firſt* of *April*, and you will ſhew him *St. James's* and all the fine folks, but *within* "the gates of his majeſty's palace" on account of his *birth*: I charge you don't let him come near any of the vulgar *mechanicks* or *baſe-born* mob of *Weſtminſter petitioners.*

For the better underſtanding of the *above card*, we have ſubjoined a *paſtoral poem*, firſt publiſhed during the late conteſted election for the *county* of *Norfolk.*

CINDA-

[41]

CINDARETTA.

A MOCK-PASTORAL POEM.

ARGUMENT.

Cindaretta, *Cook-maid to Colonel* Hurlo-Thrumbo (*so called from a famous speech made at a county meeting, in which he "hurl'd defiance" in the face of his electors,) being enamoured of his fine parts and august deportment, after having borne him two children, complains of his long absence on the annual exercise of the Norfolk militia, where he commanded in person.*

DOWN dropt her brush; the dish-clout thrown aside,
And lost was all the kitchen's silver pride;
Scarce would the deep majestic bellows blow,
The labouring jack would hardly, hardly go;
Dull was the brass, unwash'd her earthen-ware,
And Tabby slept neglected in the chair:
Love wrought the change, 'twas Love that had betray'd,
When thus in doleful dumps bewail'd the maid:
"Go, gentle gales! and bear my sighs away,
"Ah! why so long does Hurlo-Thrumbo stay?

" Why form'd Dame Nature women's love ſo *ſtrong*,
" Or, why art thou ſo *tempting* and ſo *long?*
" Reſound my tubs, my hollow tubs reſound;
" Ah me! that love ſhould give ſo deep a wound?
" Why in that houſe * ſhould'ſt thou ſo ſtrive to ſhine,
" Is it more *clean* or better *kept* than mine?
" Alas! I'm told (but they are lies, I ween)
" That *dirty* houſe no mortal yet could *clean:*
" Rub as they will, and poliſh as they can,
" Penſions and bribes will *iron-mould* the man:
" Go, gentle gales! and bear my ſighs away!
" Ah! why ſo long does Hurlo-Thrumbo ſtay?

" Why ſeeks my ſoldier forts or city walls,
" When I can make my love leſs hurtful balls?
" Why to the camp muſt Hurlo-Thrumbo fly,
" When I can raiſe, and you beſiege a pye?
" If thou muſt fight, for thou art born to weild,
" O! fight in paſte the heroes of the field:
" Go, gentle gales! and bear my ſighs away!
" Ah! why ſo long does Hurlo-Thrumbo ſtay?

" When yeſter morn I turn'd my jack around,
" The ſalt-box fell portentous to the ground:
" Thrice mew'd the cat, and thrice ſhe flew on Tray;
" Oh! think on this, and thy election day!
" Die, Cinderetta! eaſe thy hateful ſmart,
" Ambition's now the miſtreſs of his heart:

† H---e of C---o--s.

" Go!

" Go, gentle gales! and bear my ſighs away!
" Ah! why ſo long does Hurlo-Thrumbo ſtay?

" Ah, me! each object that theſe eyes can view,
" Brings to my mind ſome pleaſing form of you:
" When in this hand the poliſh'd ſpit I hold,
" Thy ſhape is here, for thou art long and cold:
" If I the cleaver take, the joint to part,
" Thy abſence then is cleaving of my heart;
" Or, if I ſtrive my kitchen fire to mend,
" Thoſe eyes are flaming at the poker's end.
" Go, gentle gales! and bear my ſighs away!
" Ah! why ſo long does Hurlo-Thrumbo ſtay?"

'Thus wail'd ſhe tearful to herſelf alone,
The hollow tubs re-echoing every groan:
When lo! her much-lov'd hero *ſtood* to view,
And her heart flutter'd as ſhe nearer drew:
She ſought the garret for her Sunday's pride,
Pinn'd on her nims, and bruſh'd the fleas aſide.
The buſy ſylphs attend the dreſſing fair,
This clears the ſcurf, and this pork-lards her hair:
This with its breath reduc'd her tear-ſwoln eye,
Another fans the pouting noſtrils dry:
Down came the damſel with ſuperior grace,
With all the ſtew-pan's radiance in her face:
So dredg'd, ſo finiſh'd, and ſo ſoft her look,
Now trips a Goddeſs, and now ſmiles a cook:
Flies to her Hero, with reſiſtleſs charms,
And claſps the long, cold Col'nel in her arms.

I M P R O M P T U.

TO THOMAS DE GREY, ESQ. MEMBER FOR NORFOLK.

TEACH us the difference to know,
Betwixt the *base* and *free-born* foe;
Left at the royal palace entry
We fhould be fhot by Scottifh centry;
Or fent to Newgate for fedition,
In figning Weftminfter's petition:
Since Thurloe fays, it matters not
Whether we die by *fhot* or *rot*.

T H E L I E.

I.

GO Truth, old-fafhion'd gueft,
To teach unwelcome news,
Thyfelf fhalt bear the teft,
When all do thee refufe.
Go both to low and high,
And give them all the Lie.

Go

II.

Go tell the ——— he's weak,
And obſtinate withal ;
Tell him (for Truth will ſpeak)
Heh's loſt the love of all :
And if he will reply,
Fear not to give the Lie.

III.

Tell ſtateſmen they're not whole,
By vice uninterrupted ;
In body and in ſoul
They're ſhamefully corrupted.
If ſtateſmen will reply,
Give ſtateſmen all the Lie.

IV.

Go tell the court it ſkreens
Knaves, murd'rers, and defaulters ;
It ſcoundrels entertains
That worthy are of halters :
And if it dare reply,
Then give it ſtraight the Lie.

V.

Go tell the church it ſlumbers,
And orders gives to fools ;
Say, churchmen there are numbers,
Who dullneſs learn by rules :

And

And if the church reply,
Dare yet to give the Lie.

VI.

Go tell the lawyer's courts,
Their lingering far worfe is,
With pleas, demurs, reports,
Than all our other curfes:
And if they dare reply,
Quick give them all the Lie.

VII.

Go tell phyficians grave,
Who boaft their mighty fkill,
Some few indeed they fave,
But many more they kill:
And if they will reply,
Fail not to give the Lie.

VIII.

Go tell the ftage directors,
True tafte with them fure fcarce is,
While they are fuch protectors
Of baby-pleafing farces:
And as they yield reply,
So give them all the Lie.

Away,

[47]

IX.

Away, and fear not, tho'
They think thee quite uncouth ;
For thou may'ſt let them know,
Thy name is *downright Truth* :
And wiſh them no reply,
For thou muſt give the Lie.

THE FOLLOWING ILLUSTRIOUS PERSONAGES WILL APPEAR IN THE UNDER-MENTIONED DRESSES AND CHARACTERS, AT THE SUBSCRIPTION MASQUERADE, AT MRS. CORNELLY'S.

HIS *M——y* in a child's frock and bib, followed by L—d N——, in the habit of an old woman, holding him in leading ſtrings.

The *Q——*, Ceres with a cornucopia.

The D—— of *Gl —— r*, in the character of Benedick the married man.

The D—— of *Cum——d*, in the character of Paris.

The P——ſs D——r of *W——es*, the witch of Endor.

The D—— of *North——d*, Trappolin, in Duke and no Duke.

The *Ducheſs*, an ale-wife.

Five

[48]

Five of the Maids of Honour, reprefenting the parable of the five foolifh virgins, carrying the lamps without oil.

Mifs *Van——t*, in the character of one of the wife Virgins.

L—y *Wald——e*, in the character of the Ifland Princefs.

The D—— of *Gr——n*, a New-Market Jockey.

L—y *Har——n*, Meffalina.

L—d *Lig—r*, an old fatyr.

Mr. *F—x*, Sir John Falftaff.

L—d *Har—g—n*, an alderman with a pair of horns in his pocket.

L—d *W—y—th*, in the character of a butcher.

L—y *Har—t Stan—e*, Sufannah.

L—d *Mar—h*, following her, in the character of one of the Elders.

L—d *Car—le*, the prodigal fon.

L—d *Tal—t*, in the character of the ftarved cook in the Mifer.

L—d *Hert—d*, Rembrandt's Gold-weigher.

L—d *Per—y*, the God Priapus.

Sir *F——r Nor—n*, the devil.

Mr. *Rig—y*, a drunken Bacchanal.

Mr. *Ver—n*, in the character of Fortune in a robe of cards, a chain of dice about his neck, and a large box on his head.

D— of *D——*, a bear in a chain.

Col. *Lut—l*, a prize-fighter.

A DIALOGUE

A DIALOGUE

BETWEEN A GENTLEMAN AND A PAINTER, AT THE EXHIBITION IN SPRING-GARDENS,

IN THE SPRING, 1770.

GENT.

MR. Painter, you joke
With us peaceable folk,
For ſurely it never can be;
That three brave ſons of Mars,
Can be talking of wars,
Whilſt like miſſes they're ſipping their tea.

PAINT.

Theſe are ſoldiers indeed,
But their trade's not to bleed,
'Tis true, they wear long ſwords and boots;
Yet they deem it no ſin
To ſleep in whole ſkin,
So ne'er venture to ſtain e'en their coats.

Should I paint them in arms,
'Midſt hoſtile alarms,
What mortals a ſmile could refuſe?

For

For tho' daggers they ſpeak,
Were their country at ſtake,
Yet, like Hamlet, Sir, none would they uſe.

'Tis theirs in the Mall
To attract the ſoft belle,
Who ev'ry day haunts the parade;
For the fair love the brave,
And ſtill firmly believe
They muſt be ſo, who wear a cockade.

GENT.

I allow your remark,
But 'tis not in the park,
That their proweſs has vanquiſh'd the fair;
There is no one but knows
How they ſlaughter'd their foes
In the battle of Bloomſbury-Square.

PAINT.

When Ulyſſes ſcot-free,
'Scap'd the ſword and the ſea,
As Ovid relateth the fable;
He deſcrib'd to his wife,
Where he ventur'd his life,
By the wine he had ſpilt on the table.

Juſt

Juſt ſo theſe repoſe,
After routing their foes,
In that bluſt'ring, bloodleſs campaign;
So now, Sir, you ſee,
With what's ſpilt of their tea,
They are fighing it over again.

" Here the troopers I led
" When the enemy fled,
" And there, Sirs, I loſt my new beaver;
" Here a taylor's aſſault
" Caus'd the firſt line to halt,
" And there I encounter'd a weaver."

BOBADIL.

PRESENT PUBLIC WISHES.

THE K—— *wiſhes* to be *quiet*.
The people *wiſh* him to be *great*.
The miniſtry *wiſh* to continue the majority.
Patriots *wiſh* for liberty.
Remonſtrants *wiſh* for redreſs.
Old maids *wiſh* for young huſbands.
Many huſbands *wiſh* for divorces.
The proprietors of Ranelagh and Vauxhall *wiſh* for fair weather.

Chairmen

Chairmen *wiſh* for foul weather.
Convicts *wiſh* for life.
Wilkes *wiſhes* no longer for his liberty.
His creditors *wiſh* him joy of it.
The *outs wiſh* to be *in*.
The *ins wiſh* to continue ſo.
Sore conſciences *wiſh* for a reſtriction on the preſs.
Players *wiſh* for good benefits.
Vagabonds *wiſh* for a revolution,
In every branch of the conſtitution.
And the writer of this rhapſody *wiſhes* he had clear,
No more, nor leſs, than juſt one thouſand pounds a year.

E P I S T L E

FROM LADY BRIDGET L***, TO LADY BAB BUTTERFLY, AT YORK.

YOU cannot imagine, my dear lady Bab,
How anxious I am all my budget to blab;
But, lord, I could tell you a thouſand times better,
Than ſcribbling my thoughts, like a clerk, in a letter:
But when we're apart, there is no other means
Of deſcribing the vulgar, and St. James's ſcenes—
Well, then to begin, my dear Bab, and be ſhort;
In the preſence I was, when the May'r came to court;

Ye

[53]

Ye Gods! what a ſhame! that the ſcum of the earth
Should dare to petition as people of birth:
Such a ſight, my dear Bab, with their gowns and broad faces,
With their vile vulgar gaits, and their ſtaves and their maces;
But, like owls in the ſun, how our king made them blink!
And then, my dear ſoul, how theſe creatures did ſtink!
I declare, *eau de luce* hardly kept me from fainting;
A plague, e'en in Turkey, was not half ſo tainting:
But the king, my dear child, who is always ſo clear,
Sent the wretches away with a flea in their ear.
You know how I ſigh'd for a prize in the lottery;
But now all my ſighs are turn'd round on the coterie:
Between you and me, I'd lay twenty to ſeven,
That many had rather go there than to heaven;
It's the ſnuggeſt affair, and the pleaſanteſt plan,
For altho' with your huſband—you may have a man;
Do you know tho', they've black-ball'd George Selwyn and March?
(That ſweet Macaroni, ſo ſtiff and ſo ſtarch)
Their reaſons I know not; but ſure it is cruel,
For of all our gay lords, ſure my lord is the jewel;
As for Selwyn, the creature has wit and good ſenſe,
Which to me, lady Bab, is a horrid offence.

E What

[54]

What you loſe, my dear creature, by not being in
town!
Foote's open, and Reynolds's paintings are ſhewn:
Enchanting Vauxhall, where the dark walks, ſo ſnug,
Afford me, at times, a dear kiſs and a hug.
Well, adieu, lady Bab, for engagements are preſſing;
I dine at Almack's—and have not begun dreſſing;
To reach the dear ſpot, I am all in a fidget,
And beg to remain, Bab—your dear little
BRIDGET.

THE STATE-COACH.

A TALE.

IN IMITATION OF THE MANNER OF DR. SWIFT.

ONCE on a time a grand lord-may'r
(No matter when, no matter where)
Kept a huge pompous coach of ſtate,
Of moſt enormous bulk and weight;
And on the times of public joy,
To wheel about the pond'rous toy;
He kept beſides a noble ſtring
Of horſes, fit to draw a king;
All of high blood, all beaſts of breeding,
But vicious from exceſs of feeding;

Of

Of courſe intractable and heady,
Yet in one point perverſely ſteady,
Viz. Each good ſteed was true and hearty
To his own intereſt and his party;
Nay, this curs'd ſpirit had poſſeſt
To ſuch degree each ſturdy beaſt,
That not a ſingle chuff would move
From threats or ſoothing, fear or love,
Unleſs in partnerſhip he drew
With thoſe of his confed'rate crew,
Though thus the clumſy and the clever,
Ill-pair'd oft hobbled on together.

Hence when the coach was order'd out,
Buck would refuſe to match with Stout,
At leaſt one inch would not proceed
Unleſs impetuous Di'mond led,
Who when of late our grand premier,
And then uncheck'd in his career,
While he tugg'd on the vaſt machine
O'er rough and ſmooth, through thick and thin,
Would often with their rapid turn
Make the wheels creak and axle burn;
Yet give the haughty devil his due,
Though bold his quarterings, they were true:
Yes, let us not his ſkill diſparage,
He never once o'erſet the carriage,
Though oft he whirl'd it, one would think,
Juſt o'er the pitfall's headlong brink;

While at each hair-breadth 'ſcape, his foes
Would cry, there, there, by G-d, it goes!
And as ſtiff Buck would ne'er ſubmit
But on theſe terms to champ the bit,
Stout in return was full as ſullen,
Nor the ſame harneſs would he pull in,
Unleſs by cautious Duke preceded,
Or by pacific Sawney headed:
The body-coachman, hence unable
To rule the refractory ſtable,
Was forc'd to leave the ſaucy brutes
To terminate their own diſputes;
And when they deign'd to wear the traces,
Chuſe their own partners and their places;
But, tir'd themſelves with theſe diſtractions,
Reſolv'd at laſt the ſeveral factions
(For in their anger all had wit)
Some terms of union to admit,
Which, that more firmly they might bind,
Drawn in this form by all were ſign'd:

We the contracting ſteeds, (expreſt
Here was the name of each prime beaſt,
As Di'mond, Sawney, Duke) however
Determin'd not to work together,
Yet by theſe preſents are agreed,
To ether peaceably to feed:
On this account then (work or play)
Let each receive his 'cuſtom'd pay:

Confirm

Confirm we by concurring votes
To each his daily peck of oats:
Befides, omit we by no means
Proportion'd quantities of beans;
Nor yet warm mafhes when we chufe 'em,
Nor Bracken's balls when pleas'd to ufe 'em;
For as 'tis likely from full feeding,
At times, difeafes may be breeding,
'Tis right for every horfe that is fick,
Who finds the food fhould find the phyfic.

These previous articles now clos'd,
Here prudent Di'mond interpos'd,
Long fam'd for his contempt of pelf,
And views which center'd not in felf,
" How chang'd at prefent?" (or no more
Wears he that mafk which once he wore.)
Quoth he, (wrapp'd round with many a clout
His greafy heels, the horfes gout)
" Snug now ourfelves and our dependants,
" Shall we neglect our dear defcendants?
" Nay e'en from fcripture we fhould learn,
" For our own houfholds due concern;
" Left we incur then, to our fhame,
" Of infidels th' accurfed name,
" Provide we next, (if fuch your will is)
" For all our prefent colts and fillies;
" No matter, though for this fupply
" We drain our mafter's coffers dry:

" Stretch we the grant too, if ye pleafe,
" E'en to the future colts of thefe;
" Then to their coltlings in entail,
" Till iffue of fuch iffue fail :
" Well, bullies, are you all content?"
Each fteed here fnorted his affent;
And, more t'exprefs their joy of heart,
All let at once th'obftreperous f—t;
The mews, through all its fpacious round,
Re-echo'd to th' unmanner'd found;
And now adjufted their pretenfions,
And thus fecur'd their long-breath'd penfions,
Like porkers fattening in the fty,
On their fat rumps at eafe they lie;
Uplitter'd to their ears in ftraw,
Yet not a fingle beaft will draw.

Dogs! to reduce you all to reafon,
I wifh, at leaft, for fome fhort feafon,
That in your prefent mafter's ftead,
Too meek to tame fo rough a breed,
Too mild to curb your factious fpirit,
Too good to treat ye as ye merit,
Stern boifterous Cromwell from the dead,
Or bluff old Hal would lift his head,
That I might fee you bound and fkip
Beneath their difciplining whip;
That I might fee your pamper'd hides
Flogg'd, 'till from out your furrow'd fides

Spun,

Spun, in each part, the ſizy blood,
Too rich from ſloth and copious food;
That thus let out at all theſe ſluices,
It may purge off its vicious juices;
While I ſhould hear you, at each jerk,
Cry, laſh no more, we'll work, we'll work.

IN THE SEASON OF 1760,

The Subſcription-Books at Bath *were opened for Prayers at the Abbey, and Gaming at the Rooms.*

In the Evening of the firſt Day, the Numbers ſtood as under:

THE church and rooms the other day,
Open'd their books for pray'r and play;
The prieſt got twelve—Hoyle ſixty-ſeven;
How great the odds for hell 'gainſt heaven!

AN ANSWER.

IF ſigning with the twelve, to heaven
The ſureſt way does ſhew,
And ſigning with the ſixty-ſeven,
As ſure to hell to go:

Tim, prithee ſay! thou knowing elf,
(For to decide I'm loth)
Where go the reſt, who with thyſelf,
Perhaps have ſign'd with both?

Thus Juſtice ſays, at her court leet,
(And Juſtice is no ſtinter)
" In heav'n you'll have a ſummer ſeat,
" In hell a houſe for winter."

EPIGRAM.

SAYS Ch—dl—gh to a certain dame,
Whom royal horners woo,
I almoſt think it is a ſhame
To talk to ſuch as you.

We both, reply'd the titled whore,
Have been a theme for laughter,
The diff'rence this, *you* felt before,
My foible happen'd after.

EPIGRAM.

OF Outs and Ins, the common ſins,
Are public peculation;
Ins have been Outs, and Outs been Ins,
And both have robb'd the nation.

Since

Since both alike one plan purſue,
Of mal-adminiſtration,
Of each ſort raiſe a choſen few
To an exalted ſtation.

My views are far from ſiniſter
To work a reformation;
I'd make Jack Ketch prime miniſter
Of each man's elevation.

ON THE OUTS AND INS.

THE Outs much like an empty ſtomach are,
That frets and keeps a coil for diet;
The Ins, to one that's full you may compare,
Which well contented is and quiet.
A veſſel full, when ſtruck, makes no replies,
But th' empty barrel always makes a noiſe:
Thus he that's in no 'ccaſion has to quarrel;
But he, that's out, is like an empty barrel.

A CHARACTER.

OF vice the ſecret friend, the foe profeſs'd,
Of every talent to deceive poſſeſs'd;
As mean in houſhold ſavings, as profuſe
In vile corruption's ſcandalous abuſe.

Mentally

Mentally blind, on whom no ray of truth
E'er glanc'd auſpicious, e'en in bloom of youth.
Perfidious, arbitrary, proud and baſe,
With all the ſins that damn'd the Stuart race,
Without one virtue to ſecure from ſhame
The flattering promiſe of an early fame,
Thou tinſel pageant of a ſummer day!
But winter ſtern ſhall tear thy maſk away;
Shall drag at once into abhorred light,
A heart beſt hid beneath the veil of night.
Nought will avail thy ſilly, ſimpering ſmile,
No artifice can his rough hand beguile;
One general indignation will be ſhewn,
Contempt, at laſt, is into hatred grown.
What, tho' inimitable Churchill's hearſe
Sav'd thee from all the vengeance of his verſe,
Macaulay ſhall in nervous proſe relate
Whence flows the venom that diſtracts the ſtate.
Thy name will ſtink in hiſt'ry's awful page,
Curs'd by thy native land from age to age:——
Sure, as that ſack-inſpir'd Whitehead ſings,
And Scotch Addreſſers hail *the—beſt of Kings*.

ALLEN'S GHOST.

The

THE ANSWER.

RISUM teneatis Amici?

TO hear your complaints I ſhall ever be ready,
And not to redreſs them I ſwear I am ſteady.
It gives me concern that you come here miſled:
Your Remonſtrance I hold is not over well-bred,
To arraign my Mama and my Minion muſt be
Diſreſpectful at leaſt both to them and to me;
Beſides 'tis injurious, tho' true, to be told
That MY P——t's bought, that the people are ſold,
For of places and penſions a monſtrous profuſion
Is plac'd in my hands by our wiſe conſtitution.

In ſpite of my modeſty too I muſt raiſe,
Since you will not do it, my own ſong of praiſe.
The law of the land to reſpect is my glory!
And as I was *born* and bred a ſtaunch Tory,
If you dare *to inſult or trifle* with law,
Like Nero, by M******S I'll keep you in awe.
I ſcorn to encroach on the one houſe or t'other;
I only c****** them; then why ſuch a pother?
Too well I remember the oath that I made,
The beſt of K—gs never your rights will invade;
From a beggarly ſpot we were call'd, and we came
Thoſe rights to defend; then may I not claim,

Since

Since the ty***t to play I ſo ſeldom endeavour,
That the cry of my People ſhould be G—e for ever?
Then *laughing* he publiſh'd this gracious command;
Inſtead of my a—ſe let them all kiſs my hand.

TO THE LORD OF THE ISLE.

Dabis, Improbe, Pœnas.

WHERE wilt thou ſtop, thou all-corrupting Thane,
Who render'ſt all the patriot's labours vain!
Who prov'ſt by titles, ribbons, or by gold,
That boaſted virtue may be bought, and ſold!
That ſtubborn pride can ſtoop to aid thy plan—
That Chatham doats, tho' Pitt was once a man!

Shall there not riſe ſome great, ſuperior force,
To check thy mad ambition in its courſe?
To drag thee, ſtruggling, from behind the throne,
And make thy head for thy falſe heart atone?
Shalt thou of goodneſs taint the pureſt ſpring,
By hell-born magic faſcinate thy King?
And ſhall not freedom's enterprizing arm
Cut through the gordian knot that binds the charm!

Bleſs'd be the man, who, virtuous, juſt, and brave,
Shall ſtretch his hand his country's rights to ſave,
Ere

Ere Albion's ſons become no longer free,
And all her chiefs unpopular, like thee!

One man ‡, like Abdiel, all thine arts hath found,
Firm 'midſt deſertion, 'midſt corruption ſound;
One whoſe quick eye can penetrate thy wiles,
Thy frowns who dreads not, nor who courts thy
ſmiles;
Who loves a Brunſwick, hates a Stuart reign,
But moſt abhors a kingdom-graſping Thane.
Beware his vengeance: For the day will come,
Big with ripe fate, and black with gath'ring doom;
When thy juſt ſov'reign, yielding to the call
Of groaning millions, urging on thy fall,
Will from thy dazzling greatneſs hurl thee down,
And vindicate the honour of his crown.

‡ Earl Temple.

E P I T A P H

FOR SIR D——Y R——R, K——T.

Here
Reſts at laſt
From all his ſanguinary Deſires,
Sir D****Y R***R, Knt.
Whoſe Love of Money
was only exceeded
By his Luſt of Puniſhment:

Form'd

[66]

Form'd by Nature for all the Chicanery
Of the Law,
Improved by the double
And deceitful Education
Of a
Presbyterian,
By unwearied Application
To his own Interest,
By prostituting his Conscience,
And
A true time-serving Spirit,
In Spite of Genius,
From the basest Original,
He acquired the immense Sum
Of Three Hundred Thousand Pounds;
And wriggled himself into the Post
Of Att——y G——l.
In the Execution of this Office,
His Heart constantly felt Affliction,
His Eye ever flow'd with Sorrow,
When the Innocent escaped unpunished.
Hence, by slavish Obedience
To M———l Mandates,
In wresting Laws to arbitrary Purposes,
He ascended the Seat
Of
Lord Ch—f J——e.
The same Thirst of Vengeance
Still waited on his Footsteps;

Those

Thoſe whom he long'd to puniſh
As Att——y,
He now condemn'd,
With Delight,
As Judge:
Truth found no Juſtice,
Virtue no Favour,
Innocence no Mercy,
When in Oppoſition to C—rt Meaſures:
Zealous to eſtabliſh Tyranny
In the Crown Law,
Againſt all but * Robbers
Of the Public Money,
To whom, from Sympathy,
He was merciful beyond Meaſure;
Enemy to Liberty,
Steady in his Country's Ruin,
Encouraged and adapted
By all the Qualities in Head and Heart,
Which diſgrace human Nature
To requeſt Nobility;
He aſked,
And it was granted.

Heaven and Monarchs
Behold with different Eyes:

* *Vide* LE--F's trial, where, after being found guilty of illegally poſſeſſing twenty thouſand pounds, he was only fined the intereſt of the money he had in his hands, ſtill preſerving all his places but one.

Him,

Him, whom his S———n ſummoned
To a Peerage,
God ſnatched to anſwer for his Crimes.
For know, the Almighty will not
Always, unreſenting,
Permit the Ambitious to receive,
Nor Kings to beſtow thoſe Honours
On the Neſarious,
Which are only the juſt Reward
Of
VIRTUE.

ON PART OF THE UNIVERSITY-CHURCH IN OXFORD BEING CONVERTED INTO A LAW-SCHOOL.

YES, yes; you may rail at the *Pope* as you pleaſe,
But truſt me that *Miracles* never will ceaſe.
See here—an event that no mortal ſuſpected!
See LAW and DIVINITY cloſely connected!
To prove the *old proverb*, which long hath ſeem'd odd,
That *the neareſt the* Church *are the fartheſt from* God.

ON A BLACK MARBLE STATUE OF A SLAVE STANDING IN ONE OF THE INNS OF COURT.

IN vain, poor ſable ſon of woe,
  Thou ſeek'ſt a tender ear;
In vain thy tears with anguiſh flow,
  For mercy dwells not here.

From cannibals thou fly'ſt in vain;
  Lawyers leſs quarter give;
The firſt won't eat you till you're ſlain,
  The laſt will do't alive.

ON SEEING A LAW-BOOK

BOUND IN UNCOLOURED CALF, AND WHITE EDGES.

WITH unſtain'd edges, and in ſpotleſs calf,
  A Law-Book bound muſt make a ſtoic laugh;
For in that ſtriking emblem you may ſee,
Not what Law *is*, but what the Law *ſhould* be:
A Law-Book thus in the Law Livery dreſt,
Is like a Jeſuit in a Layman's veſt;

'Tis like a ſtrumpet cloath'd in ſpotleſs white,
'Tis like a bitter apple, fair to ſight;
'Tis like a ſimple quaker, plain and neat,
That with his yeas and noes is ſure to cheat;
'Tis like a pirate, that falſe colours ſhows,
Or Hecla's flames conceal'd in virgin ſnows;
'Tis like—in ſhort, 'tis like Dan Milton's ſin;
All fair without, but monſtrous foul within.

WRITTEN UNDER A PICTURE OF KITTY FISHER,

DRAWN IN THE CHARACTER OF CLEOPATRA.

TO this fam'd character how juſt thy right!
Thy mind as wanton, and thy form as bright.

THE PETTICOAT ADMINISTRATION.

Peace, idiot man, WOMAN ſhall ever rule;
How oft to her, you've prov'd yourſelf a fool.

LONG have the men triumphant reign'd,
Over this giddy nation;
But neither law or truth maintain'd,
Tho' each maintain'd his ſtation.

In

In government there is no truth,
  Lord Egmont ſwears, odd rat 'em,
'Tis prov'd by Jemmy Twitcher's mouth,
  And by the Earl of Chatham.

The outs they rail at thoſe who're in;
  The ins at thoſe who're out;
Whigs roar to-day for Wilkes and Glynn,
  And then for John of Bute.

No cod-ſmack ſhifts her ſails ſo quick,
  Nor makes ſo many tacks;
They lie, they ſwear, at nothing ſtick,
  At Arthur's or Almack's.

The ribband I this day had given,
  'Twas yeſterday to two;
To-morrow 'twill be hung on ſeven,
  And then, the Lord knows how.

Away with *ſalique* law and rule;
  Why, give it to our war-ſons?
Inſtead of dangling on a fool—
  Pray hang it on Miſs Parſons.

But now, to cut the matter ſhort,
  Grieve not that all are mad,
When lying is the maſter's *fort*,
  Servants will be as bad.

I therefore to the world propofe,
No more of Wilkes and Bute,
Let them be friends, who've long been foes,
In *Air* Sir Fletcher mute.

Senate! attend; I have a plan
Drawn up by hands not common;
That government may end in man,
And now commence in woman.

I think I fee the ftatefman ftare,
The law and clergy fpar,
While foldiers bend unto the fair,
And like the fofter war.

I know no man dare difapprove
The plan which now I draw;
CHARLOTTE, fhe is the queen we love,
Of England and her law.

G——n the prefident fhall be
Of council, for fhe's able;
Then you'll have cards and burgundy,
Down to the chaplain's table.

The treafury let King——n take;
Yet, that is fcarce enough
Two paltry fireworks to make,
And buy her pins and fnuff.

Thy

Thy daughters Har——n and thee,
What little poſt will charm ye?
The navy treaſurer one ſhall be,
The other pay the army.

North——d maſter of the horſe
Aſtride ſhall nobly paſs;
And, to help out her gen'rous purſe,
Shew too the queen's fine aſs.

One for the houſhold we muſt find,
There Ch—d—s let us hitch in;
She's of a plain and homely mind,
And fit to fill a kitchen.

Th' exchequer, who's ſo fit to grace
As lovely Mrs. P—t;
Eſpecially ſince ſhe's out place,
And loves to pick a bit.

Sweet lady Sarah, ſhe ſhall rule
Where ſhe can move and feel;
She ſhall command each am'rous fool,
And have the privy ſeal.

Let's for a lord chief juſtice look—
What for the Common Pleas?
There ſhove my lady B—lb—ke,
She can divorce with eaſe.

[74]

Poor lady V—e, I'm much afraid
  Penſion or place can't hold;
Unleſs 'tis at the board of trade,
  And ſhe's for trade too old.

If Richmond's ranger will but pleaſe
  Great lady E——e's rigg,
Let her plough up the park for peaſe
  To feed her fav'rite pig.

For maids of honour, we muſt choofe
  Men who are ſtrong and ſtout;
When ladies call that won't refuſe,
  Nor ſlur what they're about.

Earl P—y then ſhall take the lead,
  That man of muckle might;
Sprung from old Chevy-chace's breed,
  And form'd for love's delight.

Sweet lady P—y ſhall no more
  Complain of loveleſs nights;
Her gentle ſpouſe ſhall be turn'd o'er
  For am'rous court delights.

M—e, V——s, A——, and Lord C—k,
  Shall cloſe this ſmirking train;
Well made for maids of honour work,
  Too delicate for pain.

Now

Now let us fill three holy fees,
Sobriety can't flur 'em,
Women can prey with as much eafe
As Briftol, York, or Durham.

V—fi—t, St—h—e, A—er, now
Supply thofe holy places;
Cards to the chaplains pray allow,
But difavow all graces.

For praying and religion too
Have got at fuch a top,
We're loft, unlefs your doctrine new,
To goodnefs puts a ftop.

Old Can——y fhall not have
A 'tifficky old grunter;
With one foot finking in the grave,
While we've a Kitty H—er.

Pem——e, fo well on honour writes,
Muft fermons make in plenty;
They'll pafs your time 'tween meals and White's,
His doctrine will relent ye.

Old lady Huntingdon, no more
Shall be reforted to;
Who won't quit Satan and threefcore,
For heaven in twenty-two.

[76]

Sweet biſhop Kitty, when you pray,
Who will refuſe to kneel?
You will reduce each ſon of clay,
Though he were ſtiff as ſteel.

For London, one both wiſe and grave
Muſt be, yet ſoft and barren;
Sir George, we muſt your goodneſs crave,
To ſpare us biſhop Warren.

To one I'll give the Admiralty,
Who'll rule it with a nod;
She ſhall an Amphitrite be,
And rule each liquid god.

Earl P—y's lady there ſhall reign,
Per terram et per mare,
And make our ſea-gulls ſtill remain
The gallant aves raræ.

As for the reſt, I wou'd'nt place
Under their ſkill a ſkuller;
Pray do you think old Neptune's face,
Was ever ſeen by Buller?

Who can controul the navy board,
Like Kn—b—es ſweet, fair, and gay;
With captains ſhe will then be ſtor'd,
And prick them of their pay.

The

[77]

The wondrous wiſe Sir Thomas Slade,
  Who other's genius mocks,
Shall fly to madam Ben—k's aid,
  To make chain-pumps and blocks.

Fair H—n—y, C—l—r, B———by,
  Shall roll in routs and cards;
They ſhall the three ſurveyors be
  Of all the royal yards.

For poet laureat we muſt chuſe
  A wench behind the curtain;
An am'rous, incoherent muſe,
  A Philippina Burton.

For ſecretaries of the ſtate,
  By heavens I'll find a ſcore,
Wiſer and of a higher date,
  Than any men in ſtore.

M'CAULAY, firſt department grace,
  Lennox ſhall then come a'ter:
If ye want Greek in ſuch a place,
  What think ye of Miſs Carter?

Now Ireland's lord lieutenant make!
  A ſpendthrift ſhe muſt be,
A giddy, gambling, gallant rake
  And lady A—b—e ſhe.

For

For this, good doctor, I'll be bail;
She cannot be revil'd,
For if the men at court ſhould fail,
She'll get you all with child.

For Mrs. Gibſon, who's ſo wiſe,
Her parts have no deception;
For youth and age ſhe will ſuffice,
And pleaſe with quick conception.

O! ſhe will give ye ſpecial ſport,
What nurſes ſhall we need!
What cradles then will wag at court,
To huſh this pretty breed!

Let L——ham command a fleet,
Boſcawen taught her how;
And ſince ſhe did the admiral beat,
The French ſhe muſt, you know.

To fight like ſome's an eaſy trade,
Our arms let G——r lead!
She'll trim ten, like the Orlean maid,
Or lord George Sackville's breed.

One ſhall command our horſe, won't flinch,
Well known to every trooper;
In charging ſhe'll not loſe an inch,
I'll warrant Lucy Cooper.

If

If ye approve this little ſketch,
  I'll end all perturbation ;
And with the aid of good Jack Ketch,
  Will calm this frantick nation.

MOLLY MACHIAVEL.

TO MISS MOLLY MACHIAVEL,

ON HER PETTICOAT ADMINISTRATION.

I.

WHAT ! all the poſts of honour gone !
  Who can refrain from laughter,
To ſee the T—wnſh—nd's left alone,
  The *mother* and the *daughter*.

II.

Long and well known to public fame,
  For gallantry and wit,
The dowager puts in her claim,
  And ſwears ſhe'll have a *bit*.

III.

With Williams, Winnington, it ſeems,
  A merry life ſhe led ;
And hackney'd in all *ways* and *means*,
  She was to *buſineſs bred*.

The

IV.

The *back-ſtairs* be her province then,
The bed-chamber without;
And but the *very beſt* of men
Will e'er get in or out.

V.

Armed with a *battle-ax* in hand,
Love's emblem in a ſtorm;
Who ſhall the *penſioners* command?
The gay, the gallant O——.

VI.

Dear Molly then for once be kind,
Their proper poſts aſſign 'em,
And if a *chaſter* pair you find,
With pleaſure they'll reſign them.

HUMOROUS ADVERTISEMENTS.

Next Month,

Will be ſold by *Inch of Candle*, to the higheſt Bidder,

The E—— of H——'s BIBLE:

(The Owner having no further Occaſion for it)

It is butefully printed in the *Minion* letter, on *royal* paper; *half bound*; *double gilt*; and has a fine *broad Phylactery* running round the borders.

With notes, comments, and illuſtrations, in manuſcript,

By *David Stuart Mac Sceptick*, Eſq;

Late Chaplain in ordinary, and Secretary of Embaſſy, and now Secretary to the Right Hon. G—— C———.

*** A conſiderable ſum has been offered for the *good-will* of this Bible, being a *lucky one*. It is admirably fitted for telling of fortunes, and diſcovering ſtolen goods, with the aid of a *Key*. On the white paper at the beginning, are the names and time of birth of his l——p's numerous and hopeful progeny, with their places, penſions, reverſions, and grants. And on the white Paper at the latter end, is a *practical* diſſertation, in his own hand-writing, on the text—*In godlineſs there is great gain.*

For further particulars enquire at the Chamberlain's Office, the borough of Orford; the Caſtle of Dublin; Kenſington Palace; the ſecretary of ſtate's office; the office of ordnance; the ſecretary of ſtate's office in Ireland, &c. &c. &c. &c. &c. &c. &c. &c. &c.

[82]

In the Preſs, and ſpeedily will be publiſhed,

Price 2*s.* 6*d.* bound in red Leather.

The CONWAY *Court Regiſter.*

In this Regiſter is contained a full account of all the offices, civil, and military; penſions, reverſions, grants, governments, titles, &c. &c. lately given to, and now held by that family and its allies, in England, Scotland, Ireland, and America. The Public may be aſſured that no pains have been ſpared to make this book complete; notwithſtanding that it has been maliciouſly aſſerted, in order to prejudice the ſale, that the number of offices, &c. has been ſo great, and ſome of the grants ſo ſecret, that no private perſon could come at the exact knowledge of them. If, after this Regiſter is printed off, any new employments ſhould be beſtowed on that family, they will be printed on a ſeparate ſheet, and given gratis to the purchaſers of this book.

N. B. By way of an Appendix, will be printed a correct Liſt of the offices from which the friends of General Conway have been lately removed.

AN

AN IMPORTANT QUESTION DECIDED.

TO break his word, or loſe his place,
Is C——y's meditation;
I own it is a weighty caſe,
And well worth conſid'ration.

But, Sir, your brother, nephew, wife,
Conſult on this occaſion;
They'll give, I vouch it on my life,
Right ſolid conſolation.

LIBERTY HALL.

OLD Homer! but what have we with him to do?
What are Grecians or Trojans to me or to you?
Such heatheniſh heroes no more I'll invoke,
Choice ſpirits aſſiſt me, attend hearts of oak,
Toll loll, &c.

Sweet peace, belov'd handmaid of ſcience and art,
Unanimity, take your Petitioners part;
Accept of my ſong, 'tis the beſt I can do—
But firſt, may it pleaſe ye, my ſervice to you.

Perhaps

[84]

Perhaps my Addrefs you may premature think;
Becaufe I have mention'd no toaft as I drink;
There are many fine toafts, but the beft of them all
Is the toaft of the times; that is, Liberty-hall.

That fine Britifh building by Alfred was fam'd,
Its grand corner-ftone Magna Charta is nam'd;
Independency came at Integrity's call,
And form'd the front pillars of Liberty-hall.

That manor our forefathers bought with their blood,
And their fons, and their fons fons, have prov'd the deeds good;
By that title we'll live, by that title we'll fall,
For life is not life out of Liberty-hall.

In her mantle of honour, each ftar-fpangled fold,
Playing bright in the funfhine, the burnifh of gold;
Truth beams on her breaft; fee, at Loyalty's call,
The genius of England in Liberty-hall.

The fweet-fmelling courtlings of ribband and lace,
The fpaniels of power, and bounty's difgrace,
So fupple, fo fervile, fo paffive ye fall;
But paffive obedience loft Liberty-hall.

But when Revolution had fettled the crown,
And natural reafon knock'd tyranny down,
No frowns cloath'd with terror appear'd to appall,
The doors were thrown open of Liberty-hall.

See

See England triumphant, her ſhips ſweep the ſea,
Her ſtandard is *Juſtice*, her watch word be *free*;
Our King is our countryman, Engliſhmen all,
GOD BLESS HIM and bleſs us in Liberty-hall.

Ou vere is des all—Monſieur wants to know;
'Tis neither at Marli, Verſailles, Fontainbleau:
'Tis a palace of no mortal architect's art,
For LIBERTY-HALL is an ENGLISHMAN'S HEART.

TO THE RIGHT HON. LORD VISCOUNT PULTENEY.

WRITTEN IN THE YEAR 1747, AT WESTMINSTER-SCHOOL.

BY GEORGE COLMAN.

TO you, my Lord, theſe lines I write,
Leſt you forget poor Coley quite,
(Who ſtill is drudging in the college,
In ſlow purſuit of further knowledge:
With many a cruel laſh his —— on,
To make him ſome time hence a parſon;
A judge, perhaps, or a phyſician,
Strolling on Ratcliff's exhibition.)

G While

While you with foreign monarchs dine,
Or ſup with princes croſs the Rhine;
Idle your hours in lazy ſtate,
Juſt as forgetful as you're great;
Ramble to ev'ry court your rounds,
Draw when you pleaſe an hundred pounds;
Deſpiſe expence, and dreſs out tawdry,
In cloaths of lace, and gay embroid'ry;
Shine at the ball, and briſkly dance,
As tho' you had been bred in France.
I hear too that your conſtant trade is
To ogle and enſnare the ladies,
Whoſe hearts unwary fire like tinder,
And waſte away by love t'a cinder,
Whilſt you are glad to ſee your pride
On all occaſions gratify'd,
And diſregard your friends at London,
Not caring tho' they're hang'd or undone.
" But hold (you cry) why this abuſe?
" Pray hearken, Sir, to my excuſe;
" Nor hurry with impetuous thought,
" To blame your friend, ere he's in fault.
" At th' Hague we had not time to reſt us,
" Diſturbances did ſo moleſt us;
" For you muſt know, theſe ſcoundrel Dutch
" Rebel, for being *tax'd* too much.
" Loyal and paſſive we obey on,
" And bear all taxes they can lay on.

" The

" The Britiſh Lion now is couchant,
" Grumbling, perhaps, but won't make much on't;
" Taking with patient reſignation,
" Whate'er's impos'd upon the nation.
" In camp too, I'd but little leiſure,
" My time was ſo fill'd up with pleaſure.
" With all old ſchool-fellows ſo dear,
" And Albemarle, and Ligonier,
" That I had ſcarce an hour to ſpare.
" The Duke too ſhew'd me a review,
" All that, at that time, he could do;
" For you muſt know, at preſent writing,
" Our armies have all done with fighting.
" From hence to Hanover we went,
" Liv'd in a round of merriment.
" I had no time to ſcribble letters,
" To you, dear Coley, or your betters."
My lord, you're right, and we from hence
Will quite o'erlook your negligence.
But, *ſans* offence, may I enquire,
In what the preſent hours expire?
What pleaſure or what ſtudy beſt
Your temper ſuits, may I requeſt?
I hear in law you're a proficient;
And other learning have ſufficient;
Can ſolve a problem mathematic;
And read with eaſe a Greek dramatic;
You're ſkill'd in hiſtory enough;
Or algebra have *quantum ſuff.*

And are, by learned men's tuition,
The quinteſſence of erudition;
So vers'd in all that can be nam'd,
Iſis and Cam are quite aſham'd,
And all their ſcholars are downright ſick,
To ſee themſelves outdone at Leipſick.
Tho' I have long with ſtudy mental
Labour'd at language Oriental,
Yet on my ſoul the Hebrew root
Has ſcarcely made one ſingle ſhoot.
I've now broke up, but have a taſk tho'
Harder than yours with Mr. Maſcow;
For mine's as knotty as the devil,
Your law and maſter both are civil;
With milder means to learning lead,
By diff'rent roads, with diff'rent ſpeed.
Douglas and you keep gently jogging,
But I muſt run the race with flogging.

ASHTED COT*.

TIR'D with the noiſe and ſmoke of town,
Its crowded ſtreets and ſumptuous fare,
To ASHTED Cot we oft ſteal down:
Who wiſh for *peace* may find her there.

* A villa belonging to T--- T---, Eſq; Aſhted is a ſmall village between Epſom and Leatherhead, in Surry.

There

There ſtretch the ample proſpects wide,
Fields, woods, down, hills and ſpires appear;
The tempting walk, the grateful ride,
Invite thro' all the varied year.

Or there, or no where can be found,
Health, ever roſy, ever gay.
Content there tills his narrow ground,
And ſings the toils of life away.

No foreign dainties glitter there;
Yet rural plenty there is known;
The home rear'd poultry's oft your fare,
And mutton fed on Banſted Down.

The garden, hemm'd in little ſpace,
Is glad its herbs and fruits to ſend:
Ne'er is forgot the thankful grace,
Nor wine to toaſt the abſent friend,

Nor *Party*'s voice, nor *Faction*'s roar,
Their baleful influence there have ſhed;
Ill-nature never op'd the door,
Nor *Spleen* once dar'd to ſhew her head.

Yet books their moral ſtore diſplay,
And ſocial wit and chat go round,
The *Muſe* there tunes her ruſtic lay,
And *Leiſure* loves th'enchanted ground.

Tho' *Pride* on humble ſcenes looks down,
And longs in pomp to paſs the hours,
There are, who gladly quit the town,
For tranquil joys in ASHTED bow'rs.

THE DYING RAKE'S SOLILOQUY.

BY DR. BARTHOLOMEW.

IN the fever of youth ev'ry pulſe in a flame,
Regardleſs of fortune, of health, and of fame,
Gay pleaſure my aim, and profuſion my pride,
No vice was untaſted, no wiſh was deny'd.
Grown headſtrong and haughty, capricious and vain,
Not decency aw'd me, nor laws could reſtrain;
The vigils of Comus and Venus I kept,
Tho' tir'd, not ſated, in ſun-ſhine I ſlept:
All my appetites pall'd, I no pleaſure enjoy'd,
Exceſs made 'em taſteleſs, their frequency cloy'd.
When my health and my fortune to riot gave way,
And my parts and my vigour felt total decay,
The doctors were ſent for, who, greedy of fees,
Engag'd that their ſkill ſhould remove the diſeaſe:
With looks moſt important each ſymptom was weigh'd,
And the farce of preſcription full gravely was play'd.
Reduc'd by their arts, and quite worn to a lath,
My carcaſe was ſent to the vultures of Bath.

When

When drench'd and well drain'd by the faculty there,
All the hope that remain'd was to try native air.
Scarce a doit in my purſe, or a drop in my veins,
To my old mortgag'd houſe they convey'd my remains;
No friend to aſſiſt, no relation to grieve,
And ſcarcely a bed my poor bones to receive;
With ſolitude curs'd, and tormented with pain,
Diſtemper'd my body, diſtracted my brain.
Thus from folly to vice, and from vice to the grave,
I ſink of my paſſions the victim and ſlave.
No longer debauch, or companions deceive,
But, alarm'd at the vengeance I'd fain diſbelieve,
With horrors foreboding deſponding I lie,
Tho' tir'd of living, yet dreading to die.

WRITTEN AT TUNBRIDGE WELLS, ON MISS TEMPLE,

AFTERWARDS LADY OF THE LATE SIR THOMAS LYTTELTON.

BY MR. CONGREVE.

NOT IN THE WORKS OF THAT POET.

LEAVE, leave the drawing-room,
Where flow'rs of beauty us'd to bloom;
The nymph that's fated to o'ercome,
Now triumphs at the Wells.

Her ſhape, and air, and eyes;
Her face, the gay, the grave, the wiſe,
The beau, in ſpite of box and dice,
Acknowledge, all excels.

Ceaſe, ceaſe, to aſk her name,
The crowned muſe's nobleſt theme,
Whoſe glory by immortal fame,
Shall only ſounded be.
But if you long to know,
Then look round yonder dazzling row,
Who moſt does like an angel ſhow,
You may be ſure 'tis ſhe.

See near thoſe ſacred ſprings,
Which cure to fell diſeaſes brings,
(As ancient fame of Ida ſings)
Three goddeſſes appear!
Wealth, Glory, two poſſeſt;
The third with charming beauty bleſt,
So fair, that heav'n and earth confeſt
She conquer'd ev'ry where.

Like her, this charmer now
Makes ev'ry love-ſick gazer bow;
Nay, e'en old age her pow'r allow,
And baniſh'd flames recal.
Wealth can no trophy rear,
Nor glory now the garland wear;
To beauty ev'ry Paris here
Devotes the golden ball.

The

The following is an Allegory on the Game of Quadrille. *It was written by Mr.* Congreve. *See* Swift's *Letters, Vol. II. Page* 198.

SUBSTANCE OF AN INFORMATION

TAKEN BEFORE ONE OF HIS MAJESTY'S JUSTICES OF THE PEACE.

THAT four ladies of quality, whom the deponent does not care to name, repair mightily to a certain convenient houfe, to meet four gallants, of the higheft rank, whom the deponent would not name, but fo far defcribed, that two of them were of a fwarthy, and two of a ruddy complexion, (but he believes they were moft abominably painted); the gallants are called, by thefe ladies, by the fond names of Hercules, Cupid, Pitts, and the Gardener.

After a plentiful fervice of the moft coftly fifh, they begin to play their tricks like the tumblers in Bartholomew Fair, upon a carpet; ftrip is the word, and it has been known, that they have lately ftrip'd a gentleman who lately came into the houfe.

At firft they begin very civilly, as Madam, by your leave, or fo, which the lady is fo good as feldom to refufe.

By

[94]

By a certain eſtabliſhed rule of precedency, every lady has, in her turn, the choice of her gallant, and ſome have been known ſo unreaſonable, that after they have had three, they have called for a fourth.

Afterwards it is ſhameful to relate the tricks that are played by the lewd pack, ſometimes they are thrown on their backs, ſometimes on their bellies, and thus they make beaſts of one another; now hickledy pickledy, and by and by you may ſee them a-top of one another.

Their diſcourſe is of a piece with their practice—The deponent has overheard them talk of their A—, with as much eaſe as they do of their hands.—I have a black one, ſays one, and names the thing directly. —Mine is better than yours, ſays another, and names it.—Muſt I be laughed at only becauſe I have a red one, ſays the third.

It is a conſtant rule, that if a lady is called upon, ſhe muſt ſhew all.

What is monſtrous; it has been known, that after a lady has had ſix—ſhe has aſked a gentleman if he could no more——and it has been known, that when the ladies have been tired with their gallants, they have called for freſh ones.—In ſhort, thoſe ladies have ſpent not only their pin-money, but their huſband's eſtates, upon Hercules, Cupid, Pitts, and the Gardener, and when they want ready money, they commonly pawn their moſt valuable jewels.

AN

AN EPISTLE TO LORD COBHAM,

BY MR. POPE †.

SIncereſt critic of my proſe or rhyme,
Tell how thy pleaſing Stowe employs thy time:
Say, Cobham, what amuſes thy retreat;
Or ſchemes of war, or ſtratagems of ſtate;
Doſt thou recal to mind, with joy or grief,
Great Marlbro's actions, that immortal chief?
Whoſe higheſt trophy rais'd in each campaign,
More than ſuffic'd to ſignalize a reign.
Does thy remembrance, riſing warm thy heart
With glory paſt, where thou thyſelf had'ſt part?
Or doſt thou grieve, indignant now to ſee
The fruitleſs end of all thy victory?
To ſee th'audacious foe ſo late ſubdu'd,
Diſpute thoſe terms for which ſo long they've ſu'd;
As if Britannia now were ſunk ſo low,
To beg that peace ſhe wonted to beſtow?
Be far that guilt, be never known that ſhame,
That England ſhould retract her rightful claim;

† This epiſtle, ſaid to be written by Mr. Pope, was publiſhed in one of the daily papers in Auguſt 1769, and there ſaid never to have been publiſhed before. As it is not in his works, we have given it a place here.

Or

Or ceafing to be dreaded and ador'd,
Stain with her pen the luftre of her fword.
Or doft thou give the winds afar to blow
Each vexing thought, and heart-devouring woe,
And fix thy mind alone, on rural fcenes,
To turn the level'd lawns to liquid plains;
To raife the creeping rills from humble beds,
And force the latent fprings to lift their heads;
On wat'ry columns, capitals to rear,
That mix their flowing curls with upper air?
Or doft thou, weary grown, thefe works neglect,
No temples, ftatues, obelifks, erect,
But with the morning breeze from fragrant meads,
Or fhun the noon-tide ray in wholfome fhades,
Or flowly walk along the mazy wood,
To meditate on all that's wife and good;
For nature bountiful in thee has join'd,
A perfon pleafing, with a worthy mind;
Not given thee form alone, but means and art,
To draw the eye, or to allure the heart.
Poor were the praife in fortune to excel,
Yet want of means to ufe that fortune well;
While thus adorn'd, while thus with virtue crown'd,
At home in peace, abroad in arms renown'd;
Graceful in form, and winning in addrefs,
While well you think what aptly you exprefs;
With health, with honour, with a fair eftate,
A table free, and elegantly neat;

What

[97]

What can be added more to mortal bliſs?
What can he want who ſtands poſſeſt of this?
What can the fondeſt wiſhing mother more,
Of heaven attentive, for her ſon implore?
And yet a happineſs remains unknown,
Or to philoſophy reveal'd alone,
A precept which, unpractis'd, renders vain
Thy flowing hopes, and pleaſure turns to pain.
Should hope, or fear, thy heart alternate tear,
Or love, or hate, or rage, or anxious care,
Whatever paſſions may thy mind infeſt,
(Where is that mind that paſſions ne'er moleſt?)
Amidſt the pangs of ſuch inteſtine ſtrife,
Still think the preſent day the laſt of life,
Defer not till to-morrow to be wiſe,
To-morrow's ſun to thee may never riſe;
Or ſhould to-morrow chance to chear the ſight,
With her enliv'ning and unlook'd-for light,
How grateful will appear her dawning rays!
As favours unexpected doubly pleaſe.
Who thus can think, and who ſuch thoughts purſues,
Content may keep his life, or calmly loſe:
All proof of this thou may'ſt thyſelf receive,
When leiſure from affairs will give thee leave.
Come, ſee thy friend retir'd without regret,
Forgetting care, or trying to forget;
In eaſy contemplation ſoothing time
With morals much, and now and then with rhyme;

Not

Not ſo robuſt in body as in mind,
And always undejected, tho' declin'd;
Not wond'ring at the world's new wicked ways,
Compar'd with thoſe of our forefathers days;
For virtue now is neither more or leſs,
And vice is only varied in the dreſs.
Believe it, men have ever been the ſame,
And all the golden age is but a dream.

S O N G.

BY THE SAME*

SAYS Phœbe, why is gentle love,
A ſtranger to that mind,
Which pity and eſteem can move,
Which can be juſt and kind?
Is it becauſe you fear to prove
The ills that love moleſt;
The jealous cares, the ſighs that move
The captivated breaſt?
Alas! by ſome degree of woe,
We ev'ry bliſs muſt gain;
That heart can ne'er a tranſport know,
That never felt a pain.

* Firſt publiſhed in one of the daily papers in Auguſt 1769.

EPILOGUE,

E P I L O G U E*,

SPOKEN BY MRS. WOFFINGTON, AT THE OPENING OF THE THEATRE IN DRURY-LANE, 1747.

BY DR. SAMUEL JOHNSON.

SWEET doings truly! we are finely fobb'd!
And at one ſtroke of all our pleaſures robb'd!
No beaux behind the ſcenes!—'tis innovation!
Under the ſpecious name of reformation!
Public Complaint, forſooth, is made a puff,
Senſe, order, decency, and ſuch like ſtuff.
But arguments like theſe are mere pretence,
The Beaux, 'tis known, ne'er give the leaſt offence,
Are men of chaſteſt conduct, and amazing ſenſe!
Each actreſs now a lock'd up nun muſt be,
And prieſtly managers muſt keep the key.
I know their ſelfiſh reaſons; tho' they tell us,
While ſmarts, and wits, and other pretty fellows,
Murmur their paſſions to our flutt'ring hearts,
The ſtage ſtands ſtill, and we neglect our parts.
But how miſtaken in this ſilly notion!
We hear 'em talk without the leaſt emotion.
Juſt, as our tea, we ſip each tender ſtrain,
Too weak to warm the heart, or reach the brain.

* See the prologue in Dodſley's collection, Vol. I.

If

[100]

If harmlefs, why are we debarr'd our rights?
Damfels diftrefs'd have ever found their knights.
Shall we, the *Dulcineas* of the ftage,
In vain afk fuccour in this fighting age?
Will you choice fpirits, who direct the town,
Suffer fuch impofitions to go down?
Can it be thought this law will ever pafs,
While doors are only wood, and windows glafs?
Befides, our play-houfe guards are paffive men:
Strike without fear; they muft not ftrike again.
Ev'n *Fribble* here, to draw his fword may venture,
May *curfe the Creters*, beat his man, and enter—
The jealous *Moor* not roars in louder ftrains,
Than all our nymphs for lofs of abfent fwains—
" We had been happy, tho' the houfe had fail'd,
" Mafters and all, had not this fcheme prevail'd.
" For ever now farewell the plumed beaux,
" Who make ambition—to confift in cloaths.
" Farewel coquettry, and all green-room joys,
" Ear-thrilling whifpers, *Deard*'s deluding toys,
" Soul-melting Flatt'ry, which ev'n prudes can move,
" Sighs—tears—and all the circumftance of love,
" Farewell!——
" But oh! ye dreadful criticks, whofe rude throats
" Can make both play'rs and mafters change their notes,
" 'Tis in your pow'r—you any lengths will run,
" Help us; or elfe—our *Occupation*'s gone.

UPON

[101]

UPON MR. MASON'S TAKING ORDERS.

BY MR. GARRICK.

TO Holdernesse, the muses three,
Of Painting, Music, Poetry,
To him, their long-lov'd patron, friend,
In grievous pet this letter send——
Give ear, my lord, while we complain,
Our sex to you ne'er sigh'd in vain.
'Tis said—A youth by you befriended,
Whom to your smiles we recommended;
Seduc'd by you, abjures our charms,
And flies for ever from our arms!
Could D'Arcy, whom we lov'd, caress'd,
In whose protection we were bless'd,
Could he, to whom our Sire imparts
That secret rare to taste our arts,
Could *he*, ungrateful, and unkind!
From us estrange our Mason's mind?
Could he, who serves and loves the nation,
So little weigh its reputation,
As in this scarcity of merit,
To damp with grace poetic spirit?
But be assur'd your scheme is vain—
He must, he shall be ours again:

Nor crape nor lawn ſhall quench his fires,
We'll fill his breaſt with new deſires.
In vain you plead his ordination,
His caſſock, gown, and grave vocation,
Whate'er he now has ſworn, he ſwore,
With ſtronger zeal to us before:
He paſs'd our forms of conſecration,
His lips receiv'd our inſpiration;
To him were all our rites reveal'd,
From him no myſt'ry was conceal'd——
Each kindred pow'r obey'd our call,
And grac'd the ſolemn feſtival!
The *Loves* forſook their *Cyprian* bow'rs,
And round his temples wreath'd their flow'rs;
The *Graces* danc'd their myſtic maze,
Our *Father* ſtruck him with his rays;
And all our *Siſters* one by one,
Gave him full draughts of Helicon!
Thus bound *our* ſervant at the ſhrine,
Ordain'd he was, and made *divine*.

ON THE ACADEMY

FOR TEACHING GROWN PEOPLE TO DANCE.

BY THE SAME.

MArſeilles no more ſhall boaſt his art,
  Which form'd the youth of France;
For you inſtruct, great *Duke* and *Hart*,
  Grown Gentlemen, to dance.

He only bends the pliant twig;
  You ſtrike a bolder ſtroke;
You ſoften rocks, make mountains jig,
  And bend the knotted oak.

ON JOHNSON'S DICTIONARY.

BY THE SAME.

TALK of war with a Briton, he'll boldly advance,
That one Engliſh ſoldier will beat ten of France;
Would we alter the boaſt from the ſword to the pen,
Our odds are ſtill greater, ſtill greater our men:

In the deep mines of ſcience tho' Frenchmen may toil,
Can their ſtrength be compar'd to Locke, Newton, and Boyle?
Let them rally their heroes, ſend forth all their pow'rs,
Their verſe-men, and proſe-men; then match them with ours!
Firſt Shakeſpeare and Milton, like gods in the fight,
Have put their whole drama and epic to flight;
In ſatires, epiſtles, and odes would they cope,
Their numbers retreat before Dryden and Pope;
And Johnſon well arm'd, like a hero of yore,
Has beat forty † French, and will beat forty more.

† The number of the French academy employed in ſettling their language.

A RIDDLE.

BY THE SAME.

KITTY, a fair, but frozen maid,
Kindled a flame I ſtill deplore;
The hood-wink'd boy I call'd in aid,
Much of his near approach afraid,
So fatal to my ſuit before.

At

At length, propitious to my pray'r,
The little urchin came ;
At once he ſought the midway air,
And ſoon he clear'd, with dextrous care,
The bitter relicks of my flame.

To Kitty, Fanny now ſucceeds,
She kindles ſlow, but laſting fires :
With care my appetite ſhe feeds ;
Each day ſome willing victim bleeds,
To ſatisfy my ſtrange deſires.

Say, by what title ‡, or what name,
Muſt I this youth addreſs ?
Cupid and he are not the ſame,
Tho' both can raiſe, or quench a flame—
I'll kiſs you, if you gueſs.

‡ The chimney-ſweeper.

SIR WILLIAM YOUNG TO HIS LADY,

ON HAVING AN EYE BEAT OUT.

HOW vain are all the joys of man,
By nature born to certain ſorrow,
Since none, not e'en the wiſeſt, can
Inſure the pleaſures of to-morrow !

Theſe eyes, ſo late my envy'd boaſt,
By Celia priz'd above all other,
See one, alas ! for ever loſt,
Its fellow weeping for its brother.

Yet ſtill I'm bleſt while one remains,
For viewing lovely Celia's beauty,
Her looks ſtill eaſe acuteſt pains,
With tendereſt love and cheerful duty.

Had I for her in battle ſtrove,
The fatal blow I'd borne with pleaſure,
And ſtill, to prove my conſtant love,
With joy I'd loſe my ſingle treaſure.

E'en then the beauties of her mind
Would amply bleſs her faithful lover,
He muſt be deaf as well as blind,
Who can't my Celia's charms diſcover.

E'en then I'd find one ſolid bliſs,
Which heav'n alone to me diſpenſes ;
Tho' deaf and blind, her balmy kiſs
Would raviſh the remaining ſenſes.

A BALLAD.

A BALLAD.

OCCASIONED BY THE ENLARGING OF THE HOUSE OF OFFICE AT THE D—— OF D—— SEAT IN SUSSEX, FOR THE ACCOMMODATION OF THREE LADIES AT ONCE, VIZ.

THE D—SS OF R——D, L—Y A——LE, AND MISS P——ST.

BY THE SAME.

I.

THE Graces were play-fellows never aſunder,
As Horace and all the old poets agree;
This being once granted, why then 'tis no wonder,
That, whene'er you ſee one, you always ſee three,
In bed, and at table,
Still inſeparable,
No mortal, or god, e'er to part them was able:
Nay, e'en to do that which goddeſſes do,
If one had occaſion, ſtill went t'other two.

II.

So, in Suſſex, three nymphs, or three graces, chooſe either,
O were I but Horace their praiſes to tell!

From morning to evening were always together,
  And did, as they ſay, that ſame thing in a quill:
    In the park, or the grove,
    Below, or above,
Not an inch e'er a one from the other would move,
One only thing grieved and vexed their ſouls,
Where there ſhould have been three, there was but
    two holes.

III.

With curt'ſy full low to the prince of the place,
  In terms the moſt moving they jointly petition,
By all that is ſacred beſeeching his grace,
  To have ſome regard on their helpleſs condition.
    The paper he read,
    And nodding his head,
Send for Smart to come over this moment, he ſaid,
For ſure, in the world there is no reaſon why,
When two friends are ſitting, the third ſhould ſtand
    by.

IV.

The chalk-pit was dug, and mortar was made,
  And bricks without number from Hampneſt there
    came,
When our architect too, who well knew his trade,
  Made by one ſingle fabric immortal his name:
    Then prithee give o'er,
    Think of builders no more,

Throw

Throw thy plummet, and trowel, and hod out of
door ;
So had done, without queftion, both Archer and Van,
Had they had the honour to furnifh the plan.

V.

Now, all you who thefe three of your zeal would
convince,
And defire that in pain they may never be long,
Congratulate them, and give thanks to the prince,
By clearing your voices, and aiding my fong:
For now when they're fat,
They may fing, laugh, and chat,
Yet all under one, without hindrance, do that;
And at the fame time their friendfhip improve
By what we all count the beginning of love.

TO SAPPHO,

A YOUNG LADY OF THIRTEEN YEARS OF AGE, 1762.

BY WM. MELMOTH, ESQ.

WHILE yet no am'rous youths around thee bow,
Nor flatt'ring verfe conveys the faithlefs vow;
To graver notes will Sappho's foul attend,
And ere fhe hears the lover hears the friend.

Let

Let maids, lefs blefs'd, employ their meaner arts
To reign proud tyrants o'er unnumber'd hearts;
May Sappho learn (for nobler triumphs born)
Thefe little conquefts of her fex to fcorn.
To form thy bofom to each gen'rous deed;
To plant thy mind with ev'ry ufeful feed;
Be thefe thy arts: nor fpare the grateful toil,
Where nature's hand had blefs'd the happy foil.
So fhall thou know, with pleafing fkill, to blend
The lovely miftrefs, and inftructive friend:
So fhall thou know, when unrelenting time
Shall fpoil thefe charms, yet op'ning to their prime,
To eafe the lofs of beauty's tranfient flow'r,
While reafon keeps what rapture gave before.
And oh! while wit, fair dawning, fpreads her ray,
Serenely rifing to a glorious day,
To hail the growing luftre, oft be mine,
Thou early fav'rite of the facred Nine!
And fhall the mufe, with blamelefs boaft pretend,
In early bloom, that Sappho call'd me friend:
That urg'd by me, fhe fhun'd the dang'rous way,
Where heedlefs maids, in endlefs error ftray;
That fcorning foon her fex's idler art,
Fair praife infpir'd, and virtue warm'd her heart;
That, fond to reach the diftant paths of fame,
I taught her infant genius where to aim?
Thus, when the feather'd choir firft tempt the fky,
And, all unfkill'd, their feeble pinions try,
The'xperienc'd fire prefcribes th'advent'rous height,
Guides the young wing, and pleas'd, attends the flight.

EPISTLE

[111]

EPISTLE TO LORD MELCOMBE.

BY RICHARD BENTLEY, ESQ.

I'VE often thought, my lord, the thing now true,
Said by lord Bute, but what I've learn'd from you;
"We ſhall loſe poetry;" in this alone
Too ſhort,—he might have added, "Wit is gone."
How came this prime delight of man thus leſſen'd
From its full orb down to a thumb-nail creſcent?
With me the caſe admits not of a doubt!
The fact is, poeſy itſelf's worn out.
To you, my lord, this notion I ſubmit,
Who knew and help'd to make this age of wit,
Mix'd with thoſe demi-gods in verſe and proſe,
Congreves, and Addiſons, and Garths, and Rowes,
Heroes of giant-limb, and high renown,
Whoſe deeds we wonder at, and hide our own;
Whom but to copy in their idle fits,
Would break the backs of puny modern wits.
To ſet this matter in the cleareſt light,
And be thyſelf th'example while I write,
Let us, my lord, if ſo it may avail,
And you have patience for a long detail,
Give the Earl's ſentence a poetic turn;
Let it run thus; "See all Parnaſſus mourn,
"Mute ev'ry muſe, ſee George's praiſe unſung,
"Their lawrels ſcatter'd, and their lyres unſtrung,
"Apollo

"Apollo veils with miſts his beamy head,
"Nay, Aganippe murmurs ſomething ſad."
Say, will this ſtile, my lord, go down or no,
Glib as it did two thouſand years ago?
I fancy ſcarce, and favour'd, if it paſs
From a raw ſchool-boy in the ſecond claſs;
The reaſon then why no diſguſt it drew,
Was, that it might be truth, for aught they knew.
Thoſe early ages no miſtruſt had ſhewn,
Ready their faith, their manners roughly hewn,
And, while both reaſon and ſuſpicion doz'd,
Prieſt, poet, prophet, patriot, impos'd.
With all that either broach'd, the world content,
Believ'd ſtill farther than they could invent,
All irrealities came forth reveal'd
By pow'rful fancy into fact congeal'd,
Then poetry had elbow-room enough,
And not reſtrain'd, as now, for want of ſtuff;
The great abyſs of fable open ſtood,
And nothing ſolid roſe above the flood.
A new religion ſpreading ev'ry where,
The ſtock of poetry fell under par;
For oracles grew dumb, as men grew wiſe,
None ſaw for thoſe, who ſaw with their own eyes.
To waſte her leaves no more the ſybil chooſes,
They and her tripod ſerve for other uſes.
No more the Jeſuit prompts her what to tell;
For to ſay Middleton and Fontenelle.

But

But the new doctrine being found too pure,
Some able doctors undertook its cure;
It ferv'd no purpofes but faving finners,
They added that by which themfelves were winners,
Ghofts, devil, witches, conjurers, in flocks
Came, like a new fubfcription, to the ftocks;
And poetry, enlarg'd with a new range,
Began to fhew her head again in change.

The world grown old, its youthful follies paft,
Reafon affumes her reign, tho' late, at laft.
By flow degrees, and labouring up the hill,
Step after ftep, yet feeming to ftand ftill,
She wins her way, where-ever fhe advances;
Satyr no more, nor Fawn nor Dryad dances,
The groves, tho' trembling to a natural breeze,
Difmifs their horrors, and fhew nought but trees.
Before her, Nonfenfe, Superftition fly;
We burn no witch, let her be e'er fo dry;
A woman now may live, tho' paft her prime,
So hallow'd and fo gracious is the time.

Bankrupt of deities, with all their train,
And fet to work without his tools in vain,
Not genius-crampt (but what can genius do
When it's tied down to one and one make two?)
How can poor poet ftir? in fuch a cafe
We muft do fomething to fupply their place.

See, at his beck, all Nouns renouncing fenfe,
Start into perfons of fome confequence.

Proud

Proud of new being, tread poetic ground
And aggregate their attributes around;
Thefe he may ufe of right, as his own growth,
In all the reft confin'd to fober truth.
To blefs a nation, fee Charlotta come,
'Twas Anfon, and not Neptune, brought her home,
A fingle Nereid ftir'd not from below,
The duce a conch did e'er one Triton blow;
But, in revenge fhe plough'd her fubject main,
With every virtue 'tending in her train.
Hark, 'tis a people's univerfal voice,
That blefs, while they approve their Sov'reign's choice.
On fuch a theme, my lord, one might extend
Far as one would, nor ftricteft truth offend,
'Twere only proper epithets to find,
To every grace of perfon and of mind;
With decent drefs, and emblem to improve
All that can merit our efteem and love.
But then to poetry where's the pretence,
Locke and Sir Ifaac write not plainer fenfe.
From the firft ages down to modern time,
Derive the pleafing ftream of verfe and rhime,
However vaft from its firft fource it rofe,
Th' inverted river dwindles as it flows.
Thus from the lunar hills fome other Nile,
Swoln with new ftores from fnows that melt the while,
Stretches his current on to fiercer funs,
And glads a thoufand nations as he runs,

Till

Till having reach'd, proud of his long career,
Thofe fands which belt the middle of our fphere,
Exhal'd, abforb'd, diverted, dry foot crofs'd,
And finger'd into rivulets, is loft.
  Fall'n cherub Simile, who erft divine,
Cloath'd with tranfcendant brightnefs didft outfhine;
Plain angel poefy, how art thou loft!
Sunk in oblivion's pit! from what height tofs'd!
  Thus to plain narrative confin'd alone,
Figure, Defcription, Simile quite gone;
The whofe affair evinc'd which we contend,
The thing has had its day, and there's an end.
With Milton, Epic drew its lateft breath,
Since Shakefpeare, tragedy puts us to death,
The affaffin Satire fheaths the keen ftiletto,
And languifhes depriv'd of the Concetto,
The age with pious eye no longer views
The great mortality of grofs abufe.
  Soft Elegy has dried up all her tears,
And Gray compofes once in feven years;
Celia's and Delia's fhine no more in fong,
Nor ballad bauls the deafen'd ftreets along.
  My lord, a little patience further ftill,
To "Wit is gone," by way of codicil;
Who but will fay the thing that hears me tell—?
The man miftakes—lord Melcombe's very well.
Suppofe I faid—O could I! war is done,
Means it there's no fuch thing, as fword, or gun?

Party

[116]

Party and faction dead, whoever grants,
Means he that every man has what he wants?
In all these cases is implied alone,
That there's no object to employ them on.
A court, my lord, and minister to hit,
And cry corruption, make all public wit;
'Tis on this sense my reason chiefly stands.
There may be cash enough in private hands.
Now where could malice bite, or envy sting,
The polish'd model of a perfect king;
Of ministers what mighty matters tell?
They give, we know, but neither buy nor sell.
Add we to what we've said this little more,
That all that can be wrote, is wrote before;
That pool of knowledge fish'd, poach'd, dragg'd, and drain'd,
Till nothing bigger than a grig remain'd;
And painful writers think it a good day,
If they can hook a news-paper essay,
And must remain so till blank years of grace,
Suspending future writing, shall take place;
Put down our piddling, bobbing, and allow
The spawn and fry of science time to grow.
But while we're on this subject, 'tis worth thinking,
How little salt has kept this world from stinking;
'Tis the same wit, at different times alive,
Sunk at Whitehall, to rise up at Queenhithe.
Born in whatever clime, whatever age,
We trace it first from the Athenian stage,

Where

Where liberty a little licence claim'd,
There, juſt as ſomewhere elſe, that ſhan't be nam'd;
Taught all her ſons this fav'rite to adore,
Much for itſelf, becauſe abuſive more;
For every comic writer braided it,
Two threads of ſcandal to one thread of wit:
O'er all, ſee Ariſtophanes preſide,
And flaſh his lightnings round on ev'ry ſide,
Struck the ſham patriot, the ſwoln poet waſted,
Alas! e'en Socrates himſelf he blaſted.
What was the burſt directly over head,
So loud its echo, now its fires ſo red,
Tho' oft thro' time's thick cloud the trembling gleam
We only catch, but miſs the vivid beam;
While half-ſeen thoughts, like meteors, twinkle
light,
And draw their lucid trails athwart the night.
Hither, to their fountain, other ſtars
Repairing, ſwell their own peculiars,
By tincture or reflection; Lucian hence,
His golden urn repleniſh'd; and long ſince
Rabelais from both his urinal drew full,
From him, and them, Swift crowded his cloſe-ſtool.
Howe'er it came, with the ſtrange paſſion ſtung,
To raiſe his choiceſt fruit on rankeſt dung,
Fully convinc'd his jeſſamine and roſe
Smelt ſweeteſt, planted by his little houſe;
Yet ſtill ſome cleaner parts diſtinguiſh'd lay,
Like cherry-ſtones upon a child's C— C—.

I The

[118]

The naſty lines, my lord, demand excuſe,
Happ'ly the times are free from that abuſe;
Our decent manners all obſceneſs flout,
And wit is at one entrance quite ſhut out.
From hence, my lord, wit took a tour about,
Reſiding in few countries on his rout,
Appear'd in places, but ne'er took his ſeat in
One ſpot of earth, except Greece, France, and Britain.
The reſt a ſingle trophy only bear,
And juſt enough to ſhow he had been there.
As nature's idcot never fails to hit,
Once in his life, on ſome ſheer ſtrokes of wit;
Then ſtoops ten thouſand fathoms down behind,
Plump in his own vacuity of mind,
A like excurſion never to repeat
To the warm regions of æthereal heat.
Yet when we look at home, my lord, at beſt
We find but little that will ſtand the teſt;
But then the boaſted days of Charles the ſecond,
Unleſs debauchery for wit is reckon'd,
Moſt that they had appears, by looking back,
A fungus growing on their butt of ſack.
E'en my good couſin Rocheſter's but barren,
From wholſome meat if you deduct the carrion.
In the next reigns how could it flouriſh much?
Bigotry, revolution, and the Dutch,
Damp'd, like wet blankets, its aſpiring flame,
And, if not quite extinguiſh'd, kept it tame,

Till

Till orient Anna lighted all its fires,
And the glad ſtars reſponſive tun'd their choirs;
Pity ſhe e'er left any in the lurch,
To follow thoſe who lighted her to church.
Then Hallifax, my lord, as you do yet,
Stood forth the friend of poetry and wit;
Sought ſilent merit in its ſecret cell,
And heav'n, nay, even man, repaid him well.
Man, in the praiſe of every grateful quill,
And heav'n in him, who bears his title ſtill,
Who on a kingdom to his virtues won,
Reflects the glories of our Britiſh ſun.

TO MR. POYNTZ,

WITH DR. SECKER'S SERMON ON EDUCATION, PREACHED BEFORE THE UNIVERSITY OF OXFORD, JULY 8, 1733.

BY LORD HERVEY.

WHILE Secker's rules in this diſcourſe I view,
How quick each maxim turns my thoughts on you!
Who in each art of education ſkill'd,
Severe in precept, yet in manner mild,
Canſt form the man, and yet not ſhock the child!

You by perſuaſion to inſtruction join'd,
Know without force to cultivate the mind;
And to rough taſks communicating eaſe,
E'en to the taught can make the teacher pleaſe;
Whilſt to a court adapting ev'ry rule,
Without enervating the ſtricteſt ſchool,
At once you ſtrengthen and adorn the heart,
With Spartan virtue, and Athenian art:
Nor vain thy toils, nor fruitleſs are thy cares,
For ſee! thy royal charge in rip'ning years,
The ſecond hope of our Auguſtan age,
Like lov'd Marcellus, ev'ry heart engage:
But to his years heav'n grant a longer date,
Nor with Marcellus' virtue give his fate!
Long may he live the glory of our iſle,
And each Minerva on his fortune ſmile:
Let this in ſenate her aſſiſtance yield,
Let that direct and guard him in the field;
In peace and war ſtill uſeful to the ſtate,
In council prudent, and in action great:
Then ev'ry rule throughout this theory ſhewn,
Shall by thy practice in this youth be known;
And the world find, by one example taught,
How well on Poyntz's conduct Secker wrote.

EXTEM-

EXTEMPORE EPIGRAM

ON THE EARL OF BURLINGTON AND HIS HOUSE AT CHISWICK.

BY LORD HERVEY.

POssess'd of one great hall for state,
Without one room to sleep or eat;
How well you build, let flatt'ry tell,
And all mankind, how ill you dwell.

VERSES

ON SECOND THOUGHTS ON THE SAME SUBJECT.

BY THE SAME.

RARE architect! in whose exotic school
Our English connoisseurs may learn by rule,
To spoil their houses, and to play the fool,
To all mankind, (could we on paper live)
What charming dwellings might thy genius give!
And tho' when executed, still we find
Thy plans have nothing to its use assign'd;
Tho' to space, light, convenience you declare
Irreconcileable, perpetual war;

With halls, where groping moles ſhould only feed,
And libraries, where lynx's eyes can't read;
With doors, to common purpoſes ſuch foes,
Some never open, others never cloſe;
Windows, inverting what they were of old,
Not form'd to let in light, or keep out cold;
Chimneys in cupboards, full of means poſſeſs'd
To fire the houſe, tho' not to warm the gueſt;
Stairs, which no mortal can go up and down,
And leaden ſkulls each emblem dome to crown;
Tho' ſuch in every ſhape, in every part,
We find thy unaccommodating art,
Yet who ſhall ſay, thy works are not divine?
When all muſt own, there is no houſe of thine,
In which (among the many have been try'd)
The devil wou'd, or mortal can reſide.

STREPHON AND COLLIN,

A DIALOGUE.

BY THE RIGHT HON. CHARLES EARL OF MIDDLESEX, AFTERWARDS DUKE OF DORSET.

STREPHON.

HAVE you not ſeen the morning ſun
 Peep over yonder hill?
Then you have ſeen my Chloe's charms,
 At beſt but painted ill.

COLLIN.

COLLIN.

Have you not ſeen a butterfly,
With colours bright and gay?
Then you have ſeen a thing leſs fine
Than Molly cloath'd in grey.

STREPHON.

The roſe, you'll ſay, of all the field,
Can boaſt the lovelieſt hue;
But, to compare with Chloe's cheeks,
It wants the lilly too.
As I ſat by her on the plain,
And talk'd the hours away,
She breath'd ſo ſweet, I thought myſelf
In fields of new-mow'd hay.

COLLIN.

Not the ſweet breath that's breath'd from cows,
With Molly's can compare;
And when ſhe ſings, the liſt'ning folks
Stand ſilent round to hear.
She ſaid, as we were walking once
Along the ſhady grove,
There's none but Collin, Molly loves,
And will for ever love.

[124]

STREPHON.

Believe not, friend, a woman's word,
Or you are much to blame;
For t'other night, behind the elms,
She ſwore to me the ſame.

COLLIN.

Yet I'll believe your Chloe's word,
As on my breaſt ſhe laid,
" This Strephon is ſo dull a clown,
" He'll think me ſtill a maid."

AN ODE

TO THE MOST UNPOPULAR MAN LIVING.

WRITTEN IN THE YEAR 1753.

SIR, while your heart with tranſport glows
To find your moſt important noſe
Loſt in your P——s ear;
Perceive you not, with ſtrange ſurprize,
How Fortune ſmiles on *ſome folks lies*,
Tho' *Truth herſelf* appear?

While your *wiſe counſels*, and your cares
Affect a nation's vaſt affairs,
A kingdom, and a ——,

I:

Is all your breaſt calm and ſerene,
As when you walk'd on * Winton's Green,
And dreamt of no ſuch thing?

Envy, you'll ſay, your worth attends
Maliciouſly, like *treach'rous friends*,
Perfidious to their truſt;
Nor may ev'n *Fortune's fav'rites* find,
That they alone, of all mankind,
Eſcape by *being juſt*.

But ſay, ſince in a luckleſs hour
You roll in wealth, and roſe to pow'r,
How reliſh you the ſcene?
Is then ambition quite as bleſt
As ſhe in *Fancy's* garb is dreſt?
—How *feel* you, Sir, *within?*

Can you reflect, without remorſe?
I *fear you can—ſo much the worſe*—
But, Sir, *How* are your *dreams?*
Free are they all from guilt, and fear?
See you not injur'd Norwich there,
Or Harcourt croſs the Thames?

Or ſeem you *lightly* ſtill to riſe
In *viſionary* dignities,
With nothing to retard?

* The family ſeat.

With

With ev'n Britannia's *council's ſet*,
To weigh your *merit* to the *ſtate*,
And give the *due reward!*

Or *wakeful* to your country's *call*,
Say rather, can't you *ſleep at all?*
—*Not ſleep* a *wink?*—Yet know
For *ſuch deſert*, a *proper* ſtate
Is fixt by the decrees of fate
—*Amongſt the ſhades below.*

† Pirithous and the ‡ Lapithæ,
Stretch'd at the royal banquet ſee———
(Thus ſung a bard of old)
A dire black ſtone, bound by a thread,
Trembled o'er each devoted head,
And all the mirth appall'd.

† Pirithous. A man who to accompliſh his ambitious views, went to hell, and was torn in pieces by Cerberus.

‡ Lapithæ. A people of Theſſaly, who violated the laws of hoſpitality, at a prince's table.

Quid memorem Lapithas, Ixonia, Pirithoumque:
Quos ſuper atra Silex jam jam lapſura, cadentique
Imminet aſſimilis. Lucent genialibus altis
Aurea fulcra toris, epulæque ante ora paratæ
Regifico luxu: Furiarum maxima juxta
Accubat, et manibus prohibet contingere menſas,
Exurgitque facem attollens, atque intonat ore.

VIR. Lib. 6.

A fury

A fury too among the reſt,
Uprear'd her dreadful ſnaky creſt,
And hiſt among the meat;
And ſtrange to tell, th' unwelcome gueſt
Quite diſcompos'd the joyous feaſt,
And ſpoilt the regal treat.

The poets ſing too, as I'm told,
(I mean they ſung in times of old)
The *dangers* of the great;
How Fortune's wheel, rolling about,
Whirls giddy mortals in, or out,
Fixt to no *ſteady* ſeat.

The lofty ſcaffold, tow'rs on high,
And climbs ambitiouſly the ſky;
One rotten plank is found—
§ Tumbles from its aërial hight
The whole, by its unlucky weight,
A ruin on the ground.

The moral hence is mighty plain,
The avaricious, falſe and vain,
(If plain the muſes ſpeak)
When they unweildy wealth deſire,
When proudly they too high aſpire,
Should look well to their NECK!

§ ---------Numeroſa parabat
Excelſæ turris tabulata, unde altier eſſet
Caſus, et impulſæ præceps immane ruinæ.
Juv. Sat. 10.

EPISTLE

[128]

EPISTLE FOR LORD LOVEL TO LORD CHESTERFIELD.

BY MR. PULTNEY, AFTERWARDS EARL OF BATH.

O Holkham! blefs'd, belov'd abode!
Productive of an annual ode,
If Chefterfield infpire:
Clio and I will club for wit,
Beneath the fpreading oak we'll fit,
And thrumb the lyric lyre.

How beauteous is this rural fcene!
With conftant verdure ever green,
How healthy, gay, and pleafant!
A clean, tho' an ungrateful foil,
Rewarding well the fportfman's toil,
With partridges and pheafant.

To you, my lord, I fend my lays,
Fondly conceiv'd in Flavia's praife,
Flavia can make a poet.
Happy the man, of choiceft tafte,
Who fees whate'er's above the waift,
Much happier, what's below it.

But

But hold ! to love I bid adieu,
A greater theme is now in view,
I feel my country's ruin :
Next winter I'll reſign my place,
Nor longer ſhare the ſad diſgrace,
And bluſh for what is doing.

The cries of an inſulted land,
Redreſs of injuries demand :
Let's out for England's glory !
I'm ready to take part with you,
And am become a patriot too,
But neither Whig nor Tory.

Let honeſt men together join,
And ſince we have it, keep that line,
Fix'd by the Revolution ;
Let us defend our ſov'reign's cauſe,
Aſſert our rights, preſerve our laws,
And ſave the conſtitution.

On me you have obtain'd your ends,
I freely now give up my friends,
As wretched politicians ;
Never to bite, yet ſhow their teeth,
In ſenſeleſs camps at Hounſlow Heath,
And Spithead expeditions.

Millions

Millions to raiſe, then arm in vain,
By fears inciting France and Spain,
(Like him of Pope's deſcribing)
Willing to hurt, afraid to ſtrike,
Juſt hint, and heſitate diſlike,
While all our ſkill is bribing.

Of filth each houſe then let us glean,
Keep thoſe Augean ſtables clean;
And ſtrike off every penſion:
Let us be ſov'reigns of the ſeas,
Our merchants ſail where'er they pleaſe,
Nor fear a new convention.

This boon alone, my lord I crave,
Many will join us, do but ſave
One ſingle ſinner for us:
Grant for our ſakes this only job,
Some mercy ſhow our old friend Bob,
Do what you will with Horace.

AN

AN EPISTLE FROM A NOBLE LORD TO MR. PULTENEY.

WRITTEN IN 1740.

Dubius non Improbus. - - - - - - - - - D. of B. Ep.

I.

HAPPY the man who with ſuch eaſe
Can different taſtes and tempers pleaſe,
Whatever be the mode, Sir:
Now charms the houſe—then ſteps to White's—
Sets down to whiſt—cuts out—indites
A letter or an ode, Sir.

II.

Thus every place, and every hour
Is witneſs to his wit and power,
Of livelieſt invention:
Old topics in his hands are new,
Spithead and Hounſlow we *review*,
And ſtart at the *convention*.

Go,

III.

Go on, my friend, the war maintain,
By various ways 'gainſt Bob † and Spain,
Tho' doubtful is the former:
Flavia, or Cheſterfield invoke,
Let off, on whom you pleaſe, your joke,
Excepting always Dormer *.

IV.

You'll take the hint as 'tis deſign'd,
Of honeſt and of tender kind;
And pardon the digreſſion:
For tho' your courage none can doubt,
No mortal *one* can hold it out,
Againſt a whole profeſſion.

V.

But why ſhould *I* in haſte incline,
To take your counſel and reſign,
And *die* by your direction:
Or, what's the ſame, myſelf turn out,
There ſtill remains an *ugly* doubt,
About a reſurrection.

VI.

So when you can that point aſſure,
And make an after-game ſecure,
Diſpatch a *ſecond letter*:

† Sir Robert Walpole. ‡ General Dormer.

But

But he deſerveth not to eat,
Who raſhly parts with *certain* ſweet,
Uncertain of a better.

VII.

The mighty æra may be near,
But that perhaps is not ſo clear,
Then you'll be in diſgrace ſtill:
There being but *one* engine more,
And that may burſt as thoſe before,
You know I mean the *place-bill.*

VIII.

The Jews, unbelieving, b'lieving nation,
Are ſtill in ſanguine expectation,
Of coming of their king, Sir;
Why ſo their fathers were before,
For ſeventeen hundred years and more,
But yet there's no ſuch thing, Sir.

IX.

I've next in view, the dog of old,
Whoſe ſtory was by Æſop told,
That politician able;
What ſad miſchance the cur befell,
At preſent I'll forbear to tell,
But profit by the fable.

X.

Expect not then, I now ſhould *ſtrike*,
But let me *heſitate diſlike*,
Till matters are more certain :
As much does on next choice depend,
I'll that event with care attend,
Before I draw the curtain.

XI.

But if, mean while, ſhould happy fate,
And ſtars benign conſent to wait,
On Cathcart's expedition :
Moſt will rejoice at the ſucceſs,
Bob's friends increaſe, and yours grow leſs—
Then farewel oppoſition.

XII.

Thus having moſt maturely weigh'd,
What may on either ſide be ſaid,
And laid my thoughts before ye :
I take my leave, and do profeſs
Myſelf Bob's friend, and yours no leſs,
Tho' neither *Whig* nor *Tory*.

ON

ON LADY T—— AT BATH,

BY THE EARL OF BATH.

PHyſick each morn is T—— care,
  Each night ſhe plays a pool;
One helps her to an elbow chair,
  The other to a ſtool.

ON DOWAGER LADY E. H——D.

BY THE SAME.

VAIN are the charms of white and red,
  Which divide the blooming fair;
Give me the nymph whoſe ſnow is ſpread,
  Not o'er her breaſt, but hair.
Of ſmoother cheeks the winning grace,
  As open forces I defy;
But in the wrinkles of her face;
  Cupids, as in ambuſh, lie.
If naked eyes ſet hearts on blaze,
  And am'rous warmth inſpire;
Thro' glaſs who darts her pointed rays,
  Lights up a fiercer fire.

Nor happy rivals, nor the train
  Of num'rous years my bliſs deſtroys,
Alive ſhe gives no jealous pain,
  And then, to pleaſe me, dies.

STRAWBERRY HILL.

BY THE SAME.

I.

SOME cry up Gunners-bury,
  For Sion ſome declare,
Some ſay that with Chiſwick-houſe
  No villa can compare;
But aſk the beaux of Middleſex,
  Who know the country well,
If Strawberry-hill, if Strawberry-hill,
  Don't bear away the bell.

II.

Some love to roll down Greenwich hill,
  For this thing and for that,
And ſome prefer ſweet Marble-hill,
  Tho' ſure 'tis ſomewhat flat;
Yet Marble-hill and Greenwich-hill,
  If Kitty Clive can tell,
From Strawberry-hill, from Strawberry-hill,
  Will never bear the bell.

Tho'

III.

Tho' Surry boafts its Oatlands,
  And Clermont kept fo jim,
And fome prefer fweet Southcoats,
  'Tis but a dainty whim;
But afk the gallant Briftol,
  Who doth in tafte excel,
If Strawberry-hill, if Strawberry-hill,
  Don't bear away the bell.

IV.

Since Denham fung of Cooper's,
  There's fcarce a hill around,
But what in fong or ditty,
  Is turn'd to fairy ground.
Ah peace be with their memory,
  I wifh them wondrous well,
But Strawberry-hill, but Strawberry-hill,
  Will ever bear the bell.

V.

Great William dwells at Windfor,
  As Edward did of old,
And many a Gaul and many a Scot
  Have found him full as bold.
On lofty hills like Windfor
  Such heroes ought to dwell,
Yet the little folks on Strawberry-hill
  Like Strawberry-hill as well.

ADVICE TO GENERAL COPE,

UPON HIS GETTING ST. ANTHONY'S FIRE BY DRINKING THE BATH WATERS, AND AT THE SAME TIME FALLING IN LOVE WITH THE GIRL THAT DIPPED THE WATER.

BY THE SAME.

SEE gentle Cope, with gout and love opprest,
Alternate torments rankling in his breast,
Tries at a cure, but tampers still in vain,
What eases one, augments the other pain.
The charming girl, who strives to lend relief,
Instead of comfort, heightens all his grief.
He drinks for health, then sighs for love, and cries,
Health's in her hand, destruction in her eyes.
She gives us water, but each look, alas!
The wicked girl electrifies the glass.
To ease the gout, we swallow draughts of love,
And then, like Ætna, burn in fires above.
Sip not, dear knight, the daughter's liquid fire,
But take the healing beverage from the sire;
'Twill ease your gout; for love no cure is known;
The god of physick could not cure his own.

ON

ON THE BISHOPS AND JUDGES,

BY P. DUKE OF WHARTON.

WHEN Y—ke to heaven ſhall lift one ſolemn eye,
And love his wife above adultery,
When godlineſs to gain ſhall be preferr'd
By more than two of the right reverend herd;
When P—rk-r ſhall pronounce upright decrees,
And H—ng—rf—rd refuſe his double fees;
When Pr—tt with juſtice ſhall diſpenſe the laws,
And King once partially decide a cauſe;
When Tracy's generous ſoul ſhall ſwell with pride,
And Eyr—s his haughtineſs ſhall lay aſide;
When honeſt Price ſhall trim and truckle under,
And P—w—s ſum a cauſe without a blunder;
When P—ge one uncorrupted finger ſhews,
And F—rt—ſcue deſerves another noſe;
Then ſhall I ceaſe my charmer to adore,
And think of love and politicks no more.

AN EPISTLE FROM JOHN SHEPHERD TO THE EARL OF MACCLESFIELD.

BY THE SAME.

WHEN curiofity led you fo far
As to fend for me, my dear lord, to the bar,
To fhew what a couple of rafcals we were;
Which nobody can deny.

You'll excufe me the freedom of writing to thee,
For the world then agreed they never did fee
A pair fo well match'd as your lordfhip and me;
Which nobody can deny.

At the prefent difgrace, my lord, never repine,
Since fame rings of nothing but thy tricks and mine,
And our names fhall alike in hiftory fhine;
Which nobody can deny.

Tho' we two have made fuch a noife upon earth,
Thy fate would now be but a fubject of mirth,
Should your death be like mine, as we're equal in both;
Which nobody can deny.

Were

Were thy virtues and mine to be weigh'd in a ſcale,
I fear, honeſt Thomas, that thine would prevail,
For you break thro' all laws, while I only break
jail;
Which nobody can deny.

Yet ſomething I hope to my merit is due,
Since there ne'er was ſo barefac'd a blunder as you,
And yet I am the more dext'rous rogue of the two;
Which nobody can deny.

We who thieve for our living, if taken, muſt die,
Thoſe who plunder poor orphans, pray anſwer me
why
They deſerve not a rope more than Blewſkin and I?
Which nobody can deny.

Tho' the maſters are raſcals, that you ſhould ſwing
for it
Is a damnable hardſhip; your lordſhip, in ſhort,
Hath been only the Jonathan Wild of the court;
Which nobody can deny.

Altho' at the helm you and Jonathan ſit,
Whilſt your myrmidons plunder, and what they can
get,
To ſave their own necks, muſt be laid at your feet;
Which nobody can deny.

Yet

Yet Jonathan's politics muſt be allow'd
To be better than thine, for he often hath ſhew'd,
He'd ſtill ſave himſelf, yet hang when he would;
Which nobody can deny.

But as thou and thy gang muſt come in for a rope,
The honour of being the firſt that's truſt up,
Is the only favour your lordſhip can hope;
Which nobody can deny.

THE TRIPLE ALLIANCE.

BY THE SAME.

IN fable all things hold diſcourſe,
Then words (no doubt) muſt talk of courſe.
Once on a time, near Channel row,
Two hoſtile adverbs, AY and NO,
Were haſt'ning to the field of fight,
Where front to front, ſtood oppoſite;
Before each general join'd the van,
AY (the more courteous knight) began:

Stop, peeviſh particle! beware,
I'm told, you are not ſuch a bear,
But ſometimes yield when offer'd fair,
Suffer yon folks a while to prattle,
'Tis we that muſt decide the battle;

Whene'er

Whene'er we war on yonder ſtage,
With various fate and equal rage,
The nation trembles at each blow
That NO gives AY, and AY gives NO;
But, in th'expenſive long contention,
We gain nor office, grant, or penſion;
Why then ſhould kinsfolks quarrel thus,
(For two of you make one of us)
To ſome wiſe ſtateſman let us go,
Where each his proper uſe may know,
He may admit two ſuch commanders,
And let thoſe wait who ſerv'd in Flanders;
Let's quarter on a great man's tongue,
A Tr——ry Lord, not maſter Y——g,
Obſequious at his high command,
AY ſhall march forth to tax the land;
Impeachments, NO can beſt reſiſt,
And AY ſupport the C—l L—t,
AY, quick as Cæſar, win the day,
And NO, like Fabius, by delay,
Sometimes in mutual ſly diſguiſe,
Let AY's ſeem NO's, and NO's ſeem AY's,
AY's be in courts, denials meant,
And NO's in B—ps, give conſent.
 Thus AY propos'd, and, for reply,
 NO, for the firſt time, anſwer'd AY;
 They parted with a thouſand kiſſes,
 And fight, e'er ſince, for pay, like Swiſſes.

ON

ON ROBBING THE EXCHEQUER.

BY THE SAME.

FROM ſun-ſet to day-break whilſt folks are aſleep,
New watch are appointed th' Exchequer to keep,
New bolts and new bars faſten every door,
And the cheſts are made three times as ſtrong as before;
Yet the thieves in the day-time the treaſures may ſeize,
For the ſame are entruſted with care of the keys;
From the night till the morning, 'tis true, all is right,
But who will ſecure it from morning till night.

ANOTHER.

BY THE SAME.

QUOTH Wild unto Walpole, make me under-taker,
I'll ſoon find the rogues that robb'd the Exchequer,
I ſha'n't look among thoſe that are us'd to purloining,
But ſhall the firſt ſearch in the chapel adjoining.

Quoth

Quoth Robin, that's right, for the caſh you will find,
Tho' I'm ſure 'twas not they, for there's ſome left behind;
But, if it were they, you could not well complain,
For what they have emptied, they'll ſoon fill again.

BY THE SAME.

DEAR Lloid, they ſay, you're Walpole's ferret,
To hunt him out poor Molly Skerrett †,
And thus are grown by views ſiniſter,
A pimp to ſuch a ſcrub miniſter;
Stick to your uſual voting trade,
Nor Chetwind's rights preſume t' invade,
To purchaſe Molly to his bed;
The booby lover fumed, and ſaid,
Spain and the galleons he'd ſacrifice,
To buy kind glances from her eyes,
Nay, ſware he'd make a plot to pay her,
At leaſt as good as that for Layer,
And bid his old tool, Delafaye
Keep Lynch and Maſon in full pay,
Paxton ‡ ſhould teach them what to ſay.
For hatching plots, and coining treaſon,
Paxton's eſteem'd, with mighty reaſon;

† Afterwards ſecond wife of the earl of Orford.
‡ Solicitor to the Treaſury.

Molly,

Molly, 'tis ſaid, by you inclin'd,
Receiv'd his offers, and reſign'd;
But Walpole long by vice decay'd,
Unable was to pleaſe the maid;
But none his fury can deſcribe,
Unlike his wretched voting tribe,
To find one Member ſcorn a bribe;
And happy were it for this land,
If corrupt Members ne'er could ſtand;
In vain were all his lying tricks,
His uſual arts in politicks;
They fail'd in one as well as t'other,
In ſpite of Townſhend and his brother.
What will become of this, poor Lloid,
When once thy maſter's pow'r's deſtroy'd,
When he refunds his unjuſt gains,
By bills of penalties and pains;
When Vaughan ſhall ſwear he did miſtake him,
And even biſhops ſhall forſake him;
Charters ſhall bully prove to bang him,
Churchill turn evidence to hang him,
Molly proclaim him fumbling imp,
And you how ill he paid his pimp.

THE

THE LYAR.

AN HEROIC TALE.

REmote from cities, in a country town,
There liv'd an honeſt, but an hapleſs clown.
Hapleſs indeed! for, if report is true,
Th'unhappy man was wedded to a ſhrew:
And what perplex'd the ill-fated ſpouſe the more,
He fear'd, from reaſon, that ſhe was a whore.
How hard his lot! who thus a wife doth wed,
At once to ſtun his ears and load his head.
How many worthy heads deſerve our pity?—
But cuſtom ſmothers evils in the city.

But to this tale.—The Muſe each name contrives,
The huſband's Jaſper; Dorcas was the wife's.
Each day gallants came ſwarming to his houſe,
Each day ſhe riots her unanſw'ring ſpouſe;
Who feels he ſuffers by th'unruly dame,
At home in ſubſtance, and abroad in fame.
He ſtrives to guard his honour and his coſt;
But gentle admonition is but loſt!
Good words he finds are thrown away in vain,
Then bad he uſes, then but bad again.
Now fully bent to ſtop this growing evil,
He plots to undermine this wily devil;
Each lover at th' accuſtom'd hour he watches,
Fix'd to diſmember every one he catches.

Fruitleſs

Fruitlefs refolve! his bufinefs he neglects,
And ftrives in vain to track the wary fex.
She fends to each gallant her private reafons,
Why love muft be deferr'd to proper feafons.
Thus all the hufband's labour'd fchemes disjointed,
And thus his cunning aims are difappointed.
Yet fo it is, that time or chance betrays
A hundred lucklefs things, a hundred ways.
'Twas on a day, when bus'nefs call'd the clown
Twenty long miles to a diftant market town,
Abroad he goes, at early morning light,
And bids her not expect him home at night.
Dorcas could ne'er let flip fuch fair occafion,
But fends a kind gallant an invitation.
He comes, he treats; when fhe, for frefh delight,
Difmifs'd one lover, for a new at night.
Mean time, jogg'd Jafper on his hobbling jade,
A fecond Rofinante, a forry fteed!
Againft whofe fides full oft the fpur was play'd,
And crofs his buttocks lafh repeated laid.
But ere on's journey he had rode half way,
Tir'd on the road the panting courfer lay:
His eafy amble having quite forgot,
Nor lafh could make him reaffume the trot:
Here then he leaves him; not too good to lofe,
And then his journey on his feet purfues.
Now Jafper was on neighbour's errand fent,
To pay his landlord certain fums of rent;

Full

Full fifteen pounds were in his pocket told,
No matter which, in ſilver or in gold.
True, ſays the proverb, as myſelf have known,
That one misfortune ſeldom comes alone:
'Twas ſo with Jaſper. Scarce his horſe was ſpent,
But robbers came and robb'd him of his rent.
He would have fought; but thinking, as I'm told,
His bones were his, and that was not the gold,
He gave it calmly up, nor further car'd;
But homeward, ſomewhat penſive, back repair'd.
Thus as he travell'd, duſky night came on,
Or dark it was, or lighted by the moon:
But to the muſe indulgent pardon ſhow,
She cannot tell you—what ſhe does not know:
But this we're told, that ere he reach'd his home,
The doleful midnight hour of twelve was come;
Much he's ſurpriz'd, at ſuch a time to catch
The door unbolted, ſhutting on the latch.
Dorcas, too, buſy with her lover's charms,
Ne'er thought of doors, but ſlept within his arms:
Now fell ſuſpicion's dart in Jaſper's brain,
Tho' glad ſo opportune he's home again:
He creeps and liſtens at the chamber door,
And overhears two ſleeping noſes ſnore:
Then from his pocket drew a ſwinging knife,
Reſolv'd to ſtab the lover or the wife;
But ſtop'd to think, before he ventur'd on,
If aught could better in the caſe be done.

L Now

[150]

Now fear ufurp'd a place in Jafper's breaft,
And thus returning reafon doth fuggeft:
Suppofe I wreak my vengeance, then may I,
Perhaps, for murder, on the gallows die;
Or on the lover only; then my wife
Would fooner take away, than fpare my life;
Or, if on both; I know not how to doubt
That proverb, "Murder fome odd time will out."
Thus reas'ning, vengeance he deferr'd till morn,
Softly retir'd, and ftroak'd each budding horn.
At neighbour's houfe he fpends the later night,
Home to return before the morning light.
At early day he thunders at his door,
But the gallant was ris'n and gone before;
From her foft fleep the treach'rous Dorcas wakes,
And thro' the broken pane in th'cafement fpeaks.
As tho' fo chafte, in th'abfence of her fpoufe,
She would admit no foul into the houfe.
Who's at the door? Pray tell me who you are?
'Tis I, quoth Jafper; I, your hufband dear.
Then up fhe gets, feems glad that he is come.
And with a Judas kifs he's welcom'd home.
Jafper moft men in temper did excel,
But when provok'd, could wield a cudgel well;
Enrag'd to fee his fpoufe her treachery,
Cries, Dorcas, who to-night did with you lie?
None, jealous monfter! with a tofs fhe cries,
And all her temper lightens in her eyes.

Aha!

Ahà ! cries Jaſper (regardleſs of her brow)
My loving faithful ſpouſe, I've caught you now.
Thus fully bent on taming of the ſhrew,
His words were ſcarce precedent to a blow.
In's hand he held a knotted taper crab,
With which he ſmartly lac'd the jilting drab.
Aloud ſhe baul'd, and begg'd him to refrain;
But ſtill he laſh'd, and ſtill ſhe begg'd in vain:
When, as it happ'd, in middle of the fray
A brother clown (that chanc'd to paſs thát way)
Ben was his name, came in to part the ſtrife,
And aſk'd, why Jaſper thus abus'd his wife.
Why ! Ben, cries Jaſper, doſt thou aſk me why?
Then laſh'd again—I've caught her in a lye.
Is lying then alone, quoth Ben, the cauſe
Of all this noiſe, and wond'rous waſte of blows?
No——not alone, quoth Jaſper, honeſt Ben,
It is becauſe ſhe lies with——other men.

A SERIO-COMIC PINDARIC.

I.

AS young in life, and young in love,
I took my roving way,
There chanc'd before my eyes to move
A female beautiful and gay,
Such as informs the wiſh, delights the dream,
The Painter's model, and the Poet's theme.

Awe-pierc'd I ſtood : and with obeiſance due
Ador'd the fairy viſion as it flew :
When lo it ſtopp'd ;—and in my tingling ear
Whiſper'd, with more melodious note
Than warbles thro' the eunuch's throat,
How do you do, my dear ?

II.

Ithaca's king ('tis ſung) could diſobey
The Syren's potent call, and keep his ſteady way ;
But how from my ſeducer fly,
She more than Syren, no Ulyſſes I ?
Pleaſures and expectations twiſted braid
Tow'd me where'er the phantom led :
The lovely phantom led me to a room,
Where the ſpread bed and artificial gloom
Bade modeſty retreat, nor dare
To damp the raptures which it cou'd not ſhare :
A pint of rack, my goddeſs calls ; and all around
The vocal waiters pints of rack reſound.

III.

Here many a ſwift-wing'd hour I lie,
Plung'd in indeſcriptive bliſs :
Then, with an eager burning kiſs,
Addreſs the partner of my ecſtacy :
Say, rapture-giving fair, O ſay,
If ſuper-human joys divine
Ought ſublunary can repay,
What recompence is thine ?

Will

Will you the avarice of glutton love
Deign to approve,
And blefs and grace your fuppliant's fide,
My faithful, my perpetual bride;
Or, if too much the rich monopoly
For any fingle he,
May I among your favour'd vaffals ftand,
With life and fortune in my ready hand,
Waiting the blifsful rotative command?—
Stoop to fenfe, and rant no more;
A one-pound-one, Sir, quits the fcore;
Returns the eafily-contented W—e.

THE CHIMNEY SWEEPER.

HOW each fond parent ftill purfues
Ambition in his children's views!
Would have his heir be fomething more,
Than what the father was before!
The Bailiff makes his fon a Proctor;
Th'Apothecary his a Doctor:
And hufband ever joins with wife,
That Tom fhould pufh himfelf in life.
A Chimney-fweeper and his *Fair*,
The footy partner of his care,
(For fair's a term, we common find
For black, and brown, and all the kind)

Indulging in their homely cheer
Of bread and cheefe, and good ftrong beer,
(For then good-nature might afford
A foaming pot to grace the board,
Ere halfpenny's advance in price
Made poor folks grow more wife than nice)
With mutual wifh, and anxious joy,
Gaz'd on their only hope, a Boy.
When the fond Dame, whom fancy led
To fafhion caftles in her head,
Bufs'd with a fmack her nown good man,
Then took a draught, and thus began:
Sure, Tommy's vaftly grown, my dear.
" Come hither, child—I fay, come here.
" Hold up thy head—Ah—he's not made
" For fuch a vaft laborious trade;
" He has not ftrength to buftle through,
" Nor writhe his body like a fkrew.
" Lard! he has genius far above
" What you and I have been, my love;
" Some gentler trade were not amifs—
" Go, child—go—give Papa a kifs."
Then looking kind at one another,
Grim firft kifs'd child, and after mother.
Why, Dame, quoth he, why all this fufs?
This Boy, our Tom, is all to us;
And ha'n't I toil'd from year to year,
But for his fake, and thine, my dear?

And

And ſhall not Tom then make a figure,
As big as father does?—aye, bigger.
For, zounds! it never ſhall be ſaid,
That Grim's own boy was baſely bred;
While Barber Scrape puts out his fool,
To learn his book at Grammar-ſchool.
Come hither, lad, look up, be bold:
Aye, there it is, my heart of gold:
Thou ſhalt complete thy father's joy,
And be a Bricklayer, my Boy;
Shalt build the chimney, and not creep
Thro' thoſe thy father us'd to ſweep.

V E R S E S

ON THE APPROACH OF WINTER.

AUtumnal leaves apace do fade,
And winter ſhows its hoary head,
With clouds and winds auſtere:
Th' enamell'd flower in earth is laid,
And lies conceal'd in Nature's bed,
'Till Sol revolves the year.

The feather'd throng prepare for flight,
The woods no ſhelter yield at night;
Unrob'd their bow'rs appear:

[156]

The ſportſman views, with true delight,
The new-reap'd fields expoſe to ſight
The haunts of tim'rous hare.

To town, my lord, with eager haſte,
Repairs, and makes his dwelling place
At Arthur's, or at White's:
Nor time her Ladyſhip doth waſte,
But ſeeks the rout ſhe oft hath grac'd,
And ſhone at whiſt whole nights.

The ſtreets ſhall now with flambeaux blaze;
The gay reſort to balls and plays,
And winter's joys poſſeſs;
While ſons of mirth in roundelays,
At feſtive board their voices raiſe,
And Bacchus' pow'r confeſs.

The ſoldier now, from direful war,
Retires with honourable ſcar,
With Cælia to engage:
While ſhe, more bright than morning ſtar,
Poſſeſs'd with ev'ry grace and air,
Unequal war doth wage.

The Pluraliſt, with ſimp'ring cheek,
And ſtall-fed ſkin ſo ſmooth and ſleek,
His tything circuit ends:

Tho'

Tho' tythes he once a year doth ſeek,
His curate preaches once a week,
    But oft with poor amends :

The rector touches all the pelf,
And curate ſtarves t' enrich himſelf,
    God's word is mammon made :
While he, a lazy pamper'd elf,
Scarce pulls a book from off the ſhelf :
    His function is a trade.

The doctor, juſt at death arriv'd,
Fearing of fee to be depriv'd,
    Ere ended is the farce,
To finiſh recipe he ſtriv'd,
That done, or live or die he's brib'd,
    Aſſur'd it is his laſt.

ON A PINCUSHION.

OF all the trinkets that the toilet grace,
The Pincuſhion deſerves the higheſt place.
When balls or operas invite the fair,
How could ſhe ſet her knots, or curl her hair ;
Did not th' important pin each air ſupply,
Subduing ſtubborn plaits that ſtand awry ?
The little pin ſtill finds an uſeful place
In mobs, in lappets, and in Bruſſels lace:

The

The modeſt pilgrim o'er the ſhoulders draws,
Or from the well-plac'd peeper gains applauſe;
In every office it performs is bleſt,
Now to her eye is neareſt, now her breaſt.

Others may to the milaner repair,
But Sylvia deigns not to be furniſh'd there:
Cupid himſelf ſupplies her magazines,
And works his pointed arrows into pins:
No wonder every look ſhould wound a heart,
Each corkin that adorns her is a dart.

ON AURELIA SLEEPING.

WRITTEN BY A YOUTH AT THE AGE OF FIFTEEN.

I.

SEE! where the bright Aurelia lies
In yonder vi'let ſmelling bow'r;
Sleep, gentle ſleep has clos'd her eyes,
Ye Cupids! guard the happy hour.

II.

Zephyrs! play ſoft around her breaſt;
Fan from her lips the ſipping fly,
That dares ſuch beauty to moleſt,
At whoſe command I live or die.

III.

Silence! ye feather'd, warbling throng!
Awhile your harmony forbear;
Awhile ſuſpend each rural ſong,
Leſt you awake my ſleeping Fair.

IV.

So may you never, never hear
The gun dread-ſounding thro' the air;
So may you never, never fear
The cruel ſchool-boy's limy ſnare.

THE GIRDLE OF VENUS.

A FABLE FROM THE GREEK,

FOR GROWN LADIES.

WHEN Jupiter's high-mettled dame
(As we read in Dan Homer the ſtory)
Had a mind his cold breaſt to inflame,
And to ſhine with additional glory.

She order'd her peacocks and car,
And then flew to the queen of the doves,
Who liv'd from her palace not far,
In the midſt of the Graces and Loves.

Dear

[160]

" Dear Venus," thus flow'd her ſmooth ſpeech,
" Prythee lend me your ceſtus to-day,
" To repair a ſmall conjugal breach;
" And be quick, for I ſoon muſt away—

" I muſt haſte to unite a good pair,
" Who took care of me when I was young;
" And each other now hardly can bear,
" Having both been by Jealouſy ſtung."

Her ſecret deſign ſhe conceal'd,
(So ſhould women act when they're marry'd)
For ſhe knew if it once was reveal'd,
It would ſoon round Olympus be carry'd—

The blythe goddeſs, not gueſſing her drift,
On her waiſt ty'd the ceſtus of pleaſure,
And the cloud-ruler's ſiſter, then ſwift
As his eagle, whirl'd off with her treaſure.

In this girdle was curiouſly ſtitch'd
The attractions which toying inſpire,
And moreover 'twas finely enrich'd
With all arts to re-kindle deſire.

In this girdle, good humour and eaſe,
Sweet words and fond looks were expreſs'd,
A perpetual endeavour to pleaſe,
And a face with gay ſmiles ever dreſs'd.

Poſſeſs'd

Poſſeſs'd of ſo rich a machine,
  She was eager in virtues to try,
And then leaving the love-darting queen,
  Shot a thouſand bright beams from each eye.

To the Thund'rer ſhe then, as by chance,
  Half her beauties with cunning diſplay'd,
From her eye ſhot a languiſhing glance,
  And then glided away like a ſhade.

But ſhe dazzl'd the eyes of grim Jove,
  Who embrac'd her with conjugal arms,
And within a delicious alcove,
  He enjoy'd with new ſpirit her charms.

Ye wives, lend an ear to this ſample
  Of the Grecian bard's ſhrewdneſs and art,
And by politic Juno's example,
  Learn to conquer a huſband's cold heart.

When the paſſion of Love's in its wane,
  And ye ceaſe to be objects of joy,
Ye muſt try the cold heart to regain,
  By thoſe beauties which never will cloy.

[162]

THE PIGEON'S CHOICE.

TO ev'ry fair a pigeon rov'd,
By ev'ry fair alike belov'd:
Where'er he flew, the female train
Practiſe their wiles his heart to gain;
Bridle the neck, and bill and coo,
And imitate what women do.
At length he found that too much joy,
Muſt ſoon his vig'rous health deſtroy;
So thought it prudent to give over,
Aſſume the huſband, drop the lover.

At firſt, the *Fan-tail* nymph he tries,
Who, in a moment, met his eyes.
Her heart exults with inward pride,
And fancy fix'd her for his bride.
Secure of conqueſt, ſhe neglected
The real charms the youth expected.
No gentle manners, no conceſſion;
All muſt be left to her diſcretion:
Whilſt vanity and affectation
Supply'd the place of ſenſe and ſtation.
" He could not anſwer to his conſcience,
" To be confin'd to pride and nonſenſe:
" A miſtreſs thus was right and civil,
" But, in a wife, they were the devil!"

So

So left the nymph to ſtrut alone,
Regardleſs of her idle moan.

The *Carrier*, a pigeon ſleek,
With ruddy bill, and ſnowy neck,
Caught his deſires; but yet the dame
Had but a ſort of doubtful fame.
He ſaw ſhe rambled round the county,
And gueſs'd ſhe might diſperſe her bounty.
He knew ſhe ſeldom kept the houſe,
And needs muſt make a wretched ſpouſe.
Never at eaſe but on the wing!
So drop'd the airy giddy thing.

The *Cropper* next, a ſtately fair!
Claim'd his affection and his care;
But to his ſorrow, ſoon he found
Her principles and mind unſound.
She boaſted much her great deſcent,
" She was not for the vulgar meant:
" Yet ſhe would yield to his requeſt,
" Provided he would make her neſt.
" Her noble limbs were quite unfit
" To do the drudg'ry of a cit."
He rais'd his head, his anger grew,
Flapping his wings, away he flew.

An hundred other ſorts he try'd,
Some promis'd fair, ſome half deny'd;

But

But what rais'd moſt his indignation,
Was pride deep fix'd by education.

Cloſe in a farmer's yard he ſaw
The *Common-Pigeon*, deep in ſtraw,
He view'd her modeſt humble mien,
Her beaut'ous feathers neat and clean :
He ſaw her earning hard her food,
And thought ſhe'd bring a healthy brood.
His judgment fix'd her in his mind,
He lov'd and courted,—ſhe prov'd kind.
Of her poſſeſs'd, he found how vain
Were all the trifling giggling train.
No gadder ſhe, no affectation!
No airs to give his mind vexation,
Her thoughts were wholly on him bent,
Studious in all to give content.
With pleaſure on his bill ſhe hung,
Then hatch'd her eggs, or fed her young.
With her he found the charms that give
The bliſs, that makes it bliſs to live.

THE

CUPID'S REVENGE.

BY THE LATE SIR JOHN VANBRUGH.

SAbina, with an angel's face,
  Ordain'd by love for joy,
Seems of the Syren's cruel race,
  To charm, and then deftroy.

The burning-glaffes of her eyes
  The fierceft flames impart,
Herfelf unhurt, the lover dies,
  Untouch'd the virgin's heart;

The God of Love, enrag'd to fee
  The Nymph elude his aim,
Pronounc'd this mercilefs decree
  Againft the haughty dame:

'Let age with double fpeed o'ertake her,
  'Let love the room of bride fupply;
'And when her lovers all forfake her,
  'A fpotlefs virgin let her die.'

[166]

THE BEGGAR.

------- inopemque paterni
Et Lari, et Fundi. HOR.

PITY the ſorrows of a poor old man!
Whoſe trembling limbs have borne him to your door,
Whoſe days are dwindled to the ſhorteſt ſpan,
Oh! give relief—and heav'n will bleſs your ſtore.

Theſe tatter'd cloaths my poverty beſpeak,
Theſe hoary locks proclaim my lengthen'd years,
And many a furrow in my grief-worn cheek,
Has been the channel to a ſtream of tears.

Yon houſe, erected on the riſing ground,
With tempting aſpect drew me from my road,
For plenty there a reſidence has found,
And grandeur a magnificent abode.

(Hard is the fate of the infirm and poor!)
Here craving for a morſel of their bread,
A pamper'd menial forc'd me from the door,
To ſeek a ſhelter in an humbler ſhed.

O! take me to your hoſpitable home,
Keen blows the wind, and piercing is the cold!
Short is my paſſage to the friendly tomb,
For I am poor—and miſerably old.

Should

Should I reveal the ſource of ev'ry grief,
If ſoft humanity e'er touch'd your breaſt,
Your hands would not withhold the kind relief,
And tears of pity could not be repreſs'd.

Heav'n ſends misfortunes—Why ſhould we repine?
'Tis heav'n has brought me to the ſtate you ſee;
And your condition may be ſoon like mine,
—The child of ſorrow—and of miſery.

A little farm was my paternal lot,
Then, like the lark, I ſprightly hail'd the morn;
But ah! oppreſſion forc'd me from my cot,
My cattle died, and blighted was my corn.

My daughter—once the comfort of my age!
Lur'd by a villain from her native home,
Is caſt abandon'd on the world's wide ſtage,
And doom'd in ſcanty poverty to roam.

My tender wife, ſweet ſoother of my care!
Struck with ſad anguiſh at the ſtern decree,
Fell—ling'ring fell a victim to deſpair,
And left the world to wretchedneſs and me.

Pity the ſorrows of a poor old man,
Whoſe trembling limbs have borne him to your door,
Whoſe days are dwindled to the ſhorteſt ſpan,
O! give relief—and heav'n will bleſs your ſtore.

A COMMON CHARACTER

AT THE OPERA-HOUSE.

WIthout an ear for muſic ſweet,
Numps at the Opera you meet:
He ſwears it is immenſely clever,
Nor knows a minim from a quaver:
With eyes ſo dim he ſcarce can ſpy—
His noſe ſo prominent and high—
Numps goes at Brunſwick's prince to ſtare,
Yet cannot ſee with all his care:
And laſtly, to complete the joke,
Numps purchaſes the Opera-book,
And ſeems to con it with wiſe look.
For notes, which never can be read,
Numps drains his purſe, to hum his head:
Strange dolt! to pay with liberal hand
For what he ne'er can underſtand!

G. B.

CUPID'S

VERSES BY MR. POPE,

ON READING A POEM, ENTITLED " A FIT OF " THE SPLEEN," BY DR. IBBOTT*.

WHat are the falling rills, the pendent ſhades,
The morning bowers, the evening colonades,
But ſoft receſſes for th' uneaſy mind,
To ſigh unheard in to the paſſing wind?
So the ſtruck deer, in ſome ſequeſter'd part,
Lies down to die—the arrow in his heart;
There hid in ſhades, and waſting day by day,
Inly he bleeds, and pants his ſoul away.

VERSES

ON THE NEW-BUILDINGS ERECTING BETWEEN BLOOMSBURY AND ST. GILES'S.

IN a doublet of ſtone, from the top of a ſteeple,
As *Brunſwick* look'd down on *the dregs of the people*,
The handſome new-buildings, the folks were erecting,
His vanity tickled, and ſet him reflecting,

* See Dodſley's collection, Vol. V. p. 202.

That ſoon he ſhould ſee, by his *Grace*'s aſſiſtance,
The *ſcum of the earth* ladled off to a diſtance.
The breed of St. Giles's, plump, tatter'd and pert,
Underſtanding his muſings, replied, from the dirt.
"Winds blaſt your hard phyz, for a weather-cock wizzard,
What is't that you grumble at thus in your gizzard?
Tho' we are ſo low, and you mounted ſo high,
Your horns, you old cuckold, don't reach to the ſky:
Then look not your haughtineſs downward ſo glum;
We can't be at once both the *dregs* and the *ſcum*.
What tho' My-Lord-Duke, your as-hard-hearted neighbour,
Would ſtarve us with nine-pence a day for our labour,
Or drive us afield, like black cattle, a grazing;
He neither can pound us, nor wall the high-ways in.
Let his bricklayers and maſons then build till they burſt,
And his ſtreets and his houſes and chapels be curſt;
While pence will, for prog, purchaſe pudding or pye,
As here we've been bred, here we'll live till we die.
Your Highneſs may vapour, with arms ſet a-kimbo,
And his Grace move the houſe to commit us to limbo:

We

We tremble as little at you as at him,
At a peace-broking peer as *a beer* brewer's whim*.
Had ſots been but ſober your worſhip had ne'er
Been raiſed thus aloft, cock-a-hoop, in the air;
To mug-houſe and mobs your high ſtation thus owing,
Keep o'er your own dunghill no longer this crowing.
Should a ſtorm ever blow that ſhould topple you down
Who, think you, would plaiſter the crack in your crown?
Your friends the True Blue ſcour'd and turn'd at the dyer's,
Old Whigs grown new tories, low-churchmen high-flyers,
By Dukes, Lords and Knights you'll be left in the lurch,
As ſure as you tumble from *Bloomſbury* church.
The ſtate in a ferment, poor *Pelham* departed,
Your Grandſon, God bleſs him, much too tender-hearted;
In faction's fierce flame party ſtill throwing oil,
'Till her long-ſimmering pot is juſt ready to boil,
Should her broth over-heated riſe up to a brimmer,
And the Devil, to cool it, be ſent with a ſkimmer,

* This ſtatue was erected at the expence of his Majeſty's brewer.

The froth and the bubbles of fortune and birth,
From the top he'd take off, as *the ſcum of the earth*;
While we, as he laughs in his ſleeve to have got'em,
The *dregs of the people*, ſink ſafe to the bottom."* * * *.

ON SEEING CAPTAIN A——

AT MRS. CORNELY'S DREST FANTASTICALLY

'TIS ſaid that our ſoldiers ſo lazy are grown,
With luxury, plenty, and eaſe,
That they more for their *carriage* than *courage* are known,
And ſcarce know the uſe of a *piece*;
Let them ſay what they will, ſince it nobody galls,
And exclaim out ſtill louder and louder;
But there ne'er was more money expended in *balls*,
Or a greater conſumption of *powder*.

THE NORFOLKE TURNIPPE.

AN AUNCIENT TALE.

SOme countyes vaunte themſelves in pyes,
And ſome in meate excelle;
For Turnippes of enormous ſize
Faire Norfolke beares the belle.

Thilke

[173]

Thilke tale an olde nurfe told to me,
Which I relate to you ;
And well I weene what nurfes fay,
Is facred all and true.

At midnighte houre a hardie knighte
Was pricking * o'er the ley ‖
The ftarres and moone had lofte their lighte,
And he had lofte his waye.

The winde full loude and fharpe did blowe,
The clouds amaine did poure,
And fuch a night, as ftoryes fhewe,
Was nivir feene before.

I vaine hee faughte full halfe the nighte,
Ne fhelter colde hee fpie :
Pitie it were fo bolde a knighte
Y-fterv'd with cold fholde dye.

Now voices ftraunge affaile his eare
And yet ne houfe was nie :
Thoughte hee, the Devil himfelfe is here,
Preferve me God on hie !

Then fummon'd hee his courage hie,
And thus aloud 'gan call ;
Fays, gyauntes, demons, come not nie,
For I defye you all !

* Riding ‖ Meadow-ground.

When

When from a hollow turnippe neare
Out jump'd a living wighte;
With friendly voice, and accent cleare,
He thus addrefs'd the knight.

Sir knighte, ne demon dwelleth here,
Ne gyaunte keepes his houfe;
But tway poor drovers, goodman Vere,
And honeft Robin Roufe.

We tweyne have taken fhelter here,
With oxen ninety-two;
And if you'll enter nivir feare,
There's room enough for you.

ON THE OAK IN PENSHURST-PARK,

PLANTED ON THE BIRTH-DAY OF SIR PHILIP SIDNEY.

AS I paffed fome weeks the laft fummer in the neighbourhood of *Penfhurft* park in *Kent*, the ancient feat of the noble family of *Sidney*, I frequently had the pleafure of riding among thofe fine old woods. Mentioning this one day among fome of my friends, a gentleman in company told us, that fome years fince, in a fall of timber that was made there for the ufe of the navy, a noble OAK,

planted

planted on the birth-day of the great Sir *Philip Sidney*, was, by miſtake, unhappily felled. We all agreed, that a tree, ſacred to the memory of ſo great a man, ought to have been preſerved inviolate from the edge of the axe.

Waller, in one of his poems written at Penſhurſt, has the following lines on this OAK:

" GO, boy, and carve this paſſion on the bark
" Of yonder tree, which ſtands the ſacred mark
" Of noble Sidney's birth; when ſuch benign,
" Such more than mortal making ſtars did ſhine,
" That there they cannot but for ever prove
" The monument and pledge of humble love.

The author of the obſervations on Mr. Waller's poems has the following note upon this paſſage—" Theſe verſes apparently refer to ſome TREE in " Penſhurſt park, planted at the birth of the famous " Sir Philip Sidney, of which there is no tradition " now remaining in the family; but we may apply " to it what Cicero ſays of the Marian Oak;" " *Manet vero, & ſemper manebit; ſata eſt enim inge-* " *nio: nullius autem agricolæ cultu ſtirps tam diuturna,* " *quam poetæ verſu ſeminari poteſt.*"

Ben Johnſon has alſo alluded to this TREE, in his Foreſt, ſpeaking of Penſhurſt:

Thou

Thou haſt thy walks for health as well as ſport,
Thy mount to which the Druids do reſort;
Where Pan and Bacchus their high feaſts have made,
Beneath the broad Beech, and a Cheſtnut ſhade;
That taller TREE, which of a Nut was ſet
At his great birth, where all the Muſes met.

But whether the tree was an Oak or a Cheſtnut, whether lately felled or ages ago, ſignifies not much: the anecdote above cited was the occaſion of the following little Ode.

QUERCUS *loquitur.*

The OAK ſpeaks.

Yes, ye muſt fall, ye fathers of the wood!
Ye, who for ages here have ſtood:
On whom an hundred wintry blaſts have beat,
Who've borne an hundred ſummers heat:
Yes, ye muſt fall, 'tis for your country's good.

The Britiſh navy ſummons now your aid;
She calls;—oh be it ever ſaid,
Each Britiſh heart, and every Britiſh oak,
Looks for the ſignal, waits the ſtroke,
And thinks the ling'ring axe too long delay'd.

Mourn

Mourn not, ye nymphs, ye Dryads of the grove,
Mourn not the ſcene of your chaſte love;
To yon wide-ſpreading ſhades of beech retreat,
There ever fix your ſylvan ſeat,
Where through the high-arch'd bow'r the Zephyrs
rove.

I, who was planted on the ſacred morn,
On which great SIDNEY here was born,
With joy exulting quit this once-lov'd plain:
I long to plunge amid the main,
And ſee the Britiſh flag my ſtrength adorn.

And thou, well pleas'd, from thy etherial throne,
Soul of great SIDNEY, oh look down!
Behold the patriot flame, that burnt in thee,
Now animates thy honour'd tree,
Who joyful meets a death ſo like thy own.

Tua Cæſar Ætas. ‡

ALL, all is Cæſar's, new-rob'd Aſton cries,
All, all is Cæſar's, the King's Bench replies.
Poor people, you have nothing left we ſee,
Since all is Cæſar's which belong'd to me,

LIBERTY.

‡ Mr. Juſtice Aſton's motto upon the rings which he diſtributed, upon being made a judge of the King's Bench.

VERSES

V E R S E S

AT LORD MELCOMBE'S, AT HAMMERSMITH,

(WRITTEN BY HIS LORDSHIP.)

FROM AN AUTHENTICK COPY.

UNDER THE BUSTO OF COMUS IN A BEAUFET.

E. AUGUST, 1750.

WHile rofy wreaths the goblet deck,
Thus COMUS fpoke, or feem'd to fpeak:
" This place, for focial hours defign'd,
" May care and bufinefs never find.
" Come, ev'ry mufe, without reftraint,
" Let genius prompt, and fancy paint;
" Let wit, and mirth, with friendly ftrife,
" Chafe the dull gloom that faddens life:
" TRUE wit, that, firm to virtue's caufe,
" Refpects religion and the laws;
" TRUE mirth, that chearfulnefs fupplies
" To modeft ears, and decent eyes;
" Let THESE indulge the livelieft fallies,
" BOTH fcorn the canker'd help of malice;
" TRUE to their country, and their friend,
" BOTH fcorn to flatter, or offend."

TWO

[179]

TWO LYRICK EPISTLES:

OR; MARGERY THE COOK-MAID TO THE CRITICAL REVIEWERS.

I write a ſad Hand but my Siſter Margery ſhe writes better.

BY the backſide!* good lack, good lack!
Chain'd to the chimney corner like a monkey,
You are as ſpiteful as a black;
That has been drinking drink for drunky.

I think I ſee my maſter leap and ſkip;
And whiſk about his tail;
Juſt like a pinnace when ſhe makes a trip,
And whiſks about her ſail.

So have I ſeen a highlander retire
And turn about to court the wind,
Shot by a cinder leaping from the fire
Amongſt his precious parts behind.

* Vide CRITICAL REVIEW for December 1761. Article, fables for grown gentlemen.

P. 461. If the *poor Highlander's backſide*, be bound in chains, we think he has ſome reaſon to complain. If the author himſelf was like a monkey chained to the chimney corner by the backſide, he might afford ſome diverſion to Margery the cook-maid but it is to be ſuppoſed he would not much reliſh the reſtraint.

Laugh!

[180]

Laugh! no he need not be afraid,
Though 'twould be comical no doubt;
To ſee him ſquatting like a maid;
And making water like a ſpout.

But I ſhould laugh at you reviewers,
If I could view your buttocks bare,
Genteelly truſs'd and pink'd with ſkewers,
And nicely larded like a hare.

Nay I could wiſh,
To ſee your backſides ſing'd and flead,
Juſt like your favourite diſh,
A ſingged hede:
To ſmell them ſavoury and reeky
Like Cocky Leaky.

And as your cook at a ſmith's forge,
Gives the fine flavour of the wool,
To a ſheep's ſkull,
Which makes you eat 'till you regorge;

So, the communication is ſo great,
Between your brains and your backſide,
Between the ſeat;
Of lazyneſs and ſeat of pride.

That tho' the brains, of all you jokers,
Never ſtruck fire, into a ſingle joke,
Yet if your bums, were ſing'd with pokers,
Your brains perhaps, might yield a little ſmoke.

Spite

Spite of your heavy jokes,
That fall upon the head ;
Like apopleƈtick ſtrokes,
Or pigs of lead.

We'll laugh, to ſee your highland ſparks,
Your highland breeding, and good manners,
To ſee them, ſtrut about the parks,
With ſhirts diſplay'd behind, like banners.

Shewing our maids, and modeſt wives,
Such modeſt ſights,
As make their huſbands, weary of their lives,
They make them paſs, ſuch reſtleſs nights.

Our lovers ſicken, and deſpair,
Dejeƈtion preys upon our beaux ;
The expeƈtations of our fair,
Are rais'd ſo highly, by ſuch ſhews.

The Indians I'm told, are more polite,
They don't produce their brawny powers,
They only ſhew their powers by candle light,
Amongſt their favourite ſquaws, at certain hours.

Good ſirs, if I aright can read,
You are deſign'd for books,
Juſt as your friends, beyond the Tweed,
For gardeners and cooks.

Your pride, and lazineſs I gueſs,
Diſorder and torment your minds,
And bring your country to diſtreſs,
For want of labourers and hinds.

I think like you, it is a ſhame,
That its beſt blood ſhould now be bleeding;
And blame,
The government, for ſuch proceeding.

I would have ſent the very worſt,
I would have ſent you all a packing;
You ſhould have gone, the very firſt,
You're good enough, for a good thwacking.

But I am weary of inditing,
Such letters;
And ſo I take my leave of writing;
And leave you to my betters.

EPISTLE THE SECOND.

YOU who aſſemble in diſguiſe;
And take your ſtands in ſecret places,
Spitting into our mouths and eyes,
With a pretence to waſh our faces!

But

But when you ſpy a Scotchman walking,
His air and manner is ſo pleaſing,
That you immediately leave hawking,
And offer him a pickle of your ſneeſing.

I do not want to rob you of your ſnuff,
Give it your countrymen, it likes me well,
But do not fright us, like Macduff,
Calling aloud, to ring the alarum bell,
Suſpend your purulence, ſwallow your ſpittle,
And liſten to an Engliſhman a little.

You know you ſpit at us, and hawk and cough,
As if you had a charter,
And alſo know we wipe it meekly off,
Like Charles the bleſſed martyr.

Whilſt you go on abuſe and rail,
As if we were not fellow creatures,
Laying about you like a flail,
And bruiſing all our Engliſh features:

If we poor Engliſhmen but ſmile,
It is high treaſon,
Tho' we are ſmiling all the while,
Both with good nature and good reaſon,

Not throwing dirt at a whole nation*
But laughing at the folly of a few,
Whofe prejudice and affectation
Become them juft as they do you.

As if they were a chofen race,
Clear and exempted by their birth ;
From all the vices that difgrace,
All other children of the earth.

I very readily excufe,
Your want of complaifance
To my ftrange mufe,
Drefs'd in the carelefs drefs of France,
A la Fontaine
A flattern but quite plain.

According to your notions,
You muft diflike the flimfy wench ;
Her drefs and all her motions
Are fo intolerably French ;
†A gracelefs copy of a gracelefs hobler,
Juft like a gouty fhoe made by a cobler.

* According to the reviewers the greateft pleafure that the whole Englifh nation enjoys, is to fee their brethren of North Britain in their theatres, reprefented as a parcel of fcoundrels.

† The reviewers fay that the verfes in the fables for grown gentlemen hobble ftrangely, from fourteen to two fyllables : that may partly be owing to their want of ears ; they muft have the fame objection to Fontaine.

You

You think the bagpipes notes are ſweeter
Than any pipe or any ſtring;
The aſs preferr'd the cuckow's ſong and metre,
To all the warblers of the ſpring,
Either the organs or the ſoul
Of you *and aſſes are ſo drole.*‡

Your ignorance and want of *Senſe*
Your want of ears I do forgive;
But unprovok'd malevolence,
I'll never pardon whilſt I live,
Such your attempt to prove me to the North
A foe to its acknowledg'd worth.

In every country I deſpiſe
A heart that's arrogant and narrow,
As much as I eſteem and prize
David Hume and David's marrow.
Now to conclude,
I am yours reviewing or review'd.

But as my fables are not to your liking,
Witneſs the fable of laſt year,*
I ſend you ſomething that's more ſtriking
Concise and clear,
I think you call it in your brogue
An apologue.

‡ Lyrick epiſtles to the reviewers.

* The aſs the cuckow and the lark.

[186]

THE APOLOGUE.

SOME folks get no more by their reading
And meditations;
Than apes and monkeys by their breeding
And obſervations:
This I agree,
May be apply'd either to you or me.

The fable that comes after,
Can only be apply'd to you,
If it excites a little laughter,
It anſwers all my view.

An ape by trade an imitator,
Had ſpent the beſt part of his days;
Like a reviewer or tranſlator
Of farces, interludes and plays,
For ever copying and itching
To ſhew his talents in the kitchen.

He would divert you if you were not nice,
And difficult to pleaſe
By cracking lice,
And catching fleas;
Which he would chaw,
And cram into a kitten's maw.

In

In ſhort,
Jacko had ſtudy'd many a trick,
Which tricks inſtead of making ſport;
Would oft'ner make you ſick:
Yet he would make you now and then;
Laugh like the fooliſheſt of men.

The cook-maid by the fire was faſt aſleep,
No kind of harm ſuſpecting,
Jacko the ape was playing at bopeep,
Reviewing and reflecting,
Whether from liquor or from whim,
The cook-maid laid in a ſtrange trim.

Hard by a raſor left upon a chair,
By Jackanapes was quickly ſeiz'd,
The cook-maid's beard expos'd and bare,
The grinning villain rub'd and greas'd;
Then ſnap'd his fingers and look'd grave,
Flouriſh'd his raſor and began to ſhave.

Jacko proceeded, without dread,
Chatter'd and did not care a fig;
Poor Margery was hack'd, and bled;
Like an aſſaſſinated pig.

Rous'd by her pains like frantick ſleepers,
She ſnatch'd a pan of boiling broth,
Bubbling and running o'er with froth,
And threw it into Jacko's peepers:

Which blinded him and ſpoil'd him, paſt all
cure,
Both for a ſhaver and reviewer.

THE SENATOR ENLIGHTENED,

OR, JULIUS CÆSAR'S SALVE.

AT Rome, in antient times, as poets ſay,
Ere the firſt Cæſar bore imperial ſway;
Patricius liv'd: no ſenator ſo juſt,
So true as he, or faithful to his truſt:
Cæſar's ambitious views he long withſtood,
And plac'd his glory on the public good:
For Roman freedom he would oft declaim,
Their rights and liberties, his conſtant aim:
By which he gain'd at length the patriot's glorious
name.
Cæſar heard, and reſolv'd to change his tone,
And by his art to make the man his own.
A ſalve he made of yellow ſhining ore,
Oft uſed in England ſince, for the ſame ſore,
Which to the patriot's palm he ſlily bound;
When lo! the wonderful effect was found:
His patriotiſm all vaniſh'd into ſmoke,
The people's liberties were now a joke:
Enlighten'd now, Patricius clearly ſaw,
What Cæſar did was right, was good, was law.

From

From Cæſar now they nothing had to fear,
He, in all Rome, was only fit to ſteer:
In Cæſar's breaſt did all the virtues meet,
Cæſar was ev'ry thing that's good and great:
He was the guardian angel of the Roman ſtate.

THE FRANTIC LOVER.

----æſtuat.ingens
Imo in corde pudor, mixtoque inſania luctu,
Et Furiis agitatus amor.----

AND ſhall then another embrace thee, my fair?
Muſt envy ſtill add to the pangs of deſpair?
Shall I live to behold the reciprocal bliſs?
Death, death is a refuge, Elyſium to this!

The ſtar of the evening now bids thee retire,—
Accurs'd be its orb, and extinguiſh'd its fire!
For it ſhews me my rival prepar'd to invade
Thoſe charms which at once I admir'd and obey'd.

Far off each forbidding incumbrance is thrown,
And, Sally, thy beauties no more are thy own;
Thy coyneſs too flies, as love brings to thy view
A trance more extatic than ſaint ever knew.

And yet I behold thee, tho' longing to die,
Approach the new Heav'n with a tear and a ſigh;

For

For oh! the fond ſigh 'midſt enjoyment will ſtray,
And a tear is the tribute which rapture muſt pay.

Still, ſtill doſt thou tremble that pleaſure to ſeek,
Which pants in thy boſom, and glows on thy cheek;
Confuſion and ſhame thy ſoft wiſhes deſtroy,
And terror cuts off the weak bloſſom of joy.

Ah! had I been bleſt with thy beauty, my fair,
With fondeſt attention, with delicate care,
My heart would have try'd all thy fears to remove,
And pluck'd every thorn from the roſes of love!

My inſolent rival, more proud of his right,
Contemns the ſweet office, that ſoul of delight;
Leſs tender he ſeizes thy lips as his prey,
And all thy dear limbs the rough ſummons obey.

Ev'n now more licentious—raſh mortal forbear!—
Reſtrain him, O Venus! let him too deſpair!—
Freeze, freeze the ſwift ſtreams which now hurry to
join,
And curſe him with paſſions unſated like mine!

How weak is my rage his fierce joy to controul!
A kiſs from thy body ſhoots life to his ſoul;
Thy froſt too diſſolv'd in one current is run,
And all thy keen feelings are blended in one.

Thy

Thy limbs from his limbs a new warmth ſhall acquire,
His paſſions from thine ſhall redouble their fire;
Till wreck'd and o'erwhelm'd in the ſtorm of delight,
Thine ears loſe their hearing, thine eyes loſe their ſight.

Here conqueſt muſt pauſe (tho' it ne'er can be cloy'd)
To view the rich plunder of beauty enjoy'd;
The treſſes diſhevell'd, the boſom diſplay'd,
And the wiſhes of years in a moment repaid.

A thouſand ſoft thoughts in thy fancy combine!
A thouſand wild horrors aſſemble in mine!
Relieve me, kind death! ſhut the ſcene from my view,
And ſave me, O ſave me, ere madneſs enſue!

A N

AN ODE

TO THE RIGHT HONOURABLE STEPHEN POYNTZ, ESQ. &c. &c.

BY THE HONOURABLE SIR CHARLES HANBURY WILLIAMS, KNIGHT OF THE BATH.

Senfere quid Mens rite, quid Indoles
Nutrita fauftis fub penetralibus
Poffet - - - -

Doctrina fed vim promovet infitam,
Rectique cultus pectora roborant.

HOR. Od. IV. Lib. IV.

I.

WHILST WILLIAM's deeds and WILLIAM's praife,
Each Englifh breaft with tranfport raife,
Each Englifh tongue employ;
Say, POYNTZ, if thy elated heart
Affumes not a fuperior part,
A larger fhare of joy?

II.

But that thy country's high affairs
Employ thy time, demand thy cares,
You fhou'd renew your flight;

You

You only ſhould this theme purſue——
Who can for WILLIAM feel like you?
Or who like you can write?

III.

Then to rehearſe the hero's praiſe,
To paint this ſunſhine of his days,
The pleaſing taſk be mine——
To think on all thy cares o'erpaid,
To view the Hero you have made,
That pleaſing part be thine.

IV.

Who firſt ſhould watch, and who call forth
This youthful prince's various worth,
You had the publick voice;
Wiſely his royal ſire conſign'd
To thee, the culture of his mind,
And England bleſt the choice.

V.

You taught him to be early known
By martial deeds of courage ſhewn:
From this near Mena's flood,
By his victorious father led,
He fleſh'd his maiden ſword, he ſhed,
And prov'd th' illuſtrious blood.

Of

VI.

Of virtue's various charms you taught,
With happineſs and glory fraught,
How her unſhaken pow'r
Is independent of ſucceſs;
That no defeat can make it leſs,
No conqueſt make it more.

VII.

This, after Tournay's fatal day,
'Midſt ſorrow, cares, and dire diſmay,
Brought calm, and ſure relief;
He ſcrutiniz'd his noble heart,
Found virtue had perform'd her part,
And peaceful ſlept the chief.

VIII.

From thee he early learnt to feel
The patriot's warmth for England's weal;
(True valour's nobleſt ſpring)
To vindicate her church diſtreſt;
To fight for liberty oppreſt;
To periſh for his king.

IX.

Yet ſay, if in thy fondeſt ſcope
Of thought, you ever dar'd to hope
That bounteous heav'n ſo ſoon

Would

Would pay thy toils, reward thy care,
Confenting bend to ev'ry pray'r,
And all thy wifhes crown.

X.

We faw a wretch, with trait'rous aid,
Our king's and church's rights invade;
And thine, fair Liberty!
We faw thy hero fly to war,
Beat down rebellion, break her fpear,
And fet the nations free.

XI.

Culloden's field, my glorious theme,
My rapture, vifion, and my dream,
Gilds the young hero's days:
Yet can there be one Englifh heart
That does not give thee, POYNTZ, thy part,
And own thy fhare of praife?

XII.

Nor is thy fame to thee decreed
For life's fhort date: When WILLIAM'S head,
For victories to come,
The frequent laurel fhall receive,
Chaplets for thee our fons fhall weave,
And hang 'em on thy tomb.

W A N T E D

An ODE to Mr. LE GRAND, on the **Tuition** of the *prefent* Duke of Cumberland.

[196]

ON SOME ENCROACHMENTS ON THE RIVER.

FOUR Scotchmen, by the names of Adams,
Who keep their *coaches*, and their *madams*,
Quoth John, in sulky mood, to Thomas,
Have stole the very river from us.
O, *Scotland!* long it has been said
Thy teeth are sharp for English bread;
What! seize our *bread* and *water* too,
And use us worse than jailors do!
'Tis true 'tis hard!—'tis hard 'tis true!
Ye friends of *George*, and friends of *James*,
Envy us not our river *Thames*:
The Pr———ss, fond of *raw-bon'd* faces,
May give you all our *posts* and *places*;
Take all—to gratify your pride,
But dip your *oatmeal* in the *Clyde*.

LONDINENSIS

F I N I S.

EDITORIAL NOTES

Notes to this edition refer to the original *New Foundling Hospital for Wit* page numbers and lines of text. References to other parts are separated by a colon; page and line references are separated by a full stop (e.g. *NFHW*, 1: 2.3 = Part 1, page 2, third line of text). For information on authors and names appearing three or more times in any one part, please see the Biographical Appendix in Volume 3 (pp. 419–35). Dashes are not always consistent, nor do they always give a clear indication of the number of missing letters. Misprints (unless substantive), unidentified allusions and references are not generally noted. See also the Abbreviations list in Volume 1 (pp. xxxix–xl).

Part 3

1.1. '*CITY LATIN*': Bonnell Thornton's critique of John Paterson's proposed Latin inscriptions for the new bridge at Blackfriars, built between 1760 and 1769, first published in London by R. Stevens in 1760 and followed by two more editions in 1761. Paterson (*c.* 1705–89), MP for Ludgershall (1761–8), spearheaded the Blackfriars Bridge project (*HWC*).

1.12–13. '*the Rev.* BUSBY BIRCH': Thornton's pseudonym, with reference to Thomas Birch (1705–66), who served as secretary to the Royal Society from 1752 to 1765. His honours include Doctor of Law, Fellow of the Royal Society, Fellow of the Antiquarian Society and Fellow of the General Council.

1.15–16. '*society … commerce*': the Royal Society for the Encouragement of Arts, Manufactures and Commerce was founded in 1754.

1.17–18. 'Quis expedivit … conari?': 'Who taught Salmasius, that French chatt'ring pie / To aim at English, and HUNDREDA cry?', the opening lines of John Milton's *Defensio secunda* (1654) in response to Claude Salmasius's *Defensio Regia pro Carlo Primo* (1649), which condemned the execution of Charles I.

1.22. 'GREAT MINISTER': William Pitt.

2.4. '*Elliptic* arches': Edinburgh architect and engineer Robert Mylne (1734–1811), whose plan for Blackfriars Bridge featuring elliptical arches won the competition over John Gwynn's semicircular design supported in the press by Samuel Johnson. Mylne worked on Blackfriars Bridge until its completion.

2.17–18. 'Ashley's motto, *pro bono publico*': Anthony Ashley Cooper, third Earl of Shaftesbury (1671–1713), whose moral philosophy – 'for the public good' – ran counter to Hobbesian self-interest.

2.24–7. 'reverend ordinary … Charter-House': i.e. the Latin inscription is faulty.

3.9. '*Anglicisms*': 'a form of speech peculiar to the English language; an English idiom' (Johnson).

5.5. 'Sir THOMAS CHITTY': Lord Mayor of the City of London in 1759.

5.11. 'MYLNE': see 2.4.

7.12. '*Stow's Survey of London*': John Stow (1525–1605), *Survey of London and Westminster* (1598).

7.25. '*Holyoak*'s dictionary': Francis Holyoake (1567–1653), whose *Dictionarium Etymologicum Latinum* (1633) was expanded by his son in 1677.

13.15. 'the Rev. *George White*': anti-Methodist Church of England preacher who published *The Miraculous Sheep's Eye … a Poem. In Two Cantos* (London: Mary Marshall, 1743; Foxon, W408) and died in 1751.

13.15–16. '*Agricola Candidus*': i.e. George White. The *ESTC* lists one item, *The High Mass. A Poem. By Agricola Candidus, Gent. Author of The Latin Mercury* (London: J. Hart, 1746; Foxon, H201).

13.n. '*Schrevelius's Lexicon*': Cornelius Schrevelius (1615–64), rector of Leiden University, whose *Lexicon Manuale Græco-Latinum et Latino-Græcum* was first published in 1654.

18.7–8. '*barbaro-latinized*': neologism for botched Latin translation.

18.18. 'Sink, ditch, bog, quagmire': synonyms for pit, i.e. Pitt.

20.21–2. 'Swift, Hastings, and On-slow': proper names chosen for this playful series of opposite terms which are given their Latin equivalents on the following page.

22.1. '*Wenman* or *Warton*': possibly Philip Wenman, sixth Viscount Wenman, the Tory MP for Oxfordshire, who contested the Whig victory in the 1754 general election; Thomas Warton, the younger (1728–90), Professor of Poetry at Oxford (1756–66).

22.8. 'NASO': Latin poet Ovid, i.e. Publius Ovidius Naso (43 BC–AD 17).

22.23. '*Racine*': Jean Baptiste Racine (1639–99), French poet and tragedian.

22.25. 'two *Corneilles*': French playwright, Pierre Corneille (1606–84), whose brother (not his son) Thomas (1625–1709) was also a noted dramatist.

23.1. 'NEPOS': Cornelius Nepos (*c.* 99–25 BC), Roman historian.

23.12–13. 'Hugger-Mugger Higgledy-Piggledy Helter-Skelter': word-play; Johnson defines 'huggermugger' as 'secrecy; bye-place', 'helter-skelter' as 'in a hurry; without order; tumultuously', and 'higgledy-piggeldy' [*sic*] as 'a cant word, corrupted from *higgle*, which denotes any confused mass, as higglers carry a huddle of provisions together'.

25.7–8. '*Stow's Survey*, or *Maitland's History of London*': for Stow, see 7.12. above; and William Maitland (*c.* 1693–1757), whose *History of London*, first printed by Samuel Richardson in 1739, went to a fifth edition in 1769.

27.2. '*My publisher*': R. Stevens, who first published *City Latin* (see 1.1).

27.3–4. 'Daily Advertiser': daily newspaper published from 1734 until the 1790s.

27.4. 'Jenour': Mathew Jenour (1707–86), printer of the *Daily Advertiser* (*HWC*).

28.2. 'Martin Marfozius': possibly a Scriblerian persona or Pasquin's Marsorio.

28.6. 'Johan. R—v—ng': possibly a satirical persona.

28.6. 'Armiger': a nobleman entitled to bear heraldic arms; a squire carrying the armour of a knight.

28.10–11. 'THIS BARG^{e} wAs buiLt': print staggered for satiric effect.

28.13. 'woodFaLL': Henry Sampson Woodfall (1739–1805), printer and journalist. His father, Henry Woodfall, was the printer of the newspaper the *Public Advertiser* from 1758 to 1793. H. S. Woodfall was apprenticed to his father, and at the age of nineteen took over the control of the *Public Advertiser*, which published the Junius letters.

28.14. 'domIne dirGe nos': 'Lord, direct us' (Latin).

28.15. '*On Mr.* Yorke's *taking a patent of Precedence*': In 1764 Charles Yorke (1722–70) applied for his old office of Attorney-General, then held by Sir Fletcher Norton, but was turned down by Grenville and had to make do with a patent of precedency before the Solicitor-General (*ODNB*).

29.14. 'Scottish thane': Bute.

29.21. 'traiterous m—s': ministers?

30.1. '*Extempore*': this and the next four verses concern 'Sir' John Hill (1714–75), author of *The Virtues of Wild Valerian* (1758) amongst many other herbal remedy guides. He supported his writing projects 'through the sale of herbal medicines such as "the essence of water-dock", "tincture of valerian", and "pectoral balsalm of honey"' (*ODNB*).

31.1. 'EPIGRAM': this appears in Garrick's letter to Dr John Hawkesworth, who reviewed *The Rout* (*GM*, 29 (1759), p. 37), *c.* January 1759, as a motto for a mezzotint (*LDG*, vol. 1, pp. 299–300).

31.3. '*Dr.* Hill's *Farce*': John Hill's two-act farce, *The Rout*, was performed at the Theatre-Royal in Drury Lane in 1758 and published in two editions in the same year. Lady Bute recommended Hill to Garrick, but the two men quarrelled over the production.

31.19. 'Jerry Sneak': a character in Samuel Foote's 1764 comedy, *The Mayor of Garret* (later *Garratt*).

32.21. 'Mons. de Bouganville': Louis Antoine, comte de Bougainville (1729–1811), General Montcalm's aide-de-camp *c.* 1758–9, the first French sailor to circumnavigate the globe (1766–9); the bougainvillaea plant is named after him, along with the largest of the Solomon Islands.

32.24–5. 'Baron de Dieskau': Jean-Armand Dieskau, Baron de Dieskau (1701–67), commander of French troops in Canada from 1755 to 1763.

34.2. '*Isle of* Thanet': off the northeast coast of Kent.

34.6. 'expiring H—d': Holland did not die until 1778.

34.7. '*Inscription for the Villa of a decay'd Statesman*': 'supposed to be written by Gray', according to an entry dated 14 April 1798 in the commonplace book of George Whittington (Special Collections, St John's College, Cambridge University (O.73)).

34.10. 'H****': Holland in recuperation.

34.14. 'Earl Goodwin': Godwine or Godwin, Earl of Wessex (d. 1053), who was banished briefly by Edward the Confessor in 1051. Blake exhibited *The Death of*

Earl Goodwin at the Royal Academy in 1780, and Ann Yearsley made him the subject of a play *c.* 1789.

35.1. 'B**e': Bute.

35.8. '*Foxes*': i.e. Henry Fox and sons, Charles James and Stephen.

35.10–11. '*Omnes congruunt … omnes noris*': 'all hanging together; when you know one, you know all', Terence, *Phormio, or The Scheming Parasite* (trans. Henry Thomas Riley), II.i.34.

35.15. 'G—m': possibly Sir Thomas Robinson (1695–1770), created Baron Grantham in 1761.

35.20. 'B—n S—e': possibly James Murray, seventh Baron Strange (1690–1764), or John Murray (1729–74) whose wife, Charlotte Murray, eighth Baroness Strange (*c.* 1731–1805), inherited the English barony of Strange and the sovereignty of the Isle of Man.

35.20. 'M—d': Mansfield.

35.23. 'H—d': Holland.

35.24. 'H—y': Robert Henley, first Earl of Northington (*c.* 1708–72), Lord Chancellor.

35.25. 'N—n': Sir Fletcher Norton.

35.25. 'W—b': Philip Carteret Webb (1702–70), barrister who assisted in the seizure of Wilkes's papers in 1763.

36.1. 'ANACR. Od. 46': This poem to John Wilkes has nothing in common with Anacreon's Ode 46 about the burgeoning of spring. It is possibly by John St John (1745/6–93), MP for Newport, Isle of Wight, from 1773, macaroni friend of George Selwyn.

36.n. 'Cet admirable maitre des muets … LAMY': Bernard Lamy (1640–1715), French philosopher. 'This admirable master of silence when he gave his first lessons, formed with his hands in their organs the disposition necessary to pronounce each letter'.

37.7. 'P—': Pitt.

37.8. 'W—s': Wilkes.

37.11. '*Epistle to* John Wilkes': Wilkes was convicted *in absentia* for publishing the *North Briton* and the *Essay on Woman* in 1764 and finally sentenced to serve two years (a year on both counts) in King's Bench prison on 14 June 1768.

37.18. 'M—d': Mansfield.

37.20. 'Y—s': Yates.

38.20. 'm—y': ministry.

39.2. 'M—' : Mansfield.

39.11. 'B—': Bute.

39.12. 'C—': council?

39.14. 'make him —': swing.

39.20. '*Ex ungue leonem*': used as the title to the second part of William Winstanley's *Protestant Almanack* for 1668, meaning out of the lion's claw.

41.7. 'HARRY *and* NAN': Henry Augustus Fitzroy, third Duke of Grafton (1735–1811), Prime Minister from 1768 to 1770, and his mistress, Nancy Parsons (*c.* 1735–1814/15).

41.8. 'TIBULLUS': Albius Tibullus (*c.* 54–19 BC), Latin elegiac poet.

42.14. 'a p—p and a wh—': a pimp and a whore.

43.11. 'bashaws': sometimes written *bassa*; 'A title of honour and command among the Turks; the viceroy of a province; the general of an army' (Johnson).

43.26. 'guttling': 'A low word', according to Johnson; the verb 'to guttle' meant 'To feed luxuriously; to gormandize'.

45.5. '*On the D. of* B—'s *Arrival in* Ireland. 1768': John Russell, fourth Duke of Bedford (1710–71), was appointed Lord Lieutenant of Ireland in 1756 and invited to return in 1768 to be installed as Chancellor of Trinity College, Dublin.

45.10. 'G*reat* PEACEMAKER': Fox acting for Bute.

46.9. 'PAM': 'the knave of clubs' (Johnson).

46.12. 'ALMA': Alma represents the virgin soul in Spenser's *Faerie Queene.*

47.8. 'on the great NEW-MARKET plain': at the horse races.

47.15. '*stock-jobbing* art': Johnson defines a 'stockjobber' as 'a low wretch who gets money by buying and selling shares in the funds'.

48.2. '*As played before the King of* Denmark': Christian VII (1749–1808), crowned in 1766, married Caroline, sister of George III, in the same year; they visited London in 1768, where he was entertained by Princess Amelia, took in a performance of *The Provok'd Wife* and became a crowd favourite because of his wild behaviour (*HWC*, vol. 23, pp. 41, 48, 57). Garrick put on Hoadly's *The Suspicious Husband* and Bickerstaffe's *Daphne and Amintor* on 18 August as well as *Macbeth* on 22 September (*LDG*, vol. 2, p. 630). In 1772 the distressed Queen of Denmark was imprisoned by her husband on suspicion of having an affair with her German doctor, John Struensee, who was treating her venereal disease. George III sent some armed vessels to the Baltic to her rescue. She died at Hanover at the age of twenty-three.

48.4. 'Wapping': just east of Tower Bridge in London, occasionally used satirically, as in an anonymous pamphlet, *To the Author of a Libel, entitled, A Letter to the Editor, &c.* (London: Webb, 1749), which asked, 'Whether you [William Warburton] are a wrangling *Wapping* Attorney, a pedantic pretender to Criticism, an impudent paradoxical Priest, or an Animal yet stranger, an heterogenous Medley of all three ...' (p. 1). In 1776, Sir John Fielding lumped it together with Rotherhithe as a place 'chiefly inhabited by sailors, [where] a man would be apt to suspect himself in another country'.

49.15. 'tar': 'A sailor; a seaman in contempt' (Johnson).

49.23. 'Banyans': 'a Hindu trader' (*OERD*).

49.25. 'bra': Scots for brave.

50.2. 'Buoy of the Nore': point of departure for the fleet, mentioned by Samuel Pepys in his diary (e.g. 18 August 1665). The Nore is a sandbank at the mouth of the Thames marked by buoys, approximately forty-seven miles below London Bridge. A warning light was placed there in 1731.

50.3. 'soldiers, like Hymen': i.e. inexperienced.

50.15. 'Mrs. Ross': Frances 'Fanny' Murray (1729–78), the courtesan and dedicatee of *An Essay on Woman*, who married actor and theatre manager David Ross (1728–90) (*ODNB*).

50.17. '*Tancred*': role played by Garrick in James Thomson's popular tragedy, *Tancred and Sigismunda* (1745), performed eighteen times between 1747 and 1776 and based on *Gil Blas* (1715–35), Le Sage's picaresque romance translated by Smollett in 1749, of the Crusader who lived from AD 1076–1112.

50.18. 'PHILIP': a guest disguised as Philip of Spain.

50.20. 'Diana from lewd Drury-lane': possibly referring to a prostitute disguised as the Roman goddess of virginity.

50.n. 'Behold in character of *Night* … Fanny has had her *Day*': possibly a parody of Isaac Watts's hymn, 'How bright these glorious spirits shine! / Whence all their white array? / How came they to the blissful seats / Of everlasting day?' (*ODQ*).

51.4. 'Epicure Mammon': the knight satirized in Ben Jonson's play, *The Alchemist*, first performed in 1610.

51.5. 'fishified': 'TO FISHIFY … to turn to fish: a cant word' (Johnson).

51.5. 'fleshified': not in Johnson; 'to turn into flesh' (*OED*).

51.6. 'jole': '1. The face or cheek [i.e. jowl]. 2. The head of a fish' (Johnson).

51.16. 'PARODY on CATO': Joseph Addison's popular tragedy went through eight editions in 1713, the year it was first performed.

51.18. 'John Glynn': John Glynn (1722–79), a lawyer and friend of Wilkes who won the controversial Middlesex by-election in 1768.

51.19. '*Sir* W. B. Proctor': Sir William Beauchamp Proctor (1722–73), one of the two sitting MPs for Middlesex in 1768 who was defeated by Wilkes after his snap decision to run five days before the election.

51.20. 'MURPHY': Arthur Murphy (1727–1805), actor, playwright, journalist, lawyer and editor of the pro-Bute *Auditor*.

52.13. '*Brentford*': violent tactics were used to intimidate Glynn's supporters at the poll in Brentford, a rural part of the county of Middlesex, in 1768. Lord Halifax was suspected of providing payment for thugs to sway voters on Proctor's behalf, but Glynn ultimately won. George Clarke, a Wilkite lawyer, died from injuries sustained in the riot. See George Rudé, *Wilkes and Liberty* (Oxford: Clarendon Press, 1962), pp. 59–61.

53.10. '*British* S—e': Senate.

54.26. 'Presumptuous man!': echoing Pope's *Essay on Man*, Epistle I.35 (*TE*, vol. 3.i, p. 17).

55.12. '*Thane*': Bute, i.e. the Scots.

55.14. 'Bareges' waters': i.e. the French; from the mineral water from the town of Barèges on the French side of the Pyrénées. Sir Christopher Meighan MD recommended its efficacious powers for the treatment of gun-shot wounds in *A Treatise of the Nature and Powers of Bareges's Baths and Waters*, self-published in 1742, expanded and reprinted by Andrew Millar in 1764.

55.18. 'Chevy Chace': one of best-known ballads dating from the fifteenth century, concerning the tragic rivalry between the English Earl Percy and the Scottish Earl Douglas; included in Edward Capell's *Prolusions* (London: J. and R. Tonson, 1760) and Thomas Percy's *Reliques* (London: J. Dodsley, 1765). Sir Philip Sidney admitted to being moved by 'Chevy Chase' in his *Defence of Poesie* (1595).

56.9. '*Horne*': John Horne Tooke (1736–1812), ardent Wilkes supporter who was elected burgess of Brentford in 1769 and soon after founded the Society of Supporters of the Bill of Rights 'to maintain and defend the *legal, constitutional liberty*' by helping to pay Wilkes's legal expenses.

57.9. 'O'M—y': no O'Malleys or O'Mahonys or variations have been found in the usual sources.

57.13. 'Count Gambler': a stock gambling figure.

58.19. '*Cardinal* De Bernis': François-Joachim de Pierre de Bernis (1715–94), whose nomination as cardinal was supported by Madame de Pompadour.

59.6–7. 'Veni Creator': Latin hymn attributed to Charlemagne, St Ambrose and Gregory, translated by Dryden as 'Veni, Creator Spiritus' ('Come Creator Spirit'), and parodied by Wilkes as 'Veni Creator; or, The Maid's Prayer'. Included here, possibly by Wilkes, to suggest that sacrilegious parodies were not confined to England. See Arthur H. Cash, *An Essay on Woman by John Wilkes and Thomas Potter: a Reconstruction of a Lost Book* (New York: AMS Press, 2000), pp. 126–7, 189–91.

59.19. 'La Pompadour': Jeanne Antoinette Poisson, Marquise de Pompadour (1721–64), mistress of Louis XV who held formidable influence over politics and the arts in France from 1745.

60.9. 'elogium': '1. an explanatory inscription; 2. = elogy [i.e. "... usually in a favourable sense, a eulogy, expression of praise"]' (*OED*); but not quite in the sense that Johnson has for 'elogy' meaning 'praise; panegyrick'.

60.13–15. '*The following ... Alderman of* London': by someone like William Beckford (1709–70), who had been elected alderman (for life) of Billingsgate ward in 1752.

60.17. '*Cretâ, an carbone notandi*': 'To be marked with white chalk or charcoal', Horace, *Satires*, II.3.246.

60.21. 'the *Auditor*': a pro-Bute, anti-Pitt periodical which ran from 1762–3, edited by Arthur Murphy (1727–1805).

60.21–2. '*North-Briton*': Wilkes's anti-Bute periodical which ran from 1762–3.

61.20–1. 'brother PAMPHLET in the *Upholsterer*': in Murphy's play, *The Upholsterer; or, What News?* (1758), Peter Pamphlet explains his ambidexterity in publishing both flattering and libellous reviews of the same person: 'Whitewash and blackball'.

63.6–7. 'candid declarations in his first number': i.e. the following quotation from *The Auditor.*

64.11–65.24. 'Duke of Cumberland ... Counsellor Jones': *North Briton* supporters in the left-hand column listed as being 'honoured with abuse' by Murphy and *The Auditor* (not included in the Biographical Appendix) are: William Wildman, second Viscount Barrington (1717–93); Frederick the Great (1712–86), King of Prussia from 1740; John Butler (1717–1802), later Bishop of Hereford, who penned an anonymous pamphlet attacking Bute entitled *An Address to the*

Cocoa Tree from a Whig (3 editions in 1762); Thomas Nuthall (d. 1775), lawyer who acted for Pitt on occasion, on whose behalf he consulted with the Duke of Newcastle in 1762 on how to bring about Bute's downfall; Arthur Beardmore, attorney who worked for Earl Temple (*HWC*); Charles Say, Almon's former employer, publisher of *The Gazetteer*; Charles Macklin (or Melaghlin, MacLaughlin; *c.* 1699–1797), actor; Edmond Hoyle (1671/2–1769), writer on card games, said to have been a barrister by profession; Arthur Pond (1701–58), artist and printseller; John Arthur (*c.* 1708–72), actor who performed in Samuel Foote's *The Devil upon Two Sticks* at the Haymarket in 1769; possibly Edward Jones (*fl.* 1771–1840), who was elected councillor for life in 1781; *Auditor* supporters in the right-hand column listed as being 'honoured with abuse' by Wilkes and *The North Briton* (not included in the Biographical Appendix) are: Augusta, Princess Dowager of Wales; John Campbell, fourth Earl of Loudoun (1705–82); George Henry Lee, third Earl of Lichfield (1718–72), politician, supporter of Bute; the Earl of Talbot's horse, which backed its rear end towards George III at his coronation, an embarrassment which Wilkes relayed to *North Briton* readers; Alexander Montgomerie, tenth Earl of Eglinton (1723–69); Richard Rigby (1722–88), MP who assisted the Duke of Bedford during the Treaty of Paris negotiations in 1763; Sir John Philips, Baronet, Tory who applied to George III for Shebbeare's pension of £200 in 1764; Samuel Touchet (*c.* 1705–73), merchant, MP and Bute supporter whose Manchester business collapsed in 1763, but was spared bankruptcy through parliamentary privilege; John Home (1722–1808), Bute's private secretary from 1757 to 1763 and recipient of a £300 pension from George III; John Burton (1696–1771), Church of England clergyman who attacked Wilkes in his encaenia oration of 1763 and was in turn satirized in Charles Churchill's *The Candidate* (ll. 716 ff.) in 1764, rather than Dr John Burton (1710–71), the supposed model for Dr Slop in *Tristram Shandy*; William Whitehead (1715–85), appointed Poet Laureate in 1757 upon the death of Colley Cibber and attacked by Charles Churchill in *The Ghost*, book III.

66.18–19. '*Peachum*': a character from Gay's *Beggar's Opera* who keeps track of his accounts from his gang of thieves in a black böok.

66.26–67.1. 'Mr. *Fitzpatrick*': Richard Fitzpatrick (1748–1813), army officer, politician and poet, whose anonymous ballad, *The Bath Picture*, was published in 1771. His uncle, the fourth Duke of Bedford, helped him to win the Okehampton election in 1770. He was a close friend of Charles James Fox and Stephen Fox's brother-in-law. His elder brother, John Fitzpatrick (1745–1818), Baron Upper Ossory, was MP for Bedfordshire, 1767–94.

67.14. 'Partridge ... Bickerstaff': John Partridge (1644–1715), astrologer whose premature death Swift satirically recounted in *The Accomplishment of the First of Mr. Bickerstaff's Predictions* (London, 1708).

67.28. 'hermaphrodites': 'an animal uniting two sexes' (Johnson).

68.3. 'Sir Anthony Branville': comic role played by David Garrick in *The Discovery* (1763) by Frances Sheridan (1724–66).

68.9. 'prince Volscius': parodic character in the 1672 play, *The Rehearsal*, by the Duke of Buckingham *et al.*, whose dilemma at falling in love at first sight with Parthenope is manifested in his stomping around on stage with one boot on. Amaryllis and Cloris exclaim simultaneously, 'How! Prince Volscius in love? Ha, ha, ha!' (III.v), a line which William Congreve makes Lady Froth repeat twenty-two years later in *The Double-Dealer* (IV.vi).

68.24–5. 'ALBUS *an* ATER *homo sit, nescio*': adapted from Catullus's Poem 93, 'Nil nimium studeo, Caesar, tibi uelle placere, nec scire utrum sis albus an ater homo': 'I have no very great desire to make myself agreeable to you, Caesar, nor to know whether your complexion is light or dark'.

69.7–16. 'Duke of Grafton ... Paul Whitehead': Names in the 'CHALK' column (not included in the Biographical Appendix) are: William Henry Cavendish-Bentinck, third Duke of Portland (1738–1809), Rockingham Whig (1762–82) and Prime Minister (1783; 1807–9); Thomas Prowse (1707–67), MP, 'a leading Tory', according to Horace Walpole (*HWC*, vol. 17, p. 385n.); Edward Popham (*c.* 1711–72), compiler of *Selecta poemata Anglorum Latina* (1774), MP for Wiltshire (1741–72) who voted with the opposition in 1768 (Namier). Names in the 'CHARCOAL' column (not included in the Biographical Appendix) are: Sir Armine Wodehouse, Baronet (*c.* 1714–77), Tory MP for Norfolk from 1737 who supported Bute and was defeated in 1768 (Namier); Sir Charles Mordaunt, sixth Baronet (*c.* 1697–1778), Tory MP for Warwickshire (1734–74) who supported the Grenville administration and voted against repealing the Stamp Act in 1767 (Namier); Welbore Ellis, first Baron Mendip (1713–1802), MP for Aylesbury (1761–8) and Petersfield (1768–74) who succeeded Sir Charles Townshend as Secretary at War (1762–5), supported the Grenville administration and voted against repealing the Stamp Act (Namier); James Oswald (1715–69), MP for Dysart Burghs (1754–68) and Scottish member of the Treasury Board whose cousin Richard Oswald made more than £125,00 from government contracts during the Seven Years' War; Richard Grosvenor, first Earl Grosvenor (1731–1802), who supported Bute's peace proposals in the House of Lords; Bamber Gascoyne (1725–91), who turned down a seat on the Board of Trade in 1762 from Bute, but accepted one the following year from Grenville on terms of independence, declaring himself to be a Pitt supporter.

70.18. 'bantlings': 'a little child: a low word' (Johnson, who cites Prior's use of the word: 'They seldom let the *bantling* roar, / In basket, at a neighbour's door'; synonymously with 'foundling').

70.21. 'pratlers': i.e. noisy ducklings.

71.6–7. '*Note of a Passage in Mr.* Churchill's Candidate': Charles Churchill's *The Candidate* was published by William Flexney, George Kearsly, C. Henderson, J. Coote, J. Gardiner, John Almon and A. Moran in May 1764. A truncated version of this note appears in *The Correspondence of the Late John Wilkes*, ed. John Almon, 5 vols (London: Richard Phillips, 1804–5), vol. 3, pp. 60–3. Some translations below have been taken from Sir Francis Dashwood, *The Dashwoods of West Wycombe* (London: Aurum Press, 1987).

71.8. 'Medmenham Abbey': early meeting place for the Knights of St Francis of Wycombe, better known as the Hell-Fire Club, founded by Sir Francis Dashwood, eleventh Baron Le Despencer (1708–81).

71.9–16. 'Whilst womanhood ... excise': *The Candidate*, ll. 695–702.

71.11. 'A nation's reckoning, like an alehouse score': Although club members liked to joke that Dashwood could scarcely tally up a round of drinks, Bute appointed him as his Chancellor of the Exchequer on 29 May 1762.

71.12. '*Paul* the aged': Paul Whitehead (1710–74), the Club secretary, also satirized in Churchill's *The Ghost* (1762), *The Conference* (1763) and *Independence* (1764).

72.1–2. 'Sir F— D— ... P—l W—d': Dashwood, Sir Thomas Stapleton, fifth Baronet Stapleton (1727–81), MP, Whitehead.

72.15. 'Eleusinian mysteries': bacchanalian rites (see *NFHW*, 1: 46.17).

72.19. '*Bona Dea*': good goddess.

72.20–1. '*sit mihi fas audita loqui*': 'may I be allowed to tell what I have heard?' (Virgil, *Aeneid*, VI.266); used by Addison as the epigraph to *Spectator* no. 31 (5 April 1711).

72.23–4. 'Rabelais' Abbey of THELEME, *Fay ce que vous voudras*': the abbey Gargantua builds at the opening of *Gargantua and Pantagruel* (1534). The Thelemites' only commandment, 'Do what you like', is adapted as a licentious motto from St Augustine's more pious advice to 'Love God and do what you like'.

72.25. '*Aude, hospes, contemnere opes*': 'Dare, my guest, to scorn riches' (Virgil, *Aeneid*, VIII.364).

72.26. 'Harpocrates': the Egyptian god Harpa-Khruti, Horus the child, represented as a naked boy sucking his finger whom the Greeks made a god of silence and secrecy.

73.1. 'Angerona': Roman goddess of silence (see *NFHW*, 1: 45.28).

73.6–7. '*Ici pâma ... heureux*': 'Here the happiest of mortals died of joy' (Dashwood, *The Dashwoods of West Wycombe*, p. 31). This and the following two quotations are from Jean de La Fontaine, 'La fiancée du roi de Garbe' (adapted from Boccaccio), *Contes et nouvelles en vers* (1664).

73.8–9. '*Mourut un amant ... sa dame*': 'a lover dies on the bosom of his lady'.

73.9–11. '*En cet endroit ... rendus*': 'in this place a thousand kisses of fire were given and a thousand others returned'.

73.12. '*Hic satyrum naïas*': 'Here the vanquished naiad overcame the conquering satyr', Dashwood, *The Dashwoods of West Wycombe*, p. 31 (original source not given).

73.17–19. '*Hic locus est ... Tartara mittit*': ''Tis here, in different Paths, the way divides: / The right, to *Pluto*'s Golden Palace guides; / The left to that unhappy Region tends / Which to the depth of *Tartarus* descends' (*Aeneid*, VI.540; trans. Dryden, VI.726–9).

73.22–4. '*Ite, agite, O juvenes ... conchæ*': 'Go into action, you youngsters; put everything you've got into it together, both of you; let not doves outdo your cooings, nor ivy your embraces, nor oysters your kisses', Dashwood, *The Dashwoods of West Wycombe*, p. 31 (original source not given).

74.1–2. '*and in his hand a reed … fire*': 'A Seraph stood, and in his hand a reed / Stood waving tipt with fire', Milton, *Paradise Lost*, VI.579–80.

74.4–6. 'PENI TENTO *non* PENI TENTI': to touch his penis, not feel guilty.

74.8. 'Trophonius's cave': In Greek mythology Trophonius disappeared into a cave in Boeotia, which subsequently became a shrine. Cult worshippers, upon descending into the cave, were frightened for their lives, but then allowed to forget their horror after drinking from the waters of Lethe. Later, priests tormented worshippers by making them drink from the waters of Mnemosyne, which made them recall their horrendous experience.

74.15. 'Cloacine': toilet.

74.18. '*Æquè pauperibus … nocebit*': Horace, *Epistles*, I.25–6, 'aeque pauperibus prodest, lucupletibus aeque, aeque neglectum pueris senibusque nocebit': '[That task, which as we follow, or despise,] / The eldest is a fool, the youngest wise: / Which done, the poorest can no wants endure, / And which not done, the richest must be poor' (Pope, *TE*, vol. 4, p. 281); the motto of *The Spectator*, no. 27 (31 March 1711).

74.24. '*goddess without eyes*': Angerona (see 73.1 above and *NFHW*, 1: 45).

74.n. 'Omne animal … fornicantem': Galen, 'Triste est omne animal post coitum': 'Every animal is sad after coitus'. Aristotle says, 'Omne animal post coitum est triste'; to which an anonymous author has given the following exception, 'praeter gallum gallinaceum, et sucerdotem gratis fornicantem', 'with the exception of the cock of the cocks and free office of a fornicating priest'. A book of Aristotle opened at 'Omne Animal Post Coitum Triste' appears on the floor after an amorous night in Hogarth's *After* (1736).

75.1. 'poured libations': '[Dashwood] shall pour, from a Communion Cup, / Libations to the Goddess without eyes, / And Hob or Nob in Cyder and excise', *The Poetical Works of Charles Churchill*, ed. Douglas Grant (Oxford: Clarendon Press, 1956), p. 369; ll. 700–2.

75.5. '*Mr.* W—s': Wilkes.

75.6. '*The* TEMPLE *of the* MUSES': the Grecian Temple at Stowe (see *NFHW*, 1: 73n.).

75.14. 'Armstrong': Dr John Armstrong, whose *Art of Preserving Health* was published in 1744 (see Biographical Appendix).

76.18. '*To* LAURA': this does not appear as the name of a mistress in Peter D. G. Thomas's *John Wilkes: A Friend to Liberty* (Oxford: Clarendon Press, 1996).

77.4. '*Daphnis*': son of Hermes, credited with writing the first pastoral poetry to his beloved shepherdess Chloe.

77.5. '*Miss* W—': Mary Wilkes, known as Polly, was born in 1750 and went to school in France.

78.11. '*Prison*': Wilkes was sentenced to two years in King's Bench Prison from 14 June 1768.

79.15. '*Schoolfellows at* Eton': Carlisle met Charles James Fox and William Wentworth Fitzwilliam, second Earl Fitzwilliam (1748–1833), who attended Eton from 1756 to 1764.

79.18. 'St. John': Frederick St John, second Viscount Bolingbroke (1732–87), who attended Eton, with a possible allusion to Henry St John, first Viscount Bolingbroke, to whom Pope dedicated *An Essay on Man* (1734).

80.8. 'Buccleugh': Henry Scott, third Duke of Buccleuch (1746–1812), whose mother married Charles Townshend in 1755 and who was sent to Eton in 1757.

80.19. 'Tully': Cicero.

80.24. 'Legge': William Legge, second Earl of Dartmouth (1731–1801), politician.

81.1. 'Ophaly': one of the FitzGeralds of Mount Ophaly, County Kildare.

81.10. 'Henry's lofty towers': Henry VI founded Eton College in 1441.

81.21. 'Storer': Anthony Morris Storer (1746–99), Etonian, politician and collector.

82.22–3. '*An* EPITAPH ... Thomas Winnington': Williams's friend Thomas Winnington died suddenly in April 1746.

83.15. 'GRAND CATHOLICON': relating to alchemy, in this case the mystical ingredients needed to create a minister.

84.8. 'Pelham': Henry Pelham (1694–1754), Prime Minister (1743–54).

84.14. 'force or fraud obtains': 'For when Success a Lover's Toil attends, / Few ask, if Fraud or Force attain'd his Ends', Pope, *Rape of the Lock*, II.33–4 (*TE*, vol. 2, p. 161).

85.6–7. '*Jam satis ... misit Pater*': 'TOO long alas, with Storms of Hail and Snow, / *Jove* has chastis'd the World below', Horace, *Odes*, I.2.1–2, trans. Arthur Maynwaring, *Odes and Satyres of Horace* (London: J. Tonson, 1717).

86.5. 'Coke upon Littleton': a standard law text; Sir Edward Coke's commentary on the *Tenures* of Sir Thomas Littleton (*c.* 1422–81), published in 1628, long the principal authority on law of real property; mentioned by Fielding in *Tom Jones*, book 3, ch. 3, p. 128.

87.2–4. 'Duke of G— ... — PARSONS': the Duke of Grafton, who was elected Chancellor of Cambridge University in 1769, and his mistress, Nancy Parsons. See 41.7.

88.6. 'T. P.': Thomas Potter.

89.13. '*On the Run of* ROMEO *and* JULIET': originally published in the *Daily Advertiser* on 12 October 1750. From 28 September, theatre-goers had a choice of two productions: John Rich's at Covent Garden and David Garrick's at Drury Lane. 'The "Battle of the Romeos", the most famous theatrical duel of the century, lasted for twelve successive performances, and by the second week in October, the town was sick and tired of it' (Ian McIntyre, *Garrick* (London: Penguin, 1999), p. 175). Garrick, who played Romeo, is said to have won.

89.17. '*Ah! pox on both your houses*': echoing Mercutio's dying curse, 'A plague o' both your houses' (*Romeo and Juliet*, III.i.91, 99, 106).

89.18–19. '*Notes on Mr.* Churchill'*s ... B— of* G—': Wilkes's notes to Charles Churchill's poem, 'The Dedication', addressed sardonically to William Warburton, Bishop of Gloucester (1698–1779), intended to preface an edition of Churchill's – more likely a compilations of his father's – *Sermons* (London: John Churchill and William Flexney, 1765). 'The Dedication' was left unfinished at Churchill's death, ending in three rows of asterisks and the phrase 'Cetera Desunt' (hence 'Fragment'). Calling it 'a virulent libel', the *Monthly*

Review reprinted 'The Dedication' in 1765 (33, pp. 101–9). See *Poetical Works*, pp. 429–35, 557–8. Wilkes's '*Notes*' were either unavailable or unwritten until Wilkes returned from his exile in 1768. The Bodleian Library's MS. Eng.lett.c.572, ff. 174–81, is a privately printed copy of these '*Notes*' with most of the blank names filled in and with substantive changes.

89.20. 'In the Manner of Mr. WILKES': these '*Notes*' are, in fact, by Wilkes according to his *Correspondence*, vol. 3, pp. 65–84.

89.21–2. 'THERE is nothing … this fragment': Wilkes parodies Warburton's editorial fulsomeness, e.g., the first footnote to Pope's *Epistle*, I.6: 'To Murray', begins: 'This piece is the most finished of all his imitations, and executed in that high manner the Italian painters call *con amore*' (Pope, *Works*, ed. William Warburton, 9 vols (London: J. and P. Knapton *et al.*, 1751), vol. 4, p. 124).

90.11. 'Mrs. W—': Gertrude Warburton (see *NFHW*, 1.11).

90.13. '*uxorius amnis*': uxorious flood (Horace, *Odes*, I.2.16).

90.15–17. 'uniformly join'd … *his* – mind': 'Thy Life and Doctrine uniformly join'd, / And flowing from that wholsome source thy mind', 'The Dedication', ll. 63–4 (*Poetical Works*, p. 432).

90.18. 'I ask no favour, not one note I crave': 'The Dedication', l. 13 (*Poetical Works*, p. 431).

90.20. 'Nor soul-gall'd *bishop* damn me with a note': Churchill's *The Candidate*, l. 144 (*Poetical Works*, p. 354).

90.21. 'My mortal journey done': 'The Dedication', l. 17 (*Poetical Works*, p. 431).

90.24. 'Thane's deputies': Bute's ministers.

91.1–3. 'Mr. Churchill … fever at Boulogne': Churchill's body was brought back to England and buried on 13 November 1764 in St Martin's churchyard, Dover. According to *ODNB*, his grave-stone was inscribed with a line from *The Candidate*: 'Life to the last enjoy'd, *here* Churchill lies'.

91.2. 'miliary fever': 'a fever that produces small eruptions' (Johnson).

91.14–16. 'Amico jucundo … merito' : 'Jocund friend, acrid poet, best citizen in a true country' (Latin).

91.19–20. 'In spirit … a bribe': 'The Dedication', ll. 24–5 (*Poetical Works*, p. 431).

91.21. 'lord H—': Holland.

91.23. 'Ayliffe's Ghost': John Ayliffe, Henry Fox's steward and agent, was executed at Tyburn for forgery in 1759. Churchill's proposed poem, 'Ayliffe's Ghost', was advertised in the *London Chronicle*, 2–5 April 1763, but it never appeared. See *NFHW*, 5: 79.

92.3. 'Let thy own offspring all thy fortunes share': 'The Dedication', l. 27 (*Poetical Works*, p. 431).

92.6–8. 'No husband, tho' he's truly wed … No father': Churchill, 'The Duellist', III.789–91 (*Poetical Works*, p. 283).

92.9–10. 'By mistaken kings … misplaced': 'The Dedication', ll. 38–9 (*Poetical Works*, p. 432).

92.13. 'secretary of state': the Earl of Sandwich.

92.14. 'steward of the houshold': Lord Talbot.

92.15. 'Mr. — the peerage': Henry Fox.

92.20–1. '— the —': George III.

92.22–3. 'right honourable lord —': Holland.

92.24–5. 'Thy open front ... lie': 'The Dedication', ll. 47–8 (*Poetical Works*, p. 432).

93.2–3. '*lætos oculis honores ... purpureum*': adapted from 'lumenque iuventae purpureum et laetos oculis adflarat honores', i.e. where Aeneas appears with 'the rosy light of youth and happy charms upon his eyes' (Virgil, *Aeneid*, I.589–91), which Dryden translates as 'His Rosy-color'd Cheeks, his radiant Eyes' (I.992).

93.25–6. '*how meek ... christian*': mocking Warburton's style.

93.27. '*Oh! what a grace ... brow*': 'See what a grace was seated on this brow', Hamlet on the image of his father (III.iv.54).

94.5. '*Potter*'s earth': using a clay analogy to suggest that Thomas Potter was the biological father of Ralph Allen Warburton (1756–75).

94.7. 'F— lord H—d': Fox, Lord Holland.

94.9. 'though the soul still sits at squat': from Pope, 'And ev'ry child hates Shylock, tho' his soul / Still sits at squat, and peeps not from its hole' ('Epistle to Cobham', ll. 55–6, 114–15; *TE*, vol. 3.ii, p. 22), which Pat Rogers notes as 'sitting in a squatting position', *The Oxford Authors: Alexander Pope* (Oxford: Oxford University Press, 1993), p. 656.

94.14. 'Mr. M—': Charles Macklin (*c.* 1699–1797), one of the best known tragic actors of the eighteenth century. According to *ODNB*, 'His origins and early years have been the subject of myth, speculation, and biographical fantasy'.

94.16. 'Mr. Quin': James Quin (1693–1766), one of the best known comic actors of the age, who often was at odds with Macklin and Garrick. Quin once put Warburton in his place by reciting some lines for Allen's benefit from Otway's *Venice Preserved*: 'Honest men / Are the soft easy cushions on which knaves / Repose and fatten' (*Oxford Book of Literary Anecdotes*, ed. James Sutherland (Oxford: Oxford University Press, 1975), p. 71.

94.17–18. '*Sir, if that fellow ... legible hand*': Fielding offers up Quin's physiognomical quip in *A Voyage to Lisbon*, part II.

94.19–23. 'Those sheep ... shou'd stray': 'The Dedication', ll. 76–8 (*Poetical Works*, p. 433).

95.4–5. 'Much did I wish ... Pope': 'The Dedication', ll. 85–6 (*Poetical Works*, p. 433).

95.8. 'duke of Chandos': James Brydges, first Duke of Chandos (1673–1744). For the satirical portrait and debate surrounding the identification of the 'puny insect, shiv'ring at a breeze!', see Pope's 'Epistle to Burlington', ll. 99–168, and F. W. Bateson's appendix, 'Timon and the Duke of Chandos' (*TE*, vol. 3.ii, pp. 142–8, 164–8).

95.13–16. 'a report ... done to me': quoted from Pope's letter to Burlington, 7 March 1731, in *Works*, ed. Warburton, vol. 8, pp. 194–5; see *The Correspondence of Alexander Pope*, ed. George Sherburn, 5 vols (Oxford: Clarendon Press, 1956), vol. 3, pp. 265–6 (here dated [January 1731/2]).

95.20–3. 'Another age shall see ... land': 'Epistle to Burlington', ll. 173–6 (*TE*, vol. 3.ii, p. 149).

95.24–96.1. 'Had the poet … filled': Warburton's footnote in *Works*, vol. 3, pp. 288–9.

96.2. 'Cannons': Brydges bought Cannons, his first wife's estate, after her death in 1712 and employed Vanbrugh and other leading architects in its renovation. Lord Burlington approved; Pope evidently did not.

96.17. 'I had no great cause to wonder': see 95.13 (Pope's letter to Burlington, *Works*, vol. 8, p. 194; *Correspondence*, vol. 3, p. 266).

97.16. 'Mr. Pitt': On 26 November 1763, at the height of the Wilkes debate in parliament, Warburton wrote to Ralph Allen that Pitt 'said that "as to that impious Man, who occasioned the dispute, and had blasphemed God & the King, he [Wilkes] ought to be thrust out of the House" and then thrust out his crouch [crutch] in the action of a man driving a noxious animal from him' (*PLL*, p. 154).

97.17. 'Duke of Newcastle': Newcastle was a long-time correspondent and patron of Warburton, who secured the deanery of Bristol for him in 1757. Warburton attempted to reconcile Newcastle with Pitt.

97.20–1. 'Might, like himself … quote a W—': 'The Dedication', ll. 111–12 (*Poetical Works*, p. 434).

97.25. 'Mr. Edwards': Thomas Edwards (d. 1757) ridiculed Warburton's edition of Shakespeare in *A Supplement* (London: M. Cooper, 1748), which he expanded and renamed *The Canons of Criticism* for the third edition (London: C. Bathurst, 1750).

98.4–5. 'Ev'n in a bishop … a heart': Pope, 'Dialogue II', ll. 70–1 (*TE*, vol. 4, p. 316). Thomas Secker (1693–1768), Bishop of Bristol (1734) and Oxford (1737), Archbishop of Canterbury (1758). Thomas Rundle (1687/8–1743), Bishop of Derry (1735).

98.6–13. 'These words … wisdom and virtue': Warburton's footnote, *Works*, vol. 4, pp. 323–4 (*TE*, vol. 3.ii, p. 149).

98.21–2. 'Virtue she finds too painful … for ever': Pope, 'To a Lady', ll. 163–4; *Works*, vol. 3, p. 205.

99.1. 'b— of Oxford': Secker.

99.3–5. 'decency is too often … defects of the mind': 'the very essence of gravity was design, and consequently deceit … it was no better, but often worse, than what a *French* wit had long ago defined it, – *viz. A mysterious carriage of the body to cover the defects of the mind*', Laurence Sterne, *The Life and Opinions of Tristram Shandy, Gentleman*, ed. Ian Campbell Ross (Oxford: Oxford University Press, 1983), p. 23; book 1, ch. 11.

99.15–16. 'Let humble Allen … fine it fame': Pope, 'Dialogue I', ll. 135–6, *Works*, vol. 4, p. 312, with a long and some might think fulsome footnote to his virtual father-in-law.

99.22–3. '*low born Allen*': the original wording Pope had in 1738. Pope explains the change to 'humble' in a letter to Allen dated 2 November 1738 (*TE*, vol. 4, p. 308n.; *Correspondence*, vol. 4, p. 145).

100.1. 'quaker-pride': referring to Allen's industry and success rather than his religion (he was an Anglican).

100.4. 'And Potter trembles even in his grave': 'The Dedication', l. 140 (*Poetical Works*, p. 434). Thomas Potter died in 1759.

100.6. 'late archbishop': John Potter (1673/4–1747), Archbishop of Canterbury from 1737.

100.12. 'parliament': Thomas Potter was MP for St Germans, Cornwall (1747–54), Aylesbury (1754–7) and Okehampton (1757–9).

100.20. 'when he was with good Mr. Allen': Potter stayed at Prior Park at various times between 1754 and 1758. Benjamin Boyce notes that Warburton went to London for two months from October 1754, leaving his wife and Potter behind in Prior Park, at which time Potter wrote to Wilkes of his intention of seducing Mrs Warburton (*The Benevolent Man: A Life of Ralph Allen of Bath* (Cambridge, Massachusetts: Harvard University Press, 1967), pp. 222–3).

101.1–4. 'liv'd with sinners ... kept not pace': 'The Duellist', III.727–30 (*Poetical Works*, p. 282).

101.6. 'race of infidelity': nothing in Warburton's biography indicates that he was inclined towards either infidelity or blasphemy.

101.8. 'This gentleman': Potter.

101.11. 'postmaster of Bath': Ralph Allen (1693–1764), patron of Pope and Fielding, who modelled Squire Alworthy in *Tom Jones* after him.

101.11–12. 'episcopa nephew': misprint for 'episcopal', referring to Warburton.

101.13. 'niece': Gertrude (*née* Tucker; 1727–96), whom Warburton married in 1746 (see *NFHW*, 1: 10).

101.15. 'Tom was vastly wild': 'The Duellist', III.783–4 (*Poetical Works*, p. 283).

101.22–3. 'not named after his father': i.e. Thomas Potter.

101.26. '*Ralph, Ralph*': after Ralph Allen.

102.1–4. 'With all the conscious ... to be true': 'The Dedication', ll. 141–4 (*Poetical Works*, p. 434).

102.5. 'what passed in the — of —': House of Lords where, on 15 November 1763, Warburton, Bishop of Gloucester, spoke against Wilkes as the alleged author of *An Essay on Woman* (the obscenity-ridden parody of Pope's *Essay on Man*, to which Warburton's name had been appended as the editor). For Warburton's version of events, see his four letters to Ralph Allen between 16 November and 1 December 1763 (*PLL*, pp. 150–5).

102.8. 'b— of p—': breach of privilege.

102.24–5. 'notes on Shakespeare and Pope': Warburton's editions of Shakespeare (London: J. and P. Knapton, 1747) and Pope (London: J. and P. Knapton *et al.*, 1751) both met with severe receptions from various critics.

103.5. '*I beg the devil's pardon*': Warburton is reported to have said, 'the blackest fiends of hell would not keep company with [Wilkes]', adding that he 'begged Satan's pardon for comparing them together' (quoted in Adrian Hamilton, *The Infamous Essay on Woman; or, John Wilkes Seated between Vice and Virtue* (London: André Deutsch, 1972), p. 118). Thomas writes, 'The Bishop of Gloucester gave intemperate vent to his feelings by denouncing Wilkes as worse than Satan' (*John Wilkes*, p. 42).

103.15. 'treatise upon Grace': *The Doctrine of Grace: or, The Office and Operations of the Holy Spirit Vindicated from the Insults of Infidelity, and the Abuses of Fanaticism*, 2 vols (London: A. Millar, and J. and R. Tonson, 1763).

103.18. 'B—': Bute.

103.20. 'Pitied himself, in turn had pitied you': 'The Dedication', l. 150 (*Poetical Works*, p. 435).

103.22. 'Lord of G— is to be pitied': actually Warburton's footnote modifying a note by Scriblerus begins, 'Seriously, *my Lord of Ely* was to be pitied', 'Epistle to Augustus' (Epistle II.i), l. 385, *Works*, vol. 4, p. 197.

104.1. 'But you, my Lord, renounced attorneyship': Warburton practised law in Newark from 1719 to 1723 before entering the clergy.

104.9–10. 'What can I now ... better guide': Pope, *The Dunciad*, I.199–200, *Works*, vol. 5, p. 101, referring to dramatist John Fletcher (1579–1625).

104.15–16. 'But what can I ... (once my better) *guide*': this couplet appears in the 1728 *Dunciad*, I.189–90, with the note as given (*TE*, vol. 5, p. 85); referring to the Roman satirist Horace (Quintus Horatius Flaccus) or Persius (Aulus Persius Flaccus).

104.19. 'Cibber': Colley Cibber, Poet Laureate whom Pope enthroned as the new king of the Dunces, replacing Lewis Theobald, in the 1743 revision.

104.22–4. '*low-born, cell-bred ... lightened dress*': *The Dunciad*, II.356 and 354 respectively, *Works*, vol. 5, p. 167 (Pope's text reads 'lengthen'd dress'); 'flamen' is a priest (Rogers (ed.), *Alexander Pope*, p. 649, note to *Essay on Man*, vol. 3, p. 265).

105.3–4. 'vile attornies': 'And vile Attorneys, now an useless race', 'Epistle to Bathurst' ('Moral Essay', III), l. 274, *Works*, vol. 3, p. 247.

105.8. 'Allen's Will': Allen died on 27 June 1764. There is no evidence to suggest that Warburton exerted a baleful influence over Allen's will. The Allens were childless, Gertrude was known to be his favourite niece, and Allen signed a codicil within hours of his death bequeathing £1,000 to William Pitt; Warburton, who had helped his wife's uncle with acquiring books, was the recipient of his library, which re-united the titles Pope had split between Allen and Warburton in 1744 (Boyce, *The Benevolent Man*, pp. 290–3).

105.10. 'Doctor, Dean, Bishop, Gloster, and my Lord': 'The Dedication', l. 163 (*Poetical Works*, p. 435), with reference to 'Dean, Drapier, Bickerstaff, or Gulliver!', Pope's *Dunciad*, I.18 (*TE*, vol. 5, pp. 62, 270 (l. 20)).

105.12–13. 'simple title of *doctor*': Both Pope and Warburton were to be awarded honorary degrees by Oxford in 1741, but when the proposal for Warburton's DD was withdrawn, Pope declined his LLD in solidarity with his new-found defender. Warburton was eventually awarded a Doctor of Divinity by the Archbishop of Canterbury, Thomas Herring, in 1754. Pope's letter to Warburton dated 12 August 1741 declares, 'I have received some chagrin at the delay of your Degree at Oxon ... I will be doctor'd with you, or not at all', *Works*, vol. 9, pp. 341–2.

105.20. 'b—k of G—': bishopric of Gloucester.

105.21. 'princess': Princess Amelia stayed with the Allens at Prior Park when taking the waters at Bath for deafness (Boyce, *The Benevolent Man*, who credits Pitt with obtaining Warburton's promotion, pp. 205–6, 253; and *PLL*, pp. 58–9).

106.1. '*Poetical Description of a* GREAT FUNERAL': a song about George II, who expired on his water closet after taking his morning chocolate on 25 October 1760. 'What an enviable death!' Horace Walpole exclaimed, later noting the Duke of Newcastle's emotional display at the funeral in Westminster Abbey on 11 November 11: 'He fell into a fit of crying the moment he came into the chapel and flung himself back in a stall, the Archbishop hovering over him with a smelling bottle, but in two minutes his curiosity got the better of his hypocrisy and he ran about the chapel with his glass to spy who was or was not there, spying with one hand and mopping his eyes with t'other. Then returned the fear of catching cold, and the Duke of Cumberland, who was sinking with heat, felt himself weighed down, and turning round, found it was the Duke of Newcastle standing upon his train to avoid the chill of the marble' (*HWC*, vol. 21, pp. 442–4; *ODNB*).

106.8. '—'s': king's.

106.9. 'd—': duke.

106.4. 'politick whore': Lady Yarmouth, George II's mistress, was amply looked after with a bequest of £6,000 along with an additional 2,000 guineas from George III.

107.10–11. 'k— c—'d': king crowned.

107.16. 'm—'d old P—': mitred old peer.

107.19. 'B— P—': possibly Baron Pelham.

107.24. 'F—': possibly Fox.

108.2. 'T—': possibly Townshend.

108.6. 'Pr—d': possibly Prebend.

108.21. 'St. P—': Westminster Abbey is the officially the Collegiate Church of St Peter.

108.22. 'Sir Isaac': presumably Newton, who was buried in Westminster Abbey, who sat on the commission to supervise the completion of St Paul's.

109.2. 'Old —': possibly Thomas, i.e. Newcastle.

109.10. 'V— … B—': Viscount … Baron.

109.18. 'half crowns and twelvers': A crown was worth five shillings; and twelver was 'a coin worth twelve pence' (*OED*).

109.24. 'Harry's chapel': Henry VII's Chapel.

109.25. '—': Frederick Cornwallis, the Archbishop of Canterbury.

110.8–10. 'CHARLES TOWNSHEND': Townshend (1725–67) married Lady Caroline Scott (1717–94) at her estate of Adderbury, Oxfordshire, in 1755.

110.24. 'savine': Johnson has 'savin. A tree'; 'a small bushy evergreen shrub' (*OED*).

111.9. '*Earl* Delawarr': see Biographical Appendix.

111.14–15. 'Miss Wrottesley … Boscawen': Queen Charlotte's maids of honour named here are: Mary Wrottesley (1761–9), Diana Beauclerk (1761–1809), Charlotte Keck (1761–74), Frances Meadows (1761–8) and Anne Boscawen (1764–88).

113.1. 'Lord Harcourt': Simon Harcourt, first Earl Harcourt (1714–77), served as Chamberlain ('without a vice') from 1763 to 1768, at which time he was appointed British ambassador to Paris.

113.19. '*posts*': ministerial positions.

114.1. 'DUCHESS *of* RUTLAND': If Chesterfield wrote this early on, he could be praising Bridget (*née* Sutton; 1699–1734), wife of John Manners, third Duke of Rutland (1696–1779).

114.16. 'P—y': William Pulteney, Earl of Bath (1684–1764), a political ally of Chesterfield.

115.1. '*On the Banishment of* CICERO': Marcus Tullius Cicero (106–43 BC), the Roman orator and consul, was exiled by the tribune Clodius in 58 BC.

115.2. '*by the Duke of* Wharton': Francis Atterbury (1663–1732), Bishop of Rochester from 1713, was exiled as a Jacobite conspirator and served as the Old Pretender's secretary of state in France.

117.15. '*Lord* CAPEL': Arthur Capel (1604–49), first Baron Capel of Hadham, royalist soldier imprisoned in the Tower of London in 1649 and beheaded. Also attributed to Sir Roger L'Estrange.

117.18. 'Boreas': the north wind.

118.1. 'Nereus': old god of the Mediterranean Sea.

118.9. 'anchoret': 'A recluse; a hermit; one that retires to the more severe duties of religion' (Johnson).

119.10. 'margarite': 'A pearl' (Johnson).

119.13. 'Retir'dness': 'Solitude; privacy; secrecy' (Johnson).

119.23. 'Jason': probably comparing an attack on the mythic leader of the Argonauts to a more recent assassination attempt.

122.7. '*Verses*': also called 'The Lie', *c.* 1592, 'now accepted as his [Raleigh's] by most, but not all, scholars' (*ODNB*).

126.7. 'ennobl'd Thief': Henry Fox, Lord Holland.

126.10. 'Ayliffe's ghost': see *NFHW*, 5: 17.

126.13. 'Scottish Thane': Bute.

126.14. 'r— lust': for Augusta, Dowager Princess of Wales.

126.25. '*Catera desunt*': 'the rest is missing' (Latin).

127.3. 'Golconda': a fortress in the south of India near Hyderabad.

129.16. 'at Eton *School*, 1729': George Lyttelton (1709–73) had already enrolled at Oxford by 1726, but references to school-mates Charles Wyndham, born in 1710, and William Pitt, born in 1708, suggest this verse was composed on a return visit.

130.11. 'LUCIAN': Syrian-born author (*c.* AD 117–180) of such satires as *Dialogues of the Dead*.

130.14. 'begirt': see 'Begird': 'To surround; to encircle; to encompass' (Johnson).

130.15–17. 'John o'Nokes ... John o'Stiles': typical property owners.

131.18. 'Seven days to labour': Sunday shopping, eighteenth-century style.

132.2. 'laylocks': obsolete or dialect form of 'lilacs' (*OED*).

132.6. 'white-thorn': 'a species of thorn' (Johnson). (Cowslip or primrose is cited but not defined by Johnson.)

132.9. 'osier': 'a tree of the willow kind ...' (Johnson).

132.16. 'Vaux-hall': the pleasure gardens opened in 1660 on the south bank of the Thames for music, dancing and fireworks.

132.17. 'cits resort to Sadler's-wells': some Londoners flock to the popular spa in Islington.

133.5. 'Bellona': Roman goddess of war.

133.12. 'Cyrus, or Darius': both Cyrus II (d. 529 BC) and Darius I (548–486 BC) were known as 'the Great' for extending the Persian empire.

133.18. 'Sophi': Sophi I was a Shah of Persia from 1628–41 and Sophi II from 1666–94.

135.13. 'B— the a—y': Bob the attorney? Robert Walpole (1650–1700) and Mary (*née* Burwell; 1654/5–1711), parents of the Prime Minister, were prominent in Houghton, Norfolk. In 1712 Walpole was found guilty by a majority of the Commons of 'a high breach of trust and notorious corruption' (*ODNB*) and spent a brief spell in the Tower. He launched an attack against the Peace of Utrecht and foreign policy in *A Short History of the Parliament* (London: T. Warner, 1713). He replaced Sunderland as First Lord of the Treasury in 1721.

135.21. 'Horace's treaties': Horatio Walpole (1678–1757), first Baron Walpole of Wolterton, who helped negotiate the 1729 Treaty of Seville.

136.5. '*Art of Coquetry*': Charlotte Lennox's poem appeared in *Poems on Several Occasions* (London: S. Paterson, 1747) and was reprinted in *GM*, 20 (1750), pp. 518–19. A thirty-two-line excerpt beginning 'First form your artful looks with studious care' (138.13) appears in Roger Lonsdale (ed.), *Eighteenth-Century Women Poets: An Oxford Anthology* (Oxford: Oxford University Press, 1989), pp. 222–3.

141.1. '*On the Death of* YORICK': the parson descended from Hamlet's dead jester in *Tristram Shandy* whose death is mourned with a black page (book 1, ch. 12).

141.17. 'poor Maria': 'Poor Maria ... is sitting upon a bank playing her vespers upon her pipe, with her little goat beside her', *Tristram Shandy*, book 9, ch. 24.

142.1. '*Epitaph on Mr.* QUIN': Garrick's epitaph on his co-star James Quin (1693–1766) was composed for his monument in Bath Abbey.

143.14–15. '*L'Homme qui ... trouvera jamais*': 'The man who cannot find himself and will never find himself', coined by Charles de Saint-Evremond (1610–1703), a French wit who fled to England in 1661 and became Charles II's keeper of the ducks in St James's Park.

144.18. '*An* INSCRIPTION': in *A Collection of Poems in Four Volumes. By Several Hands* (London: G. Pearch, 1770), vol. 4, pp. 261–2; possibly by Michael Wodhull (1740–1816). Ham Walks was across the Thames from Pope's villa in Twickenham.

149.4. '*Gens de bien*': 'good people' (French).

149.13. 'Fielding': Sir John Fielding, the novelist's half-brother, who was a Bow Street magistrate.

150.17. 'Friseur': hairdresser.

150.23. 'Vat be de matter': mimicking a French accent.

150.25. 'Ragou': or ragout, 'meat stewed and highly seasoned' (Johnson).

150.26. 'drudger': or dredger: 'a box with a perforated lid for sprinkling powder over anything' (*OED*).

151.2. 'spitted': roasted on a spit.

151.3. 'Janton': possibly Janeton Auretti, a dancer who performed at Drury Lane from 1748 to 1754 (*LDG*, vol. 1, p. 187n.).

151.10. 'Maitre Trotte': perhaps one who trots around, or John Trott-Plaid, Henry Fielding's nom-de-plume for the *Jacobite's Journal*.

151.14. '*quelles barbares ... Anglois*': 'what barbarians, what fools the English' (French).

152.1. '*Fripon, poltron*': 'rogue, coward' (French).

152.22. '*degagé*': 'casual' (French).

153.6. 'Scandalum magnatum': 'giant scandal' (Latin).

153.10. '*habeas corpus*': 'A writ, the which, a man indicted of some trespass, being laid in prison for the same, may have out of the King's Bench, thereby to remove himself thither at his own costs, and to answer the cause there' (Johnson).

155.3. 'Temple beau': title of a play by Henry Fielding performed at Goodman's Fields in 1730.

155.15. 'Ned Shuter at Whitefield's': Edward Shuter (*c.* 1728–76), the colourful actor who sought salvation at George Whitefield's Methodist tabernacle in Tottenham Court Road.

155.26. 'hollow': see holla, 'to shout; to hoot' (Johnson).

156.1. 'TEMPORA MUTANTUR': '... et nos mutamur in illis', 'Times change and we change with them', Ovid, *Epistulae ex ponto*, IV.10.

156.3. 'Grafton': As Prime Minister, the Duke of Grafton refused to allow his former friend Wilkes to hold a seat in parliament as the member for Middlesex, even though he had been elected three times.

156.7. 'Wildman's': the opposition's Club.

156.10. 'With Temple, and with Wilkes was seen': 'In May 1763, following Temple's lead, he [Grafton] attempted to visit John Wilkes in the Tower, an action significant not only as evidence of his association with Temple, but also because of the sentiments which prompted him to go ...' (*ODNB*).

157.4. 'And Wilkes again be free': Wilkes was released in April 1770.

158.20. '*Her R— H— the P. D. of W.*': perhaps a misguided attempt to appeal to Princess Augusta as a patron. Cunningham had published *A Poetical Essay, In Manner of Elegy, on the Lamented Death of ... George II* (Newcastle: R. Marchbank *et al.*, [1760]) with little success.

159.1. '*Lines to Mr.* WILKES': Lloyd died on 15 December 1764 in the Fleet prison.

159.19. 'Great G—': George I, who made the second of his six return visits to Hanover in 1719.

159.20. 'concubine': possibly Melusine von der Schulenburg, one of the mistresses George I brought to England.

160.10. 'phiz': 'the face, in a sense of contempt' (Johnson).

161.1. '*An* ODE *upon the present Period of Time*': the late 1760s.

161.2. '*By the Author of the Ode to Lord C—m*': the author of 'To Lord C[hatha]m. An Ode', in *NFHW*, 1: 118, is anonymous.

161.20. 'Grenville': George Grenville (1712–70).

164.12. 'Alike have stabbed her breast': see frontispiece to *NFHW*, 2.

164.22. 'B—df—ds': Bedfords.

165.19. 'Quintus': perhaps Quintus Sertorius (d. 72 BC), Roman general and politician who led the Iberian revolt against their Roman occupiers.

166.16. 'Townly to Fletcher': Francis Towneley (1709–46) and George Fletcher (d. 1746) were executed as rebels after the Jacobite Rising; theirs were the last heads to be displayed on the spikes of Temple Bar.

167.8. 'Eddy B—': Edward Bangham, politician and Thomas Harley's father-in-law.

167.9. 'Charley': Prince Charles Edward Stuart.

167.10–11. 'W—s, and H—l—y': Wilkes and Thomas Harley (1730–1804), politician and banker.

167.17–18. 'The man that seiz'd petticoat, gibbet, and boot': Bute.

167.19. 'woundy': 'Excessive. A low bad word' (Johnson).

168.14. 'Mac Quirk': Edward McQuirk, 'an experienced election hooligan' whose followers intimidated voters at the Brentford polls in 1768; later convicted, along with Laurence Balse, of the murder of Wilkite lawyer George Clarke (Thomas, *John Wilkes*, p. 88).

169.15. ''Change': the Royal Exchange, London's centre of commerce and finance in Cornhill.

Part 4

5.1–13. 'MR. GARRICK ... VERSES': see Biographical Appendix for David Garrick. A comic poem about a visit the Garricks made in 1768 at the invitation of the Earl of Warwick where they were offered light refreshment and a book, but no dinner.

5.14. 'Warwick's kind earl': Francis Greville (1719–73), created first Earl Brooke of Warwick Castle in 1746.

5.n. 'One or two persons': Garrick may have taken his wife and a family member.

6.5. 'Guy's pot': cooking utensil of legendary hero, Guy of Warwick, which ironically contains nothing of sustenance for the hungry narrator.

6.13. 'hist'ry of Greville and Brooke': possibly a privately printed family history; nothing readily emerges from the *ESTC*. Fulke Greville, first Baron Brooke (1554–1628), poet, biographer of Sir Philip Sidney (1652) and author of *Remains* (London: H. Herringham, 1670).

6.18. 'AN INSCRIPTION': dated 1768, Garrick continues the theme of the above *Verses*.

6.19. 'Neville': Richard Neville, Earl of Warwick (1428–71), known as 'Kingmaker' during the War of the Roses.

6.25. '*This earl*': Francis Greville (1719–73), created first Earl Brooke of Warwick Castle in 1746.

6.27. 'book': see 6.13 above.

7.1. 'NATURE AND GARRICK': a dialogue between Garrick and personified Nature, who comically maintains Shakespeare plagiarized her works.

7.22. 'EXTEMPORE': General James Wolfe was killed during the British capture of Quebec in 1759, an event commemorated in the heraldic painting by Benjamin West. Henry Fox, first Baron Holland, led Bute's government and was commonly thought to have taken bribes to expedite the Treaty of Paris in 1763. According to *ODNB*, 'His reputation plummeted, both because he abandoned all care for his public image and because his residual ambitions made him appear sufficiently dangerous to be worth blackening'.

8.1–4. 'ODE … CHANCELLOR OF THE UNIVERSITY OF CAMBRIDGE': Otherwise known as *Ode for Music*, this was performed at the installation of the Duke of Grafton as Chancellor on 1 July 1769. Grafton served as Prime Minister from 1768 to 1770. Thomas Gray (1716–71) was appointed Regius Professor of Modern History at Cambridge in 1768 with some help from Richard Stonehewer, the Duke of Grafton's secretary. As Gray died in 1771 (the same year this part of *NFHW* appeared), he may not have known that his *Ode* would run parallel with its 'Travestie' and be followed by 'Another' (p. 18). Gray's 'Ode' and its parody appeared in *St James's Chronicle or British Evening Post* (11/15 July 1769).

8.8. 'Comus': In John Milton's 1634 masque, Comus, a shepherd, is the son of Circe and Bacchus. *Comus* was adapted in 1738 for the stage by John Dalton.

9.5. 'Wilkes': see Biographical Appendix for John Wilkes.

9.7. 'modern *Algernons*': an Old French name derived from *aux gernons* 'having a moustache'. Relatively modern ones include Algernon Sidney (1622–83), Algernon Seymour, seventh Duke of Somerset (d. 1750) and Algernon Percy (1750–1830).

9.8. 'Alcaic': a classical Greek poetic stanza, also used by Horace in his Latin *Odes*.

9.11. 'Philippic weeds': verbal attacks.

11.12. 'N—st—e': Thomas Pelham-Holles, Duke of Newcastle (see Biographical Appendix).

11.19. 'Camus': Latin name for Cambridge's river Cam.

11.22. '*Bute*': John Stuart, Earl of Bute, Tory Prime Minister from 1762–3. 'Northern light' refers to his native Scotland.

12.4–5. 'High Potentates … mitred fathers': referring to Cambridge benefactors mentioned in the following lines.

12.6. 'Great Edward': Edward III, founder of King's Hall, later incorporated in Trinity College. He added the fleur-de-lys of France to the arms of England, in consequence of his claim to the French throne.

12.7. 'Gallia': France.

12.8. 'sad Chatillon': Mary de Valentia, Countess of Pembroke, daughter of Guy de Chatillon, founded Pembroke College in 1343. Her husband had been killed in a tournament on their wedding day twenty years earlier.

12.9. 'princely Clare': Elizabeth de Burg, Countess of Clare, refounded University Hall as Clare Hall *c.* 1342.

12.10. 'Anjou's heroine': Margaret of Anjou, who founded Queen's College in 1448.

12.10. 'paler rose': Elizabeth Widville or Woodville, wife of Edward IV; as a member of the House of York, she was regarded as the paler rose. She added to the foundation of Queen's.

12.12. 'either Henry': Henry VI, who founded King's College, or Henry VIII, who was a great benefactor to Trinity College.

12.13. 'murdered saint': Henry VI.

12.13–14. 'majestic lord ... bonds of Rome': Henry VIII.

12.19. 'Granta': Latin name for Cambridge.

12.22. 'Fitzroy': see Biographical Appendix for Grafton.

13.6. 'Great G—': the Duke of Grafton (see 8.1 above).

13.8. 'W—y': Elizabeth Wrottesley, the Duke of Grafton's second wife.

13.9. 'B—d': possibly John Russell, fourth Duke of Bedford (1710–71), involved in the Treaty of Paris negotiations in 1762–3; he supported the Grafton administration, but without office, in 1767.

13.10. 'False M—ue': John Montagu, fourth Earl of Sandwich, former friend who turned against Wilkes in the 1763 *Essay on Woman* scandal.

13.13. 'm—l l—ds': possibly 'ministerial [as four syllables] lords' to fit the pentameter.

13.22. 'F—y': Fitzroy.

13.23. 'Camus': see 11.19 above.

14.12–16. 'Margaret ... Beaufort's grace': Lady Margaret Beaufort, mother of Henry VII, founded Christ's in 1505 and St John's in 1508. The Duke of Grafton was descended from Henry Fitzroy, an illegitimate son of Charles II, and therefore connected through Margaret Tudor, sister of Henry VIII and wife of James IV of Scotland, to the Tudors and Beauforts (see 8.1 above).

15.19. 'h—l—t': harlot.

16.9. 'Cecil': William Cecil, Lord Burleigh, minister to Elizabeth I and Chancellor of Cambridge.

16.19. 'Brunswick': the Hanoverians, who occupied the British throne after the death of Queen Anne in 1714.

18.14. 'stern-sy'd F—tz—y': i.e. stern-eyed Fitzroy.

19.3. 'N—t—n': Sir Fletcher Norton, first Baron Grantley (1716–89), Solicitor-General (1762); Attorney-General (1763); Speaker of the House of Commons (1770).

19.5. 'Sp—k—r': Arthur Onslow served as Speaker of the House of Commons from 1728–61; he was followed by Sir John Cust and then Sir Fletcher Norton.

19.15. 'N—ncy': Anne 'Nancy' Parsons, alias Mrs Houghton, with whom the Duke of Grafton had a well-publicized affair. He left his wife to live with her in 1764. Lady Grafton carried on affairs with the Duke of Portland and the Earl of Upper Ossory, with whom she eloped. Parsons's and Grafton's images were linked in 'The Female Pilot. A Prime Minister', *Town and Country Magazine* (March 1769), see Cindy McCreery, *The Satirical Gaze: Prints of Women in Late Eighteenth-Century England* (Oxford: Oxford University Press, 2004), p. 92.

19.21. 'N—th': Lord North.

19.22. 'Gr—nv—lle': Grenville, Earl Temple.

19.23. 'F—tzp—ck': Fitzpatrick.

19.24. 'D—nd—s': possibly Henry Dundas, first Viscount Melville (1742–1811), Solicitor-General for Scotland, 1766.

19.25. 'Dy—n': Jeremiah Dyson (1722–76), Edinburgh-educated Lord of the Treasury, 1768–74 (see 34.21 below).

19.25. 'B—ke': Edmund Burke (1729–97), MP for Wendover, 1765–74; his *Thoughts on the Present Discontents* (23 April 1770) criticized the government for censoring public opinion.

19.27. 'Ons—w': George Onslow, first Earl of Onslow (1731–1814), MP for Surrey, 1761–74. He opposed Wilkes's election as MP for Middlesex in 1769.

20.1. 'Sp—k—r': Speaker.

20.5. 'Tha—s D—tt—n': Thames Dutton, Surrey.

20.5. 'O—kh—m': Oakham, Leicestershire.

20.10. 'F—tz—y': Fitzroy.

20.18. 'D—nd—s': Dundas (see 19.24 above).

20.19. 'Cli—e': Robert Clive, Baron Clive (1725–74), who went from rags to riches in India, becoming Governor of Bengal in 1765; MP for Shrewsbury, 1760–74. Following a parliamentary inquiry, he became addicted to opium and committed suicide.

20.20. 'H—ll—d': Holland (see 7.22 above).

20.24. 'Gert—de': the Hon. Gertrude Leveson-Gower, wife of John Russell, fourth Duke of Bedford (see 13.9 above).

21.2. 'A R—ss—'s fire, a Wr—ttsl—y's grace': possibly Lady Caroline Russell (1743–1811), whom Queen Charlotte described as 'the proudest woman in England' (G. E. Cokayne, Vicary Gibbs, H. A. Doubleday *et al.* (eds), *The Complete Peerage of England, Scotland, Ireland, Great Britain and the United Kingdom* ..., new edn, 13 vols in 14 (1910–59), vol. 8, p. 500), and Elizabeth Wrottesley (see 13.8 above).

21.6. 'Newmarket': where horse races were (and still are) held.

21.8. 'White's': White's chocolate house, founded in 1693, in St James's Street. According to the first number of The *Tatler* (12 April 1709), it was the place of choice to go for '*All Accounts* of Gallantry, Pleasure, *and* Entertainment'. After the fire in 1733, which gamblers are oblivious to in plate 6 of Hogarth's *Rake's Progress* (1735), it moved next to St James's coffee house. It became a private club from 1755.

21.20. 'N—ncy': Anne 'Nancy' Parsons, Grafton's mistress (see 19.15 above).

22.2. 'S—rt': Stuart.

22.3. 'horrors of the axe': referring to the execution of Charles I.

22.4. 'SHAKESPEARE'S FEAST': a parody of Dryden's 1697 poem, 'Alexander's Feast' (beginning ''Twas at the royal feast, for Persia won / By Philip's warlike son'), attributed to George Steevens, *Public Advertiser* (5 August 1769), satirizing the Shakespeare Jubilee at Stratford in 1769 organized by Garrick. Reprinted in the *St James's Chronicle* (7 June 1800), which noted: 'The following Parody, on Dryden's celebrated Ode, was the production of the late celebrated George

Steevens: It was occasioned by the Shakspeare Jubilee, at Stratford upon Avon, in the year 1769; and appeared in one of the periodical publications of that day'.

22.24. 'bard of FERNEY': i.e. Voltaire, who bought the chateau of Ferney near Geneva in 1758 and moved there in 1761 (replacing Timotheus, Alexander the Great's music teacher, in Dryden's original).

23.3. 'G—K': Garrick.

23.4. 'LITCHFILD': Lichfield, which Samuel Johnson left with his star pupil Garrick in 1737 to make their names in London.

23.6. 'RICHARD's crooked form': Shakespeare's *Richard III*, in which Garrick starred at Goodman's Field in 1741.

23.11. 'HASTINGS': Garrick played the role of Hastings in Nicholas Rowe's *Jane Shore* (1743–55; 1758–73).

23.11. 'PRITCHARD': Hannah Pritchard (1711–68) starred opposite Garrick for two decades from 1747 at Drury Lane.

23.13. 'DRUGGER': Abel Drugger was the ambitious tobacconist, a role played by Garrick, in Ben Jonson's *The Alchemist*.

23.16. 'A present SHAKESPEARE': referring to Garrick as an actor and playwright.

24.20. 'TYBURN': place of execution in London.

24.22. 'deer-stealer': one of the legends surrounding Shakespeare's early years.

25.7. 'Pactolian': referring to the Pactolus river in ancient Lydia, famous for its golden sands.

25.10. 'bard of FERNEY': Voltaire (see 22.24 above).

25.17. 'Sillabub': 'curds made by milking upon vinegar' (Johnson). Now 'syllabub': 'a dessert made of cream or milk flavoured, sweetened, and whipped to thicken it' (*OED*).

26.4. 'b—t': burst.

26.17–18. 'See the volumes ... curl hair': suggesting that the pages Voltaire's critics fill are useful only for tearing out for hair-curlers. See, for example, Hogarth's *Marriage A-la-Mode*, plate 4 (1745), 'The Levee', which shows a dandy with paper curlers in his hair.

26.25. 'Clare-court, Drury-lane': theatre district where book stalls carried unsold volumes of criticism.

27.1. 'CLOACINA's abode': suggesting that critics' pages should also be recycled as toilet paper.

27.4. 'CAPEL's edition': Edward Capell's ten-volume edition of Shakespeare was published in 1768. The rhyme for 'hit on' I leave for the discerning reader to figure out.

27.7. 'H—l—y': Robert Henley, first Earl of Northington (*c.* 1708–72), Lord Chancellor, 1761; a close friend of George III.

27.8. 'North Briton': Wilkes's journal, whose forty-fifth number caused a major furore in 1763.

27.9. 'G—K': Garrick.

27.13. 'ON THE BIRTH-DAY OF SHAKESPEARE': traditionally 23 April 1564.

27.14. 'CENTO': 'a composition formed by joining scraps from other authors' (Johnson).

27.17–18. 'Natura ipsa valere … spiritu afflari': 'strong by nature herself and stirred by the strength of his own mind and inspired, as it were, by divine spirit / breath, so to speak', Cicero defending Archias, his old teacher and poet, *Pro Archia*, I.18.

28.6. 'To hold thy mirror up': 'for any thing so o'erdone is from the purpose of playing, / whose end, both at the first and now, was and is, to hold, / as 'twere, the mirror up to nature', Shakespeare, *Hamlet*, III.ii.19–22.

28.20–1. 'What a piece … infinite in reason': 'What a piece of work is a man! / how noble in reason! how infinite in faculty!', *Hamlet*, II.ii.303–4.

28.26. 'To the last syllable of recorded time': 'To-morrow, and to-morrow, and to-morrow, / Creeps in this petty pace from day to day, / To the last syllable of recorded time', *Macbeth*, V.v.19–21.

28.28–9. 'For if we take him … like again': 'He was a man, take him for all in all, / I shall not look upon his like again', *Hamlet*, I.ii.187–8.

29.1. 'ODE TO COLONEL L—': Henry Lawes Luttrell, second Earl of Carhampton (1743–1821), soldier and MP for Bossiney (1768–9 and 1774–84). Even though he lost against Wilkes in the 1768 Middlesex election, the House of Commons declared Luttrell the victor, thus infuriating voters.

29.2–3. 'Quis novus … pectore & armis!': 'Who is this stranger guest come to our house? / How confident he looks, how strong his chest and arms!', Virgil, *Aeneid*, IV.11–12.

29.7. 'Alcides': one of Hercules's epithets. As a son of Zeus by Alcmena, wife of Amphitryon, he was sometimes called Alcides, after Alcaeus, father of Amphitryon.

29.13. 'G—ft—n': the Duke of Grafton, who often enjoyed horse racing, was a founding member of the Jockey Club, established in 1752 with its racecourse at Newmarket.

29.17. 'M—d': possibly William Murray, first Earl of Mansfield (1705–93), lawyer; Attorney-General, 1754; Lord Chief Justice and created baron, 1756; he reversed Wilkes's outlawry because of a technical error, and imposed a sentence of twenty-two months as well as a fine.

29.17. 'H—d': Lord Holland (see 7.22 above).

29.19. 'N—rt—n': Sir Fletcher Norton (see 19.3 above).

29.20. 'Henley': John 'Orator' Henley (1692–1756), who preached from a 'gilt tub', as Pope mentioned in the *Dunciad* (II.2; *TE*, vol. 5, p. 96).

29.20. 'Ryder': Sir Dudley Ryder (1691–1756), knighted, 1740; Solicitor-General, 1733; Attorney-General, 1737; Lord Chief Justice of the King's Bench, 1754. See his 'Epitaph' on p. 65 below.

30.2. 'G—ft—n': the Duke of Grafton (see Biographical Appendix).

30.5. 'Fl—tch—r': Sir Fletcher Norton (see 19.3 above).

30.17. 'p—': pox, venereal disease.

30.18. 'miss —': generic bisyllabic girl's name, e.g. Fanny.

30.22. 'patriot Glynn': John Glynn (1722–79), Serjeant-at-Law, 1763, who defended Wilkes and worked with him when he became MP for Middlesex, 1768–79.

30.23. 'Burke': see 19.25 above.

31.13. 'B—df—d': Bedford (see 13.9 above).

31.16. 'R—gby': Richard Rigby (1722–88), MP who accompanied the Duke of Bedford to Ireland as his secretary in 1758; he opposed Wilkes in 1769.

31.20. 'vet'ran Bullface': Sir Fletcher Norton's nickname was 'Sir Bull-face Double Fee'.

31.22. 'Billingsgate': London fishmarket.

32.2. 'Bl—cks—e': Sir William Blackstone (1723–80), judge, MP for Westbury, Wiltshire (1768). His published lectures, the *Commentaries on the Laws of England* (4 vols, 1765–9), became the standard reference on English law. When Blackstone opposed Wilkes's right to hold his elected seat in parliament, George Grenville cited Blackstone's own grounds for disqualification in the *Commentaries* to contradict his reasons.

32.3. 'Th—rl—e': Edward Thurlow (or Thurloe), first Baron Thurlow (1731–1806), Solicitor-General, 1770; Attorney-General, 1771; Lord Chancellor, 1778.

32.4. 'N—s': Sir George Nares (1716–86), judge, MP for Oxford, 1768; Justice of Common Pleas, 1771.

32.5. 'M—rt—n': Samuel Martin, Secretary to the Treasury (with Dyson; 1762–3), who wounded Wilkes in a duel in 1763.

32.7. 'D—nning': John Dunning, first Baron Ashburton (1731–83), Solicitor-General, 1768–70; elected Whig MP for Calne, 1768, 1774 and 1780. Author of *Inquiry into the Doctrines lately Promulgated concerning Juries, Libels, &c.* (1764); he opposed the growing influence of the crown.

32.7. 'Y—rke': Charles Yorke.

32.11. 'W—rb—rn': Alexander Wedderburn, first Baron Loughborough and first Earl of Rosslyn (1733–1805). He supported Wilkes in 1769, attacked the North administration in 1770, but returned to the Tory fold in 1771 when he was appointed Solicitor-General.

32.15. 'Mungo': Jeremiah Dyson's nickname.

32.16. 'Cl—re': Sir Thomas Pelham-Holles was also first Earl of the third creation of Clare (see 11.12 above).

32.19. 'W—ym—th': Thomas Thynne, third Viscount Weymouth (1734–96), Secretary for Northern Department under Grafton; instrumental in suppressing the Wilkes riots in 1768; he left office in 1770 over the Falkland Islands dispute with Spain.

32.19. 'B—rr—gt—n': William Wildman Barrington, second Viscount Barrington (1717–93), Secretary at War, 1765–78.

32.23. 'G—ft—n': the Duke of Grafton (see 8.1 above).

33.1. 'Allen's fall': William Allen was killed at the St George's Fields 'massacre' in 1768.

33.5–6. 'Admit the sword … Stuart reign'd': referring to the English Civil War to oust Charles I.

33.8. 'Charles's age': reign of Charles I, from 1625, ending with his execution in 1649.

33.19. 'DARGO': the name appears in James Macpherson's 1760 Ossian 'discovery': 'They killed mighty Dargo in the field: Dargo who never fled in war', *Fragments of Ancient Poetry collected in the Highlands of Scotland, and translated from the Gaelic or Erse Language.*

34.1. 'ON MR. SECRETARY BRADSHAW': Thomas Bradshaw was secretary to the Treasury with Grey Cooper from 1766–70. On 29 January 1770, Bradshaw was pensioned off at £1,500 per annum.

34.2. 'caprich': Johnson doubles 'caprice' (from the same word in French) and 'caprichio' (from the Spanish 'capricho'), meaning 'freak; fancy; whim; sudden change of humour', in the 1755 *Dictionary*; by 1771 this would seem an affectation.

34.12. 'Aye, there's the question': a variation on Hamlet's 'To be, or not to be, that is the question' (III.i.55).

34.21. '*Jerry Dyson*': see 19.25 above.

34.23. 'Nimming Ned': a member of Macheath's gang in John Gay's *Beggar's Opera* (1728) whose talent lies in stealing goods from burning buildings. Nimming is slang for stealing.

35.10. '*sinecure*': 'an office which has revenue without any employment' (Johnson).

35.12. 'as one would an apple': possibly quoted from a report on the ease of accepting money.

36.6. 'Chloe': a generic female name, usually linked with her young lover Strephon. 'Cloe' is used by Pope in *Of the Characters of Women: To a Lady* (1735), l. 157. For Henry William Bunbury's satirical sketch of an aged Strephon and Chloe, engraved and published by J. Bretherton (1772), see McCreery, *The Satirical Gaze*, p. 220.

36.7. 'St. Thomas': i.e. 21 December, the winter solstice, the joke being, the newly wedded bride will have the longest night of the year to enjoy her honeymoon.

36.12. '*Luttrell ... Wilkes*': see 29.1 above.

36.14. 'K—': King.

36.n. '*l—d C—m*': William Pitt, first Earl of Chatham (1708–78): see Biographical Appendix.

37.10. 'G—ft—n': the Duke of Grafton (see 8.1 above).

37.16. 'Dowdeswell': William Dowdeswell (1721–75), MP for Worcester, 1761–75; Chancellor of the Exchequer, 1765–6.

37.n. 'Ille robur & æs duplex. HOR.': 'for him [there was] oak and bronze twofold', a variation on Horace's *Odes*, I.3: 'Illi robur et aes triplex circa pectus erat ...'.

38.4. 'Sp—k—r': Speaker (of the House of Commons).

38.10. 'B—r—gt—n': Barrington (see 32.19 above).

38.11. 'De G—y the old, and Fox the young': William de Grey, first Baron Walsingham (1719–81), Attorney-General, 1766–71, Chief Justice of Common Pleas, 1771–80; and Charles James Fox (1749–1806), elected MP for Midhurst at age nineteen and appointed junior Lord of the Admiralty by Lord North, 1770.

38.13. 'P—l—ms—n ... Cl—re': Henry Temple, second Viscount Palmerston (1739–1802), MP for Southampton, 1768–74, Lord of the Admiralty, 1766; for Clare see 32.16 above.

38.14. '*Mungo*': Dyson (see 32.15 above).

38.15. 'Th—r—oe': Thurlow (see 32.3 above).

38.17. 'R—g—y': Rigby (see 31.16 above).

38.19. 'E—l—t': Sir Gilbert Elliot, third Baronet of Minto (1722–77), MP for Roxburghshire, 1765–77; Treasurer of the Navy, 1770. His 'broad and strong' accent would have been lowland Scots.

38.20. 'J—k—s—n': Richard Jackson (d. 1787), politician, 1770.

38.22. 'Ellis and St—ge': Welbore Ellis, first Baron Mendip (1713–1802), MP for Weymouth intermittently between 1747–84, Secretary at War, 1762–5; and Sir John Strange (1696–1754), Solicitor-General, 1737–42, and Master of the Rolls, 1750–4.

38.23. 'O—sl—w': Onslow (see 19.5 above).

39.1. 'Priam's son': Hector.

39.4. 'Swiss': the Swiss had an army for hire.

39.7. 'G—ft—n': Grafton.

39.10. 'W—m—th': Weymouth (see 32.19 above).

39.10. 'Richmond's duke': Charles Lennox, third Duke of Richmond (1735–1806), soldier, Secretary of State for the southern department (1766–7).

39.11. 'S—dw—ch': Sandwich (see 13.10 above).

39.12. 'Rockingham and Camden': Charles Watson-Wentworth, second Marquis of Rockingham (1730–82), dismissed as premier of a coalition ministry in 1765 after repealing the Stamp Act and opposing general warrants; leader of the opposition in the House of Lords, 1768–81, Prime Minister, 1782. Charles Pratt, first Earl Camden (1714–94), Attorney-General under Pitt, 1757; as Chief Justice of Common Pleas, he found in the case of Wilkes in 1763 that general warrants were illegal and in 1765 that the Stamp Act was unconstitutional; he was Lord Chancellor 1766–70.

39.13. 'p—rs': peers.

39.16. 'M—sf—d': Mansfield (see 29.17 above).

39.17. 'M—hm—t': Hugh Hume, third Earl of Marchmont (1708–94).

39.18. '*Erse*': the Gaelic language.

40.4. 'Hurlo-Thrumbo': Samuel 'Maggoty' Johnson (1691–1773) of Cheshire starred as Lord Flame in the 1729 production of his play *Hurlothrumbo: or The Supernatural*, which ran for thirty nights at the Haymarket Theatre and was satirized by Fielding in *The Author's Farce*. Not in the *OED*, it is listed in *Roget's International Thesaurus* (1922) under 'object of fear' along with other dreadfuls like bugbear, Gorgon, hobgoblin, ogre and *bête noire*.

40.5–6. '*base-born* electors of Westminster': italicized slurs evidently refer to adverse comments made by Thomas de Grey, MP for Norfolk; see similar phrases in 'Impromptu', p. 44 below.

40.17. '*pastoral poem*': i.e. 'Cindaretta'.

41.1–2. 'CINDARETTA, A MOCK-PASTORAL': this was published in *The Middlesex Journal* (3 February 1770).

42.n. 'H—e of C—s': House of Commons.

43.18. 'Pinn'd on her nims': nimb is a halo (*OED*); perhaps a cant phrase for trying to look one's best.

43.19–20. 'The busy sylphs … her hair': a parody of 'The busy *Sylphs* surround their darling Care; / These set the Head, and those divide the Hair' (Pope, *Rape of the Lock*, I.145–6; *TE*, vol. 2, pp. 157–8).

43.26. 'Now trips a Goddess … a cook' : a parody of 'Now trips a Lady, and now struts a Lord' (Pope's portrait of Sporus in *An Epistle to Dr. Arbuthnot*, l. 329; *TE*, vol. 4, p. 119).

44.7. 'centry': misprint for 'sentry'.

45.2. '—': king; 'the Lie' descends the social ladder in each verse.

45.5. 'Heh's': misprint for 'he's'.

47.11–12. 'MRS. CORNELLY': Theresa Cornelys (1723–97), dancer and singer; she hosted balls and masquerades at Carlisle House, Soho Square, 1760–72, and concerts, 1764–72.

47.13. '*M—y*': Majesty.

47.14. 'L—d N—': Lord North.

47.16. '*Q*—, Ceres': Queen; Ceres is the Roman goddess of the harvest.

47.17–18. '*D— of Gl—r* … Benedick': Duke of Gloucester; Benedick is Beatrice's sparring partner in Shakespeare's *Much Ado about Nothing.*

47.19–20. '*D— of Cum—d* … Paris': Duke of Cumberland; Paris is Helen's kidnapper in the *Iliad*, or the hapless courtier in *Romeo and Juliet.*

47.21. 'P—ss D—r of *W—es*': Princess Dowager of Wales.

47.23. 'D— of *North—d*, Trappolin': Sir Hugh Percy, originally Smithson (1712–86), created first Duke of Northumberland of the third creation in 1766, aligned with Bute; Lord-Lieutenant under Grenville, 1763–5; opposed Wilkes's election in 1768. As John Cannon notes, 'During the Wilkite riots of 1769 he was accused of hiring an election mob and threatened with a prosecution' (*ODNB*). Trappolin is the leading character in Sir Aston Cokain's *Trappolin Creduto Principe, or Trappolin Suppos'd a Prince* (1685), revised by Nahum Tate as *Duke and No Duke* (1693) and revived in 1758.

48.4. 'Miss *Van—t*': Miss Vansittart, an attendant of the Princess Dowager of Wales at whose house in Sackville Street her highness secretly met with the Earl of Bute (John Clarke, *The Life and Times of George III* (London: Weidenfeld and Nicolson, 1972), p. 60). Henry Vansittart (1732–70), the governor of Bengal, was married to Emilia Morse in 1754; they had five sons and two daughters. They returned to England in 1764. The name of Miss Vansittart appears between those of Arthur Vansittart, Esq., and Edward Vansittart, Esq., of Winchester, in the list of subscribers to Helen Maria Williams's *Poems* (London: T. Cadell, 1786); Elizabeth Carter included 'Mrs. Vansittart's Dream' in her *Memoirs* (London: Rivington, 1808).

48.6. 'L—y *Wald—e*': Maria Walpole (1736–1807) became Countess of Waldegrave upon her marriage to James Waldegrave, second Earl of Waldegrave, in 1759. Three years after his death in 1763, she married William Henry Hanover, first Duke of Gloucester.

48.8. 'D— of *Gr—n*': Duke (or duchess as cross-dressing jockey?) of Grafton.

48.9. 'L—y *Har—n* … Messalina': Lady Caroline Fitzroy (1722–84), the beautiful wife of William Stanhope (known as 'Peter Shambles'), second Earl of Harrington (1719–79) and friend of Horace Walpole, who said 'she had a very bad character'; Messalina was the unfaithful wife of the Emperor Claudius.

48.10. 'L—d *Lig—r*': John or Jean Louis Ligonier, first Earl Ligonier (1680–1770), French-born soldier in the British army; MP for Bath, 1748; created Earl Ligonier of Ripley, Surrey, in 1766, the same year he was promoted to the rank of field marshal.

48.11. 'Mr. *F—x*': Henry Fox.

48.12. 'L—d *Har—g—n*': second Earl of Harrington (see 48.9 above). His wife conducted an affair with George Townshend, fourth Viscount Townshend (*HWC*, vol. 30, p. 84; vol. 37, pp. 194, 196–7).

48.14. 'L—d *W—y—th*': Lord Weymouth (see 32.19 above).

48.15. 'L—y *Har—t Stan—e*': Lady Harriet Stanhope (1750–81); mentioned often in Horace Walpole's letters.

48.16. 'L—d *Mar—h*': William Douglas, third Earl of March (1724–1810), 'notorious for his escapades and dissolute life' (*DNB*); representative peer for Scotland, 1761; Vice-Admiral of Scotland, 1767–76; later satirized by Robert Burns.

48.18. 'L—d *Car—le*': Frederick Howard, fifth Earl of Carlisle (1748–1825), who succeeded to earldom in 1758; he was a friend of Charles James Fox.

48.19. 'L—d *Tal—t*': Lord Talbot, Lord High Steward, whose horse approached George III rump first at the royal coronation in 1761 (Clarke, *George III*, p. 32).

48.21. 'L—d *Hert—d*': Francis Seymour Conway (1719–94), created Earl of Hertford, 1750; Lord Chamberlain, 1766–82.

48.23. 'L—d *Per—y*': Sir Hugh Percy (see 47.23 above).

48.24. 'Sir *F—r Nor—n*': Sir Fletcher Norton (see 19.3 above).

48.25. 'Mr. *Rig—y*': Richard Rigby (see 31.16 above).

48.26. 'Mr. *Ver—n*': most likely, Richard Vernon (1726–1800), 'father of the turf', MP, and, like Grafton, a founding member of the Jockey Club. Alternatively Joseph Vernon (*c.* 1738–82), actor and singer at Drury Lane (1762–81).

48.29. 'D— of *D—*': William Cavendish, fifth Duke of Devonshire (1748–1811), who married Georgiana Spencer in 1774.

48.30. 'Col. *Lut—l*': Luttrell (see 29.1 above).

49.9. 'three brave sons of Mars': i.e. soldiers, rather than Romans.

50.1. 'For tho' daggers they speak': adapted from 'I will speak daggers to her' (*Hamlet*, III.ii.421).

50.16. 'battle of Bloomsbury-Square': the site of a duel (*HWC*, vol. 15, p. 180n.), possibly referring to Lord Mansfield's house, which may have been targeted during the Wilkes riots of 1768 (*HWC*, vol. 29, p. 57n.; vol. 35, p. 505), and was later burned in the 1780 riots.

51.9. 'beaver': i.e. a beaver hat.

51.13. 'BOBADIL': after the cowardly old braggart, Captain Bobadill, in Ben Jonson's *Every Man in his Humour* (1598). Also, a satire on 'Dr' John Hill, *Dr. Bobadil's Monody by Quinbus Flestrin* (what Lilliputians call Gulliver), which was published in 1752.

51.15. 'K—': king.

51.22. 'Ranelagh and Vauxhall': public gardens with evening entertainments.

53.11. '*eau de luce*': 'a medical preparation of alcohol, ammonia, and oil of amber, used in India as an antidote to snake-bites, and in England sometimes as smelling salts' (*OED*; used in *GM* in 1756).

53.22–3. 'they've black-ball'd George Selwyn and March': for Selwyn, see Biographical Appendix. For the Earl of March, see 48.16 above.

54.3. 'Foote's open ... Reynolds's paintings': the Haymarket theatre. Samuel Foote (1720–77), Oxford-educated actor who held the patent for a theatre in Westminster by way of compensation after losing his leg; he built new Haymarket in 1767, which he ran until 1777. Sir Joshua Reynolds was chosen as first president of the Royal Academy upon its opening in 1768.

54.7. 'Almack's': a London gaming club, founded in 1764, frequented by the Fox brothers, Charles James and Stephen, who won and lost fortunes overnight.

56.24. 'Sawney': derisive name for a Scot.

57.6. 'Bracken's balls': possibly connected to horseshoe expert, Henry Bracken (1697–1764), author of the much reprinted *Farriery Improved* (London: J. Clarke, J. Shuckburgh, 1737).

58.8. 'f—t': fart.

59.1. 'sizy': 'viscous, glutinous' (Johnson).

59.14. 'Hoyle': Edmond Hoyle's *Laws* was the ultimate authority over games of whist from 1760. In other words, parishioners are abandoning church for the gaming table.

60.10. 'Ch—dl—gh': Elizabeth Chudleigh, Countess of Bristol (1720–88), who secretly married Augustus John Hervey in 1744, lived with Evelyn Pierrepont, second Duke of Kingston in 1760, denied her earlier marriage in 1769, promptly married the duke, and was found guilty of bigamy by the House of Lords in 1776.

60.11. 'horners': adulterers; not Johnson's 'one that works in horn, and sells horns', but the *OED*'s 'one who cuckolds; a cuckold-maker', considered obsolete (last citation dated 1717 by Christopher Bullock, *Woman is a Riddle* (Dublin: Thomas Hume, *c.* 1717)).

60.16. 'felt': perhaps a misprint for 'fell'.

60.19. 'Outs and Ins': opposition and ruling parties; in the Whig-dominated century, the Tories were in power for less than a year under Bute in 1762–3; Lord North's Tory administration began its dozen years in power in 1770.

61.7. 'Jack Ketch': John Ketch (d. 1686), whose name became synonymous with the role of public executioner throughout the eighteenth century.

62.15. 'Churchill': Charles Churchill (see Biographical Appendix).

62.17. 'Macaulay': Catharine Macaulay (1731–91). The first of eight volumes of her *History of England* were published in 1763, completed in 1783.

62.21. 'Whitehead': Paul Whitehead (1710–74), satirical poet and member of the Hell-Fire Club; attacked by Charles Churchill.

62.23. 'ALLEN'S GHOST': see 33.1.

63.2. 'RISUM teneatis Amici?': 'spectatum admissi risum teneatis, amici?': Could you, my friends, if favoured with a private view, refrain from laughing?', Horace, *Ars Poetica*, l. 5, Loeb edn, trans. H. R. Fairclough.

63.10. 'P—t's': perhaps Parliament's.
63.18. 'M******S': perhaps Majesties.
63.20. 'c******': perhaps condemn.
63.22. 'K—gs': Kings.
64.1. 'ty***t': tyrant.
64.2. 'G—e': George.
64.4. 'a—se': arse.
64.5. 'TO THE LORD OF THE ISLE': by John Almon, according to the 1786 edition of *NFHW*, 3: 261.
64.6. 'Dabis, Improbe, Pænas': 'You will pay [for this], shameless [one]', Virgil, *Aeneid*, IV.386.
64.8. 'Thane': Bute.
64.13. 'Chatham doats, tho' Pitt was once a man': suggesting that gaining a title changed Pitt.
64.21. 'gordian knot': the Gordian knot could not be untied, so Alexander the Great cut it.
65.3. 'Abdiel': Abdiel appears in Milton's *Paradise Lost*, V.805, as one of the angelic seraphim who remains in God's service after Satan's rebellion.
65.8. 'Who loves a Brunswick, hates a Stuart reign': who enjoys freedom under the Hanoverian Georges rather than suffering under the royal prerogatives under Charles I.
65.n. 'Earl Temple': see 19.22.
65.17–18. 'SIR D—Y R—R': Sir Dudley Ryder (see 29.20 above).
66.17. 'Att—y G—l': Attorney-General.
66.23. 'M—l': perhaps Ministerial.
66.27. 'Ch—f J—e': Chief Justice.
67.2. 'Att—y': Attorney.
67.9. 'C—rt': Court.
67.n. 'Le—p's trial': Peter Leheup (d. 1774), an under clerk at the accession of George II, was investigated by the House of Commons for financial irregularities in connection with a lottery intended to raise funds to purchase the collection of Sir Hans Sloane for the British Museum in 1754, the last year in which Sir Dudley Ryder served as Attorney-General. Leheup was fined £1,000.
68.1. 'S—n': Sovereign.
69.1–2. 'ON A BLACK MARBLE … INNS OF COURT': the same verse (with slight changes in accidentals) appears under the title 'Written upon the Wall of Clements-Inn, when the Dial was put up which is supported by a black Slave in a kneeling Posture', in *The Merry-Thought: or, The Glass-Window and Bog-House Miscellany. Published by Hurlo Thrumbo*, 2nd edn (London: J. Roberts, *c.* 1733), part 2. Clement's Inn, an inn of Chancery from the reign of Edward II, was named after the Church of St Clement Danes. This verse was later reprinted in Vicesimus Knox's *Elegant Extracts* (London: Charles Dilly, 1784), and Leigh Hunt's *The Town: Its Memorable Characters and Events. St Paul's to St James's* (London: Smith, Elder, 1848), ch. 4.
70.6. 'Hecla': a volcano in Iceland which erupted in 1768.

70.7. 'Dan': deriving from 'dominus', Latin for 'lord', 'the old term of honour for men; as we now say *master*' (Johnson). *OED* adds, 'its modern affected application to poets appears to be after Spenser's "Dan Chaucer"'. See also the satiric 'Dan Homer', p. 159 below.

70.10. 'KITTY FISHER': Catherine Mary Fisher (or Fischer; *c.* 1738–67), well-known courtesan who later married John Norris of Benenden, MP for Rye, and was painted as Cleopatra by Reynolds *c.* 1759. See Marcia Pointon, 'The Lives of Kitty Fisher', *British Journal for Eighteenth-Century Studies*, 27 (2004), pp. 78–97; pp. 79–83. See also the Appendix of Satiric Texts about Kitty Fisher (pp. 93–4). Also, McCreery, *The Satirical Gaze*, pp. 86–99.

70.15. 'Peace, idiot man … yourself a fool': untraced.

71.2. 'Lord Egmont': Sir John Perceval, second Earl of Egmont (1711–70), allied with Frederick, Prince of Wales, 1748–9; MP for Bridgwater, 1754 and 1761; first Lord of the Admiralty, 1763–6, who resigned over disagreements with Pitt. He published several political pamphlets.

71.3. 'Jemmy Twitcher': a member of Macheath's gang in John Gay's *Beggar's Opera* whose name was applied to Sir Robert Walpole. To twitch meant to snatch (Johnson).

71.4. 'Earl of Chatham': William Pitt the elder.

71.7. 'Wilkes and Glynn': see 30.22 above.

71.8. 'John of Bute': see Biographical Appendix.

71.9. 'cod-smack': 'a vessel engaged in cod-fishing' (*OED*).

71.12. 'Arthur's or Almack's': two London clubs. Arthur's, in St James's Street, was established in 1765. For Almack's, see 54.7.

71.16. 'how': misprint for 'who'.

71.17. '*salique* law': Salic law, which forbids female succession to the throne, as applied by the French to deny Edward III's claim to their throne, based upon his maternal descent.

71.20. 'Miss Parsons': 'Nancy' Parsons (see 19.15 above).

72.2. 'Wilkes and Bute': see Biographical Appendix.

72.4. 'Sir Fletcher': Sir Fletcher Norton (see 19.3 above).

72.15. 'CHARLOTTE': George III's queen.

72.17. 'G—n': Grafton (see Biographical Appendix).

72.21. 'King—n': Kingston (see 60.10 above).

73.1. 'Har—n': Lady Harrington (see 48.9 above).

73.5. 'North—d': Elizabeth Seymour, Duchess of Northumberland (1716–76). For the duke, see 47.23 above.

73.10. 'Ch—d—s': Anne, Duchess of Chandos, formerly a chambermaid at the Pelican Inn in Newbury who, according to an 1870 article in *Notes and Queries*, was sold to Henry Bridges, second Duke of Chandos, by Jeffries the ostler, her first husband.

73.14. 'Mrs. P—t': William Pitt the elder married Hester Grenville, sister of Earl Temple and George Grenville in 1754. She was twenty-three years his junior. They had three sons, the second of whom was William Pitt the younger, and two daughters.

73.17. 'lady Sarah': Lady Sarah Lennox (1745–1826). George III was smitten with her before he married Charlotte. She was one of the queen's bridesmaids, and married Sir Charles Bunbury in 1762; they were divorced in 1776.

73.23. 'lady B—lb—ke': Lady Diana Spencer (1734–1808) married Frederick St John, second Viscount Bolingbroke, in 1757. They were divorced in 1768; she married Topham Beauclerk (with whom she had eloped) in the same year.

74.1. 'lady V—e': Frances Anne Vane, Viscountess Vane (1713–88), eldest daughter of Lord Barnard, Maid of Honour at court, and mistress of William Stanhope, Lord Hervey and the Prince of Wales, by whom she had a son.

74.5. 'Richmond's ranger': Bute was appointed Ranger of Richmond Park in 1761.

74.6. 'lady E—e': Lady Eyre, wife of Sir James Eyre (1734–99), who defended Wilkes against Wood in 1763; Chief Justice of Common Pleas, 1770.

74.13. 'Earl P—y': Sir Hugh Percy, Earl Percy (1742–1817), son of the Duke of Northumberland (see 47.23 above); MP for Westminster, 1763–76.

74.14. 'muckle': Scots for much or great.

74.17. 'lady P—y': Lady Percy, wife of Sir Hugh (see 47.23 above).

74.21. 'M—e, V—s, A—, and Lord C—k': perhaps Melville; Lady Elizabeth Villiers (d. 1782); Mary, Duchess of Ancaster (Mistress of the Robes, 1761); Edmund Boyle, seventh Earl of Cork and seventh Earl of Orrery (1742–98).

75.4. 'Bristol, York, or Durham': three of the more lucrative bishoprics.

75.5. 'V—si—t, St—h—e, A—er': perhaps Miss Vansittart (see 48.4 above); Lady Harrington (Stanhope; see 48.9 above); Lady Elizabeth Archer (1741–1801), parodied by Englefield (*HWC*, vol. 33, p. 500).

75.13. 'Old Can—y': Frederick Cornwallis, Archbishop of Canterbury (1713–83), confirmed in 1768.

75.14. ''tissicky old grunter': Johnson has for 'grunter', 'he that grunts'; 'tisical' and 'tisick', 'corrupted from phthisick', meaning 'Consumption; morbid waste'. (Possibly the origin of the phrase 'to get in a tizzy'?)

75.16. 'Kitty H—er': Elizabeth Catherine Hunter (d. 1795), daughter of Thomas Orby Hunter, MP and Lord of the Admiralty. She eloped with the Earl of Pembroke in 1762 and married Sir Alured Clarke in 1770.

75.17. 'Pem—e': Henry Herbert, tenth Earl of Pembroke (1734–94), general; Lord of the Bedchamber, 1769.

75.19. 'White's': a club (see 21.8 above).

75.21. 'Old lady Huntingdon': Selina Hastings, Countess of Huntingdon (1707–91), friend of the Wesleys and Whitefield; an active Methodist.

76.1. 'bishop Kitty': Kitty Hunter (see 75.16 above).

76.7. 'Sir George': Sir George Nares (see 32.4 above).

76.8. 'bishop Warren': John Warren, Bishop of Bangor (1730–1800).

76.11. 'Amphitrite': Greek sea-goddess, wife of Poseidon and mother of Triton.

76.13. 'Earl P—y's lady': Lady Percy.

76.14. 'Per terram et per mare': 'through earth and through sea' (Latin); perhaps a family motto.

76.16. 'aves raræ': 'rare birds' (Latin).

76.20. 'Buller': Sir Francis Buller (1746–1800), judge.

76.22. 'Kn—b—es': Knee-buckles, nickname used by Walpole's friend Sir Horatio Mann of Prince Marc de Beauvau (*HWC*, vol. 17, p. 95).
77.1. 'Sir Thomas Slade': Surveyor of the Navy from 1755–71, credited with making great advances in the fleet.
77.3. 'Ben—k': William Henry Cavendish Bentinck, third Duke of Portland (1738–1809) (see 19.15 above).
77.5. 'H—n—y, C—l—r, B—by': perhaps Henley; Culpepper; Boothby.
77.12. 'Philippina Burton': Philippina Hill, also known as Burton, playwright (*fl.* 1768).
77.17. 'M'CAULAY': Catharine Macaulay (see 62.17 above).
77.18. 'Lennox': Charlotte Lennox (1720–1804), American-born English author of *The Female Quixote* (1752); friend of Johnson.
77.20. 'Miss Carter': Elizabeth Carter (1717–1806), poet, translator of Epictetus (1758); friend of Johnson.
77.21. 'Ireland's lord lieutenant': George Townshend, fourth Viscount Townshend (1724–1807), Lord Lieutenant of Ireland from 1767 to 1772.
77.24. 'Lady A—b—e': Lady Anne Lennox, Countess of Albemarle (1703–89).
78.5. 'Mrs. Gibson': perhaps Anne Gibson (d. 1777), wife of Sir Thomas Webb.
78.13. 'L—ham': perhaps Mrs Janet Lessingham (d. 1783), who acted at Drury Lane in 1756 and Covent Garden 1765–7 (*LDG*, vol. 2, p. 565).
78.14. 'Boscawen': Edward Boscawen (1711–61), admiral.
78.18. 'G—r': Duchess of Gloucester.
78.19. 'Orlean maid': Joan of Arc.
78.20. 'lord George Sackville': George Sackville Germain, first Viscount Sackville (1716–85), soldier and statesman; MP for Dover, 1741–61.
78.24. 'Lucy Cooper': perhaps Elizabeth Cooper (d. 1809) (*LDG*, vol. 2, p. 729).
79.3. 'Jack Ketch': see 61.7 above.
79.11–12. 'T—wnsh—nd's ... *daughter*': family of Charles Townshend (1725–67), Chancellor of the Exchequer.
79.16. 'dowager': Princess Dowager of Wales.
79.19. 'Williams, Winnington': Thomas Winnington (1696–1746) was at odds with Viscountess Townshend (*HWC*, vol. 37, p. 232). Or possibly Sir Charles Hanbury Williams and his widow, Lady Winnington.
80.10. 'O—': Robert Orme (1728–1801), historiographer to the East India Company; friend of Johnson.
80.19. 'E— of H—': perhaps the Earl of Home, whom Hume was related to.
81.1. 'butefully': play on Bute's name.
81.1. 'Minion letter': in printing, 'the name of a type intermediate in size between "nonpareil" and "brevier"' (*OED*).
81.6. '*David Stuart Mac Sceptick*': David Hume, famous for his scepticism.
81.9. 'G— C—': General Conway (see *NFHW*, 1: 69.5).
81.15. 'l—p': lordship.
83.4. 'C—y': Conway.
85.5. '*Ou vere is des all*': Frenchified English for 'where is this hall'.
85.6. 'Marli, Versailles, Fountainbleau': all places in France.

85.10. 'PULTENEY': see Biographical Appendix.
85.13. 'GEORGE COLMAN': see Biographical Appendix.
85.15. 'Coley': Colman's nickname.
85.18. '— on': something that rhymes with 'parson'.
85.21. 'Ratcliff': Radcliffe Camera at Oxford.
87.1. 'British Lion now is couchant': in terms of heraldry, resting, i.e. Britain is at peace.
87.8. 'Albemarle, and Ligonier': old generals; William Anne Keppel, second Earl of Albemarle (1702–54), and John Ligonier, Earl Ligonier (1680–1770).
87.10. 'Duke': Thomas Pelham-Holles, Duke of Newcastle, is listed as an old Westminster pupil.
87.17. 'Coley': see 85.15.
87.20. '*sans*': 'without' (French).
87.29. '*quantum suff.*': '*quantum sufficit*', 'sufficient quantity' (Latin).
88.4. 'Isis and Cam': the rivers in Oxford and Cambridge.
88.12. 'Mr. Mascow': mentioned by the Earl of Chesterfield in a letter to his son who stayed with him in Leipsig, dated London, 13 December 1748 (OS): 'Mr. Mascow is much known and esteemed in the republic of letters' (Chesterfield, *Letters to His Son* (London: J. Dodsley, 1774), Letter LIX.
88.17. 'Douglas': perhaps Charles Douglas, third Duke of Queensberry and second Duke of Dover (1698–1778), who, along with his wife, supported John Gay.
88.n. 'T— T—': untraced.
89.12. 'Bansted Down': mentioned by Pope in *Satires*, II.ii.143 (*TE*, vol. 4, p. 67).
90.6. 'DR. BARTHOLOMEW': see Biographical Appendix.
90.13. 'vigils of Comus and Venus': i.e., revelry, the son of Circe and Bacchus carousing with the goddess of love.
90.24. 'vultures of Bath': quacks.
91.3. 'doit': 'a small piece of money' (Johnson).
91.16. 'MISS TEMPLE': Christian Temple (1688–1759), daughter of Sir Richard Temple and sister of Richard Temple, first Viscount Cobham, who married Sir Thomas Lyttelton, fourth Baronet (1685–1751), of Hagley, Worcestershire.
91.19. 'CONGREVE': see Biographical Appendix.
92.15. 'Ida': Greek mountain range.
93.1. 'Quadrille': 'A game at cards' (Johnson). 'The Game of Quadrille' (*c.* 1726) is attributed to Thomas Woolston in the *ETSC* (t096953). Congreve is also assumed to have written 'A Ballad of Quadrille' (1727). It was included by Edmund Curll in the 1730 collection, *Mr. Congreve's Last Will and Testament.* See 'William Congreve: *The Game of Quadrille*', *The Book Collector*, 34 (1985), p. 209.
93.7–8. 'deponent': 'One that deposes his testimony in a court of justice; an evidence; a witness' (Johnson).
93.15. 'Hercules, Cupid, Pitts, and the Gardener': names or card-faces chosen perhaps for their humourous incongruity.
93.18. 'Bartholomew Fair': circus in London, commemorated by Ben Jonson.
93.18. 'Strip is the word': perhaps an early version of strip poker.

94.9. 'hickledy pickledy': see note to 3: 23.12 above.

94.12. 'A—': presumably their posteriors.

95.1–2. 'AN EPISTLE TO LORD COBHAM, BY MR. POPE': spurious; not mentioned in the Twickenham edition.

95.n. 'published in one of the daily papers in August 1769': presumably also in the October 1769 issue of *The Scots Magazine* (as below).

98.9–10. 'SONG. BY THE SAME': spurious; attributed to Pope in *The Scots Magazine* (October 1769) and *The Annual Register*, vol. 12 (*TE*, vol. 6, p. 461 and n.).

99.1–5. 'EPILOGUE ... SAMUEL JOHNSON': while Johnson wrote the 'Prologue' for Garrick's first night at Drury Lane, the 'Epilogue' was in fact written by Garrick (*The Poems of Samuel Johnson*, ed. David Nichol Smith and Edward L. McAdam, 2nd edn (Oxford: Clarendon Press, 1974), p. 462). Margaret 'Peg' Woffington (*c.* 1714–60) started acting in Dublin from the age of ten; she played at Covent Garden in 1740, then Drury Lane in the following year; starring as Lady Anne opposite Garrick's Richard III in 1742. She was engaged to Garrick, and she stabbed Mrs Bellamy during the production of her play, *Statira*.

99.n. 'prologue in Dodsley's collection, Vol. I': Robert Dodsley's popular *Collection of Poems by Several Hands* first appeared in three volumes in 1748, four volumes in 1749, and expanded to six volumes in 1758.

100.3. '*Dulcined*': Don Quixote's beloved.

100.11. '*Fribble*': 'To trifle' (Johnson); 'a frivolous, contemptible fellow; a fop' (*OED*).

100. 12. '*curse the Creters*': possibly slang for 'creatures'.

100.13. 'jealous *Moor*': Othello.

100.20. '*Deard's*': a clothing and novelty shop mentioned in Lady Mary Wortley Montagu's poem, 'Lady M. M—'s Farewel to Bath', published in *GM*, 1 (1731), p. 305; Geoffrey Tillotson, Paul Fussell, Marshall Waingrow *et al.* (eds), *Eighteenth-Century English Literature* (New York: Harcourt, Brace & World, 1969), p. 817.

101.1–2. 'UPON MR. MASON'S TAKING ORDERS': William Mason (1724–97), poet, clergyman, friend of William Warburton, Richard Hurd, Horace Walpole and Thomas Gray. He became a vicar of Aston, Yorkshire, in 1754 and canon of York in 1762.

101.4. 'Holdernesse': Robert D'Arcy, fourth Earl of Holderness (1718–78), diplomat, appointed Secretary of State in 1751; dismissed in 1761.

103.6. '*Duke* and *Hart*': Hart and Dukes was a dancing academy; mentioned by Garrick in a letter to George Colman, 25 December [1765] (*LDG*, vol. 2, pp. 485–6).

103.12. 'ON JOHNSON'S DICTIONARY': Johnson's *Dictionary*, first published in 1755, had become a symbol of national pride.

104.6. 'verse-men and prose-men': 'Verse-man or Prose-man, term me which you will', Pope, *Satires*, II.i.64; *TE*, vol. 4, p. 11).

104.16. 'A RIDDLE': cited in Jane Austen's *Emma*. See Jill Heydt-Stevenson, '"Slipping into the Ha-Ha": Bawdy Humor and Body Politics in Jane Austen's Novels', *Nineteenth-Century Literature*, 55 (2000), pp. 316–18.

105.17. 'SIR WILLIAM YOUNG TO HIS LADY': Mary Yonge was accused of committing adultery in 1724 by her profligate husband; George I granted a divorce settlement which allowed Sir William to keep much of his wife's fortune. See Lady Mary Wortley Montagu's 'Epistle from Mrs. Yonge to Her Husband', written in the same year but not published until after her death. Sir William Yonge (*c.* 1693–1755) was a prominent Whig whose name, according to Lord Hervey, represented 'everything pitiful, corrupt and contemptible' (*TE*, vol. 4, p. 394).

106.2. 'Celia': any lady.

106.4. 'Its fellow weeping for its brother': a variation on Regan's reason for having Gloucester's other eye put out, 'One side will mock another', *King Lear* (III.vii.69).

107.3. 'D— OF D—': Charles Sackville, second Duke of Dorset (1711–69), MP for Sussex (1742–7).

107.6–7. 'D—SS OF R—D, LADY A—LE, AND MISS P—ST': Lady Mary Bruce, Duchess of Richmond (1740–96); Lady Anne Lennox, Countess of Albemarle (1703–89); and, perhaps, Miss Parkhurst.

108.16. 'Smart': presumably a friend.

108.22. 'Hampness': the name of a brickyard, perhaps in West Hampness, listed as a variant of Westhampnett, Sussex.

109.3. 'Archer and Van': presumably a pair of architects.

109.16. 'TO SAPPHO': early seventh-century BC Greek poet from the isle of Lesbos; the name was used by Pope in reference to Lady Mary Wortley Montagu *c.* 1733.

109.19. 'WM. MELMOTH': Melmoth's first wife died in 1761; he remarried Miss M. Ogle (birth date unavailable) in 1762 and they moved to Bath.

111.1. 'LORD MELCOMBE': George Bubb Dodington, Baron Melcombe (*c.* 1690–1762).

111.14. 'Congreves ... Rowes': the 'greats' from bygone days. For Congreve, see Biographical Appendix; Joseph Addison (1672–1719), best known for *The Spectator* (1711–12); Sir Samuel Garth (1661–1719) whose poem, *The Dispensary* (1699), influenced Pope; and Nicholas Rowe (1674–1718), appointed Poet Laureate in 1715.

111.25. 'George': George III.

112.2. 'Aganippe': a spring on Mount Helicon sacred to the Muses.

112.15. 'irrealities': rare form of 'unreality' (*OED*).

112.28. 'Middleton and Fontenelle': Conyers Middleton (1683–1750), Church of England clergyman who engaged in a heated pamphlet war and legal battle with the elder Richard Bentley at Cambridge and wrote on the lure of Roman Catholicism; Bernard le Bovier, Sieur de Fontenelle (1657–1757).

114.5–6. 'Charlotta ... Anson': Sophia Charlotte, the seventeen-year-old Princess of Mecklenburg-Strelitz (1744–1818), was escorted by Admiral George Anson,

Baron Anson (1697–1762), through rough seas to Harwich (instead of the intended destination of Greenwich) to meet her soon-to-be husband George III in 1761. Her dramatic voyage was the subject of a painting, *The Royal Yacht Bringing Queen Charlotte to England in a Storm* (*c.* 1761), by Richard Wright.

114.8. 'duce': an obsolete form of 'deuce' (*OED*).

114.20. 'Locke and Sir Isaac': The elder Richard Bentley (1662–1742) formed a club in London in 1697 whose members included Sir Christopher Wren, John Locke (1632–1704) and his colleague at Cambridge, Sir Isaac Newton.

115.16. 'Concetto': 'concept' (Italian).

115.20. 'And Gray composes once in seven years': Gray was known for taking a long time to polish his verse.

116.17. 'grig': '1. It seems originally to have signified any thing below the natural size. 2. A small eel. 3. A merry creature' (Johnson).

116.27. 'Sunk at Whitehall, to rise up at Queenhithe': i.e. what fails to pass as wit with politicians may succeed with stevedores and vice versa; Whitehall is the main political avenue; the docks at Queenhithe in London on the Thames date back to Alfred the Great.

117.20. 'Lucian': Syrian-born rhetorician whose satires took the form of dialogues (AD *c.* 117–*c.* 180).

117.22–3. 'Rabelais ... Swift': writers known to possess scatological candour.

117.26. 'jessamine': 'another form of jasmine' (*OED*).

117.29. 'C—C—': i.e. 'cock' spelled out.

118.27. 'Bigotry, revolution, and the Dutch': referring to the Glorious or Bloodless Revolution of 1688 which ousted the Roman Catholic King, James II, replacing him with the Dutch King, William of Orange, and Mary.

119.1. 'orient': 'often a vague poetic epithet: Precious, excellent ...' (*OED*), here applied to Queen Anne.

119.5. 'Hallifax': the Earl of Halifax.

119.13–14. 'TO MR. POYNTZ, WITH DR. SECKER'S SERMON ON EDUCATION': Stephen Poyntz (1685–1750); referring to a sermon preached at Oxford in 1733, 'On the Advantages and Duties of an Academical Education', by Thomas Secker (1693–1768), who became the Archbishop of Canterbury in 1758.

120.12. 'lov'd Marcellus': Augustus Caesar hoped for a successor in his adopted son Marcellus (43–23 BC), the tragedy of whose early death was told by Virgil in the *Aeneid*, VI.861–87.

120.16. 'Minerva': Roman goddess of war and handicrafts.

121.1–3. 'EXTEMPORE EPIGRAM ... HOUSE AT CHISWICK': Chiswick House, a model of Palladian architecture in the west of London, built in 1726–9 by Richard Boyle, third Earl of Burlington and fourth Earl of Cork (1694–1753), the architect celebrated by Pope (*TE*, vol. 3.ii, p. 130).

121.12. 'RARE architect': Andrea Palladio (1508–80).

121.15. 'could we on paper live': i.e. architectural blueprints drawn up according to geometrical ideals vs human needs.

122.1–2. 'groping moles ... lynx's eyes': i.e. really dark.

122.17. 'STREPHON AND COLLIN': note Swift's inversion of the pastoral persona in 'Strephon and Chloe'; here a sophisticated urbanite and country bumpkin have a boasting contest over their lovers' beauty.

124.11–12. 'AN ODE TO THE MOST UNPOPULAR MAN LIVING': The *ESTC* notes the manuscript addition of the words, 'Address'd to Mr. Stone', in the BL copy of this volume (n042003). In the winter of 1752–3, Andrew Stone (1703–73) was accused by Lord Harcourt and Thomas Hayter of attempting to convert the Prince of Wales to Tory principles and Jacobitism (see *NFHW*, 1: 10.14).

124.16. 'P—s': Prince's.

124.22. 'a —': a king.

125.2. 'Winton's Green': Winton Green is near King's Cross in north London.

125.20. 'injur'd Norwich': Hayter was Bishop of Norwich.

126.1. 'Britannia's *council*': i.e. parliament.

126.10. 'Pirithöus and the Lapithæ': referring to a battle between the Lapithae and the Centaurs, who attempted to kidnap Hippodamia, the bride of Pirithöus, at her royal wedding feast.

126.n. 'Quid memorem ... intonant ore'. Dryden translates this passage as:

> *Ixion* and *Perithous* I cou'd name;
> And more *Thessalian* Chiefs of mighty Fame.
> High o're their Heads a mould'ring Rock is plac'd,
> That promises a fall, and shakes at ev'ry Blast.
> They lye below, on Golden Beds display'd,
> And genial Feasts with Regal Pomp are made.
> The Queen of Furies by their sides is set;
> And snatches from their Mouths th' untasted Meat.
> Which, if they touch, her hissing Snakes she rears:
> Tossing her Torch, and thund'ring in their Ears.
> (*Aeneid*, VI.814–23; p. 169).

127.n. 'Numerosa parabat ... ruinæ': 'numerosa parabat / excelsae turris tabulata, unde altior esset / casus et inpulsae praeceps inmane ruinae': 'Swooping naked out of the sky with spear and shield – fit sight / For a dying foreman ...', Juvenal, *The Sixteen Satires*, trans Peter Green (Harmondsworth: Penguin, 1967), X.107–9; p. 230.

128.1–2. 'EPISTLE FOR LORD LOVEL TO LORD CHESTERFIELD': *An Epistle from Lord L—l to Lord C—d. By Mr. P—* (London: T. Cooper, 1740) (Foxon, P1160; *ESTC* t090920) (*HWC*, vol. 37, p. 82); see next poem.

128.4. 'Holkham': Holkham Hall, a Palladian-style mansion in Norfolk, designed by the Earl of Burlington and William Kent, built between 1734 and 1764 by Thomas Coke (1697–1759), created Baron Lovel (1728), first Earl of Leicester (1744), who died before its completion.

128.7. 'Clio': Muse of history.

128.17. 'Flavia': 'Flavia's a Wit, has too much sense to Pray, / To Toast our wants and wishes, is her way' (possibly based on Sarah Churchill, Duchess of Marlborough (1660–1744)), Pope, *Epistle to a Lady*, ll. 87–8 (*TE*, vol. 3.ii, pp. 55–6).

128.19. 'Happy the man': the opening to Pope's 'Ode on Solitude': 'Happy the man, whose wish and care / A few paternal acres bound, / Content to breathe his native air, / In his own ground' (*TE*, vol. 6, p. 3).

129.23. 'In senseless camps at Hounslow Heath': presumably the army and navy awaiting instructions.

130.3. 'Like him of Pope's describing': Joseph Addison.

130.4. 'Willing … strike': 'Willing to hurt, and yet afraid to strike, / Just hint a fault, and hesitate dislike', from Pope's description of 'Atticus' in *An Epistle to Dr. Arbuthnot*, ll. 203–4 (*TE*, vol. 4, p. 110).

130.8. 'Augean stables': One of Hercules's twelve labours was to clean the Augean stables.

130.12. 'new convention': Sir Robert Walpole supported the Convention of Pardo, a trade agreement between England and Spain, signed in January 1739, opposition to which became so strong that war was declared the following October. William Pitt joined in the effort to shame Walpole, and Pulteney's pro-war stance brought him much popularity.

130.17. 'Bob': Walpole.

131.4. 'Dubius non Improbus … D. of B. Ep.': epitaph on the tomb of John Sheffield, first Duke of Buckingham and Normanby (1647–1721), in Westminster Abbey meaning 'doubtful, not wicked'.

131.6. 'HAPPY the man': see 128.19 above.

131.9. 'White's': coffee house (see *NFHW*, 1: 9.33).

131.17–18. 'Spithead and Hounslow … *convention*': see 129.23 above.

132.3. 'Bob and Spain': see 130.12 above.

132.4. 'Flavia': see 128.17 above.

132.7. '*Dormer*': James Dormer (1679–1741), appointed Lieutenant-General in 1735; member of the Kit-Cat Club.

133.10. '*place-bill*': Baron Sandys's Place Bill for securing the freedom of parliament by limiting the number of civil and military officers in the house was defeated on 29 January 1740.

133.19. 'dog of old … Æsop told': perhaps 'The Dogs and the Hides', about ravenous dogs who attempt to drink a river dry in order to reach some cowhides, then burst.

134.2. '*hesitate dislike*': see 130.4 above.

134.11. 'Cathcart's expedition': Charles Cathcart, eighth Lord Cathcart (*c.* 1685–1740), Brigadier-General who was appointed Commander-in-Chief during the War of Jenkins's Ear in 1739, but died from dysentery in December 1740 while sailing to the West Indies.

134.13. 'Bob's friends': the Walpole administration.

135.1. 'ON LADY T— AT BATH': possibly Lady Etheldreda Townshend (*c.* 1708–88) who is mentioned by Horace Walpole in a letter to John Chute (30 April 1754) as entertaining Pulteney and Charles Stanhope (*HWC*, vol. 35, p. 80).

135.7. 'ON DOWAGER LADY E. H—D': possibly Lady Elizabeth Howard (d. 1739), whose first husband, Baron Lechmere, died in 1727; she married Sir Thomas Robinson in the following year.

136.5. 'STRAWBERRY HILL': all places in this poem are meant to pale by comparison to Strawberry Hill, 500 yards up the road from Pope's villa in Twickenham, where Horace Walpole lived from 1748.

136.22. 'Kitty Clive': Catherine 'Kitty' Clive (1711–85), a well-known actress who worked with Fielding and Garrick; a neighbour and friend of Horace Walpole from *c.* 1749; 'easily one of the most talented and most famous actresses of her generation' (*ODNB*).

137.3. 'jim': obsolete for 'gim', meaning 'smart, spruce' (*OED*).

137.11. 'Cooper's': Sir John Denham's 'Cooper's Hill' (1642; rev. 1655) celebrates the panorama of Windsor, London and the Thames from eighteen miles away in Egham.

138.1. 'GENERAL COPE': General Sir John Cope (1690–1760).

138.19. 'Ætna': a volcano in Sicily.

138.23. 'god of physick': Apollo.

139.3. 'Y—ke': Lancelot Blackburne, Archbishop of York (1658–1743), whose 'reputation was that of a man of pleasure and as a womanizer' (Rogers (ed.), *Alexander Pope*, p. 715). In Pope's *Sober Advice from Horace* (1734), the 'Lord of *L—n*' tells 'a *noted* Dean' caught fornicating in the park, 'Better than lust for Boys, with *Pope* and *Turk*, / Or others Spouses, like my Lord of — [York]' (ll. 43–4; *TE*, vol. 4, p. 79).

139.8. 'P—rk—r': Thomas Parker, first Earl of Macclesfield (1667–1732), Lord Chancellor (1718–25).

139.9. 'H—ng—rf—rd': John Hungerford (*c.* 1657–1729), Tory MP for Scarborough (1692) and lawyer who defended the printer John Matthews in 1719. See Pat Rogers, 'Alexander Pope and "Duke upon Duke": Satiric Content, Aims, and Means', *Modern Language Review*, 99 (2004), p. 880.

139.10. 'Pr—tt': Sir John Pratt (1657–1725), judge.

139.11. 'King': Peter King, first Baron King (1669–1734), Lord Chancellor (1725–33).

139.12. 'Tracy': Robert Tracy (1655–1735), judge.

139.13. 'Eyr—s': Sir Robert Eyre (also called 'Eyres'; 1666–1735), judge.

139.14. 'honest Price': Robert Price (1655–1733), judge.

139.15. 'P—w—s': Sir Thomas Powys (1649–1719), judge and MP.

139.16. 'P—ge': Sir Francis Page (*c.* 1660–1741), remembered by Pope in 1733: 'Hard Words or Hanging, if your Judge be *Page*', *Satires*, II.i.82 (*TE*, vol. 4, p. 13).

139.17. 'F—rt—scue': William Fortescue (1687–1749), judge; Pope's friend and *adversarius* in *Satire*, II.i (*TE*, vol. 4, p. 4).

140.1–2. 'JOHN SHEPHERD TO THE EARL OF MACCLESFIELD': Jack Sheppard (b. 1702), a notorious thief who made several daring prison escapes; a few weeks after his execution on 16 November 1724, before a huge crowd at Tyburn, the Lord Chancellor, Thomas Parker, first Earl of Macclesfield (1667–

1732), was accused of misappropriating funds amounting to £60,000, accepting bribes and other corrupt practices. Many Londoners were outraged at the perceived legal disparity between rich and poor when Macclesfield, who was found guilty, was fined £30,000 and spent six weeks in the Tower.

140.7. 'Which nobody can deny': this shares the same refrain as 'The Protecting Brewer', which parodied 'The Brewer' in Thomas d'Urfey's *Pills to Purge Melancholy* (1682):

> Some Christian kings began to quake,
> And said With the brewer no quarrel we'll make,
> We'll let him alone; as he brews let him bake;
> Which nobody can deny.

'For He's a Jolly Good Fellow' (which in another version is complemented by 'And so say all of us') became popular after the Duke of Marlborough's victory at Malplaquet in 1709.

141.2. 'honest Thomas': the Earl of Macclesfield.

141.13. 'Blewskin': The *Daily Journal* for 3 October 1724 reported the capture of Sheppard's accomplice, Joseph Blake (b. 1700), alias Blueskin, by Jonathan Wild. Shortly before his execution at Tyburn on 11 November 1724, Blake tried to kill Wild by cutting his throat.

141.18. 'Jonathan Wild': born in 1683, this thief-taker and roguish entrepreneur of criminals recovered from Blueskin's blade in time for his own execution on 24 May 1725; his story made for a bestseller by Henry Fielding in 1743.

141.21. 'myrmidons': i.e. thieves, highwaymen, after followers of Achilles.

142.6. 'trust up': i.e. trussed up for hanging.

142.9. 'TRIPLE ALLIANCE': between England and France in 1716, joined by Holland in the following year, to keep Philip V of Spain at bay.

143.14. 'Tr—ry Lord ... Y—g': Treasury; perhaps Sir William Yonge (*c.* 1693–1755).

143.18. 'C—l L—t': Council List.

143.20. 'Fabius': Fabius 'Cunctator', 'the Delayer', who avoided direct confrontation with Hannibal *c.* 217 BC: the subject of a biography by Plutarch.

143.24. 'B—ps': Bishops.

143.28. 'Swisses': i.e. mercenary army (see 39.4).

144.16. 'Wild unto Walpole': Jonathan Wild and Sir Robert (Robin) Walpole, Earl of Orford.

145.7. 'Lloid': perhaps Sir Richard Lloyd (*c.* 1696–1761).

145.8. 'Molly Skerrett': Maria Skerrett (1702–38), Walpole's mistress, possibly introduced by Lady Mary Wortley Montagu at her house in Twickenham in 1724; he married her shortly after the death of his first wife in 1737; she died a few months later from a miscarriage.

145.12. 'Chetwind': perhaps the Hon. William Richard Chetwynd (*c.* 1683–1770).

145.18. 'Layer': Christopher Layer, who was implicated in the Atterbury plot.

145.19. 'Delafaye': Charles Delafaye, Under-Secretary of State; Walpole's envoy in Paris in 1732 (Maynard Mack, *Alexander Pope: A Life* (New York: Norton, 1985), p. 572).

145.20. 'Lynch and Mason': perhaps Colonel John Lynch (d. 1733), High Sheriff for Kent (1714), and another soldier; a Hugh Mason was appointed as porter at 'His Majesty's Royal Palace of Somerset House' in 1734 (*ODNB*).

145.21. 'Paxton': Nicholas Paxton (d. 1744), Solicitor to the Treasury (*HWC*, vol. 17, p. 502).

146.13. 'Townshend': Charles Townshend, third Viscount Townshend (1700–64); and the Hon. Thomas Townshend (1701–80), politician.

146.18. 'Vaughan': perhaps William Vaughan, MP for Merioneth; or Wilmot Vaughan, third Viscount Lisburne (m. 1727; d. 1766).

146.20. 'Charters': Francis Chartres or Charteris (*c.* 1665–1732), condemned for rape more than once, he received a royal pardon from George II; a gambler and rake mentioned by Pope: 'And something said of *Chartres* much too rough', *Satires*, II.i.4 (*TE*, vol. 4, p. 5), with the implication that nothing said could be too rough.

146.21. 'Churchill': perhaps Lieutenant-General Charles Churchill (*c.* 1678–1745).

148.18. 'Rosinante': Don Quixote's ungainly horse.

150.8. 'Murder some odd time will out': the proverb 'Murder will out' dates from the early fourteenth century and was a used by Chaucer in 'The Nun's Priest's Tale', *The Canterbury Tales*, l. 3052.

151.5. 'knotted taper crab': i.e. a walking stick like the one wielded by Partridge in Fielding's *Joseph Andrews*.

151.14–18. 'I've caught her in a lye … she lies with – other men.': echoing Iago's double entendres in *Othello*, IV.i.33–5.

152.8. 'Ithaca's king': Ulysses.

152.9. 'Syren's potent call': After plugging his crew's ears with wax, Ulysses had himself lashed to the mast so he could hear the Sirens' song, which usually lured sailors to their deaths.

152.18–19. '*A pint of rack* … pints of rack resound': an echo device similar to that used in Pope's *Rape of the Lock*.

153.12. 'W—e': Whore.

153.22. 'THE CHIMNEY SWEEPER': a parental wish for children's upward mobility.

154.11. 'Buss'd … nown': kissed; own.

154.13. '*Sure, Tommy's vastly grown, my dear*': perhaps alluding to Churchill's *The Duellist*, III.784 (see *NFHW*, 3: 101.17).

154.24. 'Grim': Grime personified.

155.5. 'Barber Scrape': perhaps following Cutbeard, the barber, in Ben Jonson's *Epicene*, or an earlier version of Phenegan M'Scrape, the barber and fiddler, in William Pearce's 1794 *Netley Abbey: an Operatic Farce*.

156.6. 'Arthur's … White's': London gambling establishments.

156.18. 'Cælia': see *NFHW*, 1: 13.20.

156.22. 'Pluralist': a clergyman with more than one living.

156.23. 'stall-fed skin': i.e. pampered.

157.6. 'mammon': greed.

157.24. 'mobs': 'A kind of female head dress' (Johnson).

157.24. 'lappets': 'The parts of a head dress that hang loose' (Johnson).

158.10. 'corkin': perhaps a shortened form of 'corking-pin', 'a pin of the largest size' (Johnson).

159.14. 'Jupiter's high-mettled dame': Juno.

159.15. 'Dan Homer': see 70.7 above.

160.2. 'cestus': 'The girdle of Venus' (Johnson); 'a belt or girdle for the waist' (*OED*).

160.15. 'cloud-ruler's sister': Juno.

161.5. 'Thund'rer': Jupiter.

163.22. 'cit': a contracted form of 'citizen', 'in an ill sense', to which Johnson adds, 'a pert low townsman; a pragmatical trader' (Johnson).

164.13. 'gadder': 'A rambler; one that runs much abroad without business' (Johnson).

165.7. 'burning-glasses': eyes.

166.2–3. 'inopemque ... Fundi': 'inopemque paterni et laris et fundi': 'beggared of paternal home and estate', Horace, *Epistles*, II.2.50–1.

168.4–6. 'Numps ... quaver': a 'strange dolt' (168.16) who goes to the opera for the first time and gawks at royalty. A minim is a half-note while a quaver is an eighth-note.

169.1–3. 'VERSES BY MR. POPE ... DR. IBBOTT': originally these formed the last eight lines of a fourteen-line poem, 'To Mr. Gay, Who wrote him a congratulatory letter on the finishing his House' (*TE*, vol. 6, pp. 225–6). Pope included a revised version of these lines in a letter to Mrs Judith Cowper (5 November 1722), whom he mistook for the author of *A Fit of Spleen*, written by the divine, Benjamin Ibbot (1680–1725). The lines appeared in *The Whitehall Evening Post* and *The London Magazine* in 1737 as well as five other publications before finding their way into *NFHW*. Ibbot was an Anglican clergyman known for his strong views against Deism.

169.n. 'See Dodsley's collection, Vol. 5, p. 202': Ibbot's 'Fit of the Spleen' appears in volume 5 of the 1782 edition (see 99.n. above).

169.13–15. 'VERSES ... BLOOMSBURY AND ST. GILES'S': Roy Porter notes that the Duke of Bedford was slow to develop Bloomsbury: 'Bedford Square – the first triumph of the 1774 Building Act, built entirely of "first-rate" houses – is now Bloomsbury's only complete Georgian Square', *London: A Social History* (Cambridge, Massachusetts: Harvard University Press, 1994), p. 112.

169.17. '*Brunswick*': the only statue of George I still adorns the spire of St George's Bloomsbury. Ridiculed for being excessively heroic in its pose, the statue appears in the background of Hogarth's *Gin Lane* (1751). The church, consecrated in 1730, was designed by Nicholas Hawksmoor.

169.17. '*dregs of the people*': this italicized phrase and '*scum of the earth*' on p. 170 are possibly quoted (a favourite expression of the king perhaps) and repeated on p. 172. 'Dregs of the people' is used by Tobias Smollett in *Humphry Clinker* (Oxford: Oxford World Classics, 1984), p. 104.

170.1. 'his *Grace*': Bedford.

170.5. 'phyz': perhaps short for 'physiognomy', 'the face; the cast of the look' (Johnson).

170.23. 'prog': 'Victuals; provision of any kind. A low word' (Johnson).

170.27. 'vapour': used as a verb.

171.4. 'cock-a-hoop': Johnson notes '*Cock on the Hoop*', meaning 'triumphant; exulting', under 'cock'.

171.13. 'True Blue': Tories.

171.21. 'Your Grandson': George III.

172.6. 'MRS. CORNELY': Teresa Cornelys (see 47.11 above).

172.21. 'NORFOLK TURNIPPE': this tall tale was printed in *Town and Country Magazine*, 2 (September 1770), pp. 493–4, two months after Thomas Chatterton (1752–70) submitted his 'Rowley' poem, 'An Excelente Balade of Charitie', to the same magazine. It was reprinted several times as late as 1826, when it appeared in *New England Galaxy*. Norfolk became famous for its turnips due to Colonel Robert Walpole of Houghton, father of the Prime Minister, who cultivated them from *c*. 1673. His son-in-law, Charles Townshend (1674–1738), second Viscount Townshend, who retired from politics to his native Norfolk in 1730, was dubbed 'Turnip Townshend' for his devotion to experimenting with the root crop, so much so that Pope made reference to 'All *Townshend's* Turnips' in *Epistles*, II.ii.273, *Imitations of Horace* (*TE*, vol. 4 , p. 185). Stith Thompson notes an American version, 'Lies about big turnips', in *Motif-Index of Folk Literature* (Bloomington: Indiana University Press, 1955), X1431.1; p. 531. Ernest W. Baughman, in *Type and Motif-Index of the Folktales of England and North America* (The Hague: Mouton, 1966), notes a tall tale out of Nebraska, dated 1943: 'Animals find shelter in great vegetable … (turnips, thousands of sheep)' (X1401 1(d); p. 535).

173.3. 'weene': know.

173.6. 'pricking o'er the ley': 'To prick' is 'To come upon the spur' (Johnson). 'A lusty knight was pricking o'er the plain' ('The Wife of Bath's Tale', l. 47, Keith Walker (ed.), *The Oxford Authors: John Dryden* (Oxford: Oxford University Press, 1987), p. 803).

174.7–8. 'goodman Vere … Robin Rouse': generic Norfolk names.

174.17. 'PENSHURST-PARK': Sir Philip Sidney (d. 1586) was born at Penshurst, near Tonbridge in Kent, on 30 November 1554.

175.2. 'unhappily felled': according to Ian Donaldson in *The Oxford Authors: Ben Jonson* (Oxford: Oxford University Press, 1985), 'An oak which still stands today at Penshurst is said to have grown from an acorn planted on the day of Sir Philip Sidney's birth' (p. 671).

175.6–12. 'Waller … humble love': Edmund Waller's 'At Penhurst' (1645), ll. 25–30.

175.20. 'Cicero … Marian Oak': Cicero's poem on General Marius.

175.21–3. '*Manet vero … seminari potest*': 'Manet vero Attice noster et semper manebit: sata est enim ingenio. Nullius autem agricolae cultu stirps tam diuturna quam poetae versu seminari potest': 'That oak lives indeed, my dear Atticus, and will live forever; for it was planted by the imagination. No tree nourished by a farmer's care can be so long lived as one planted by the imagination' (Loeb edn, trans. Clinton Walker Keyes), spoken by Quintus at the start of Cicero's *De Legibus* (I.1).

175.24. 'Ben Johnson': Jonson's 'To Penhurst', in 'The Forest', ll. 9–14, written *c.* 1612, in *The Works of Benjamin Jonson* (London: R. Meighen, 1616).

176.11. '*QUERCUS loquitur*': i.e. the following title.

177.17. 'Tua Cæsar Ætas': '… Fruges et agris rettulit uberes', 'Thy age, great Caesar, has restored to squalid fields the plenteous grain', proclaiming that Augustus has defined his age, Horace, *Odes*, IV.15.

177.n. 'Justice Aston': Sir Richard Aston (1717–78) was one of the judges under Lord Mansfield who reversed Wilkes's outlawry on a technicality in 1768.

178.1–2. 'VERSES AT LORD MELCOMBE'S': see 111.1 above. Melcombe spent much of his retirement from 1749 holding forth at La Trappe, his riverside villa in Hammersmith (*ODNB*).

178.6. 'BUSTO OF COMUS IN A BEAUFET': Comus, son of Bacchus and Circe, who presides over feasts and riotry, applied to Milton's 1634 masque. 'Beaufet' is a variant form of 'buffet'.

179.1–3. 'TWO LYRICK EPISTLES … CRITICAL REVIEWERS': published anonymously in 1762; by John Hall-Stevenson (*ODNB*).

179.n. 'Vide CRITICAL REVIEW': *The Critical Review* (December 1761), p. 461, ran a negative review of his *Fables for Grown Gentlemen* (in *NFHW*, 2: 127).

180.14. 'Cocky Leaky': Johnson lists the ingredients separately: 'cockbroath' ('broath made by boiling a cock') and 'leek' (he allows quotations to suffice for the definition of the Welsh national emblem which the Scots use in 'cock-a-leekie' or 'cocky-leeky' soup).

181.23. 'beyond the Tweed': the river that marks part of the boundary between England and Scotland.

183.4. 'pickle of your sneezing': snot.

183.7. 'Macduff': Macbeth's vanquisher.

183.14. 'Charles the blessed martyr': Charles I, the Stuart King executed in 1649.

184.13. 'Fontaine': Jean de la Fontaine (see *NFHW*, 2: 122.2).

184.19. 'hobler': i.e. one who hobbles in an 'uneven awkward gait' (Johnson).

185.16. 'David Hume and David's marrow': the Scottish philosopher; a bizarre juxtaposition.

185.24. 'apologue': i.e. the next allegorical poem.

185.n. 'Lyrick epistles': see 179.1 above.

185.n. 'The ass, the cuckow and the lark': not one of Hall-Stevenson's; perhaps a variation on Aesop.

187.9. 'bopeep': a nursery game like peek-a-boo.

187.21. 'Poor Margery': see 179.1 above.

188.8. 'Patricius': an early Roman senator who honoured the republican ideal.

189.7–9. 'æstuat ingens … agitatus amor': 'Aestuat ingens Imo in corde pudor, mixtoque insania luctu, Et furiis agitatus amor, et conscia virtus': 'Deep in her inmost heart is stirred the immense shame, and madness with commingled grief, and love agitated by rage, and conscious virtue', Virgil, *Aeneid*, X.571–3.

192.1–2. 'AN ODE TO THE RIGHT HONOURABLE STEPHEN POYNTZ': published under Williams's name by Robert Dodsley in 1746 (Foxon, W492–93). Poyntz (1685–1750) was in charge of running the household of the young Duke of Cumberland.

192.6–10. 'Sensere quid Mens … roborant': the opening lines of the seventh and ninth verses of Horace's *Odes*, IV.4:

> What prowess dwells in boyish hearts
> Rear'd in the shrine of a pure home,
> What strength Augustus' love imparts
> To Nero's seed, the hope of Rome.
> Good sons and brave good sires approve:
> Strong bullocks, fiery colts, attest
> Their fathers' worth, nor weakling dove
> Is hatch'd in savage eagle's nest.
> But care draws forth the power within,
> And cultured minds are strong for good …

192.13. 'WILLIAM's deeds': In 1743, at the age of twenty-two, Prince William sustained a leg wound which left him with a permanent limp, at the Battle of Dettingen in Germany, led by his father, George II.

193.21. 'Mena's flood': Dettingen lies on the north bank of the Main River.

194.9. 'Tournay's fatal day': Tournai in Flanders was captured by the allied forces in 1709.

195.12. 'Culloden's field': The Jacobites' last stand against the Hanoverians was at Culloden Moor near Inverness on 16 April 1746.

195.20. 'WILLIAM's head': i.e. Prince William, Duke of Cumberland (1721–65).

195.26. 'Mr. LE GRAND': Edward Legrand (d. 1781), who was tutor to Prince Henry Frederick, Duke of Gloucester (1743–1805), but apparently did not teach spelling to Prince Henry, Duke of Cumberland and Strathearn (1745–90) (*HWC*, vol. 23, p. 230n.).

196.3–5. 'Adams … Thomas': perhaps an oblique reference to the Kirkcaldy-born Adam brothers, John (1721–92), Robert (1728–92) and James (1732–94), who made their mark on London architecture from 1758 and started work on the Adelphi in 1768.

196.11. ''Tis true 'tis hard! – 'tis hard 'tis true': echoing Polonius, 'That he is mad, 'tis true; 'tis true 'tis pity / And pity 'tis 'tis true' (*Hamlet*, II.ii.98–9).

196.14. 'Pr—ss': a dig at Augusta, Princess Dowager of Wales, and Bute.

196.17. '*Clyde*': the river that runs through Glasgow.

196.18. 'LONDINENSIS': the Roman name for a Londoner.